DAILY LIFE OF

ARAB AMERICANS IN THE 21st CENTURY

**Recent Titles in
The Greenwood Press Daily Life Through History Series**

Civil War in America, Second Edition
Dorothy Denneen Volo and James M. Volo

Elizabethan England, Second Edition
Jeffrey L. Forgeng

The New Americans: Immigration since 1965
Christoph Strobel

The New Inuit
Pamela R. Stern

The Indian Wars
Clarissa W. Confer

The Reformation
James M. Anderson

The Aztecs, Second Edition
David Carrasco and Scott Sessions

The Progressive Era
Steven L. Piott

Women during the Civil Rights Era
Danelle Moon

Colonial Latin America
Ann Jefferson and Paul Lokken

The Ottoman Empire
Mehrdad Kia

Pirates
David F. Marley

DAILY LIFE OF

ARAB AMERICANS IN THE 21ST CENTURY

ANAN AMERI AND HOLLY ARIDA, EDITORS

Published under the auspices of the Arab American National Museum

The Greenwood Press Daily Life Through History Series

 GREENWOOD

AN IMPRINT OF ABC-CLIO, LLC
Santa Barbara, California • Denver, Colorado • Oxford, England

Library of Congress Cataloging-in-Publication Data

Daily life of Arab Americans in the 21st century / Anan Ameri and Holly Arida, editors.

     p. cm. — (Greenwood Press daily life through history series)
  "Published under the auspices of the Arab American National Museum."
  Includes bibliographical references and index.
  ISBN 978-0-313-37714-3 (hardcopy : acid-free paper) — ISBN 978-0-313-37715-0 (ebook)   1. Arab Americans—Social life and customs—21st century.   2. Arab Americans—Social conditions—21st century.   3. United States—Ethnic relations—History—21st century.   I. Ameri, Anan.   II. Arida, Holly.
III. Arab American National Museum (Dearborn, Mich.)
  E184.A65D35   2012
  305.892'7073—dc23   2011048338

ISBN: 978-0-313-37714-3
EISBN: 978-0-313-37715-0

16 15 14 13 12   1 2 3 4 5

This book is also available on the World Wide Web as an eBook. Visit www.abc-clio.com for details.

Greenwood
An Imprint of ABC-CLIO, LLC

ABC-CLIO, LLC
130 Cremona Drive, P.O. Box 1911
Santa Barbara, California 93116-1911

This book is printed on acid-free paper ∞

Manufactured in the United States of America

CONTENTS

ACKNOWLEDGMENTS

Bringing this publication to fruition could not have happened without the valuable contributions of a number of people, especially the authors of the various chapters of this book. To each of them we owe a special debt of gratitude for their timely submissions and for the high quality of their work: Marvin Wingfield, Randa Kayyali, Dr. Janice J. Terry, Kathleen Marker, and Helen Samhan.

We would also like to extend our heartfelt thanks and appreciation to Denyse Sabagh, Nadeen Aljijakli, and Noel Saleh for sharing their valuable knowledge and experience about 9/11 and immigration laws for the immigration chapter. Our warm gratitude goes to the artists in the Arab American art movement and the organizations and publications that support them for the art included in the art chapter.

Our deepest appreciation and heartfelt gratitude goes out to the Arab American National Museum staff members who helped with this project: Janice Freij for her contribution to the timeline and glossary; Celia Shallal for helping with research and for her technical assistance; Fay Saad for her help in proofreading and the many logistics associated with putting an edited book together; Arleen Wood and Kristin Lalonde at the Museum Library and Resource Center for their support in finding the resources necessary for this publication; Suzy Mazloum and Kim Silarski for their help in securing images for the publication; and Lama Mansour for sharing her expertise on the Arab American art community. We thank Sonya Kassis for sharing with us her personal experience of her family's celebration of Easter and Nadia Bazzy for her story about being an Arab American student today. Special thanks go to our copy editor Cindy Bohn for her outstanding work.

We are indebted to the American-Arab Anti-Discrimination Committee (ADC), the Arab American Institute (AAI), and the Arab Community Center for Economic and Social Services (ACCESS) for sharing many of the resources used in the book.

Anan Ameri and Holly Arida

INTRODUCTION: ARAB AMERICAN LIFE AND CULTURE TODAY

Holly Arida

Today, Arab American life and culture is very much shaped by the political landscape in the United States and the Arab world. The terrorist attacks of 9/11 had a significant impact on Arab Americans—some perished in the attacks, many stepped forward as heroes in the aftermath, and many have suffered from undue suspicion, prejudice, collective blame, or fear of reprisals as America processed the tragedy. Following 9/11, many more immigrants from Arabic-speaking countries and their descendants began to assert their ethnic identity as Arab American. Why? As the Arab Canadian writer Joanne Kadi puts it, this "allows us to reclaim the word Arab, to force people to hear and say a word that has become synonymous with 'crazy Muslim terrorists.' It affirms our identity and links us to our brothers and sisters in Arab countries."[1] This book explores the many dimensions of Arab American life today, beginning with the immigrant experience. Subsequent chapters cover in depth the political, family, religious, educational, professional, public, and artistic aspects of the Arab American experience, taking particular care to explore how that experience is impacted by political events both here in America and in the Arab world.

Since the 1970s, hyphenated terms have often been used to name subgroups of the American mosaic. Around that same time, the hybrid "Arab-American" identity began to take form in response to politics in the Arab world, specifically the 1967 war between Israel and the surrounding Arab states. Americans of Arab origin began to organize politically and to establish new organizations and institutions. This effort coincided with the arrival of a new wave of immigrants who came to America from the war-torn countries of Lebanon and Palestine and, later, Iraq. Some of these newly arrived Arab immigrants settled in existing Arab American ethnic enclaves that had been established in the early part of the 20th century, and their presence served to reinforce and rejuvenate Arab American identity in those communities. Before the terrorist attacks of 9/11, some immigrants and their descendants identified only with the specific Arab country from which they or their ancestors had come—perhaps Lebanon or Egypt—and some still do. But for many Americans of Arab origin, shared interests and experiences have given rise to a sense of unity.

Who are Arab Americans? The simple answer is either immigrants or descendants of immigrants who trace their national origins to one of the 22 Arabic-speaking countries. Some of these descendants have assimilated over the generations and do not maintain cultural connections to their Arab homeland. And those who do identify as Arab Americans are not monolithic—they come from a region that has shifting national boundaries and identities, a multitude of religious practices, and strong and varied local cultures, whether centered on city, town, or village. Although there will be some discussion in this book about the overall Muslim American experience, the Arab world is distinct from the Muslim world. There are an estimated 1.2 to 1.5 billion Muslims in the world, the majority of whom are not Arabs. The largest Muslim population lives in the non-Arab countries of Indonesia, Pakistan, India, and Bangladesh; and the Arab world includes a significant population of Christians. In other words, all Arabs are not Muslims, and certainly, all Muslims are not Arabs.

The majority of Arab Americans are, in fact, Christians whose ancestors immigrated generations ago from Syria, Lebanon, and historic Palestine. The most recent wave of Arab immigration, which began in the 1970s, has, however, been predominantly Muslim, originating not only from the three countries just mentioned but also from Iraq, Egypt, and Jordan. Arab Americans live in all 50 states but reside predominantly in major metropolitan areas, such as Chicago, Detroit, Los Angeles, New York, and Washington, D.C., which are also home to Arab American ethnic enclaves.

While this book focuses on Arab American culture *today*, references to earlier times are sometimes necessary in order to illuminate the current daily life of Arab Americans. In the same way, because Arab Americans were uniquely affected by the events of 9/11, the impact of that tragedy is an unavoidable touchstone for understanding the Arab American experience. Arab Americans shared the shock, fear, and loss felt by all Americans, and indeed the global community, but Arab Americans also became victims when they were treated as if they were responsible for what had happened: they had to defend themselves against collective blame and prejudice and struggle with the larger community's lack of knowledge about what it means to be Arab or Muslim.

As the contributors to this book show, the level to which 9/11 has impacted Arab Americans varies across the many aspects of their lives. Anan Ameri explains that while immigration rates from Arab countries have not drastically fluctuated, the circumstances and processes surrounding immigration have changed. Middle East politics and the United States' relationship with various Arab countries have always shadowed the lives of Arab Americans, and Marvin Wingfield puts the impact of 9/11 in the context of that history. The effects on family life and typical Arab American interconnectedness are more subtle, and yet Randa Kayyali discerns some recent changes. Religious life remains a powerful component of the Arab American experience, irrespective of religious affiliation, but the scrutiny and suspicion faced by Muslim Americans has called forth a response from Muslim American organizations, which Anan Ameri explores in detail. Many students and teachers have faced new challenges in their educational life since 9/11, and Janice J. Terry shows that education has the power to raise awareness and combat stereotypes. For Arab Americans, life in the workplace has sometimes meant facing ignorance and discrimination, but according to Kathleen Marker, many have found purpose in educating their coworkers and have enjoyed support and acceptance from those with whom they work. Helen Samhan examines how 9/11 brought unprecedented challenges to the leaders of Arab American organizations, causing them to build on their history of successfully representing Arab Americans in public life and to forge new partnerships to promote understanding. The final chapter, by Holly Arida, outlines how the curiosity about the Arab world and Arab Americans that came out of 9/11 galvanized an art movement that led Arab Americans to collaborate more intentionally with each other and to use their artistic mediums to enlighten their audiences about Arab American life today.

Chapter 1, "Arab American Immigration," provides a short history of Arab migration to America. What were the forces that drew Arabs to this place and what were the circumstances of their early settlement here? The chapter defines key features of the major waves of migration, which often correspond to periods of war and economic uncertainty in the Arab world, and explores the ways Arabs have embraced the political freedom and economic opportunity that America represents. While generations of Arabs have assimilated and integrated into the fabric of American society, like many ethnic American communities, Arab Americans have also established their own ethnic enclaves. This chapter explores the dynamics of the immigrant experience, both in these self-sustaining communities and in the mainstream.

Chapter 2, "The Impact of 9/11, Middle East Conflicts, and Anti-Arab Discrimination," speaks to how American policy in the Middle East and U.S. relationships with the Arab world have long had an influence on how Arab Americans are perceived and how that perception affects their treatment by their fellow citizens, the government, and the media. Although Afghanistan and Iran are not part of the Arab world, they are considered part of the geopolitical region known as the Middle East. U.S. political and military involvement in these non-Arab countries, as well as in the Arab-Israeli conflict, the Iraq War, and Lebanon, has played out negatively in Arab American lives for decades. But while prejudice, discrimination, hate crimes, and increased scrutiny and surveillance against Arab Americans are part of this story, so, too, is the positive response by government, support from fellow citizens, and the ability of Arab Americans and their organizations to affirm their rights and combat bigotry.

Chapter 3, "The Family," addresses the fact that the relatively small size of the Arab American population, estimated at 4.2 million, makes it difficult to quantify and qualify statistics on Arab American families. Relying upon information from the U.S. Census Bureau and the smaller American Community Survey (ACS), as well as personal observation and scholarly assessment, this chapter synthesizes available data on the average Arab American household and compares trends in dating, marriage, and child-rearing to the national averages. This examination of Arab American family life explains patterns of matriarchy, patriarchy, and the rituals that surround weddings, births, deaths, and funerals. Levels of assimilation and where families live impact the retention of Arab traditions in American life. The Arab American family is unique in terms of its interconnectivity with unusually strong bonds within the nuclear family and among extended family members. A strong sense of family remains a central feature of Arab American life and culture today.

Chapter 4, "Religious Life," outlines the rich diversity of Arab American religious practices and traditions. Christianity was founded in what became the Arab world; so many Arab immigrants have brought with them some of Christianity's earliest traditions. Coming from a variety of denominations, early Arab American immigrants founded their own churches, a situation that has been a long-standing feature of Arab American life and explains the propensity of immigrants to settle in areas already established by early waves of Arab immigrants. While the percentage of Arab Muslim immigrants was relatively small, they, too, established their own houses of worship, building a few mosques in the early 20th century. As their number increased since the 1970s, they founded more mosques and Islamic centers in various U.S. cities, both so they could practice their faith and as a means to stay connected. Arab American religious practices are varied but remain a strong foundation for maintaining their faith and building relationships with members of their community.

Chapter 5, "Arab Americans and the American Educational System," examines a number of trends in education and the resistance to anti-Arab discrimination that has occurred in places of learning, particularly since 9/11. Both Arab and Arab American culture place a great emphasis on education, and Arab Americans tend to have higher educational levels than the national average. At the postsecondary level, there are many educational centers at universities and colleges throughout the country that are dedicated entirely to the study of the Arab world, some of which have been in existence for a long time. More recently new centers that focus on Arab Americans have also been established in many universities. Arab American intellectuals have contributed in a number of ways to academic organizations that serve both students and graduates; these have developed over several decades, and many remain active as new organizations have emerged to meet changing times. Following 9/11, Arab Americans faced dramatically increased discrimination at schools and universities. In particular, centers for Middle East studies, as well as professors, have been scrutinized and attacked on a regular basis. Arab American scholars and intellectuals have been combating stereotyping of Arab Americans for a long time but their efforts and those of Arab and Muslim student organizations have intensified. The need to educate Americans about the Arab world and Arab Americans also goes on outside of institutions of higher learning; many Arab American organizations have played a vital role through their educational outreach programs that are being used in a variety of learning environments.

Chapter 6, "Professional Life," investigates the expansion of Arab American contributions to the American economy and workforce. At the turn of the 20th century, early Arab American immigrants had little formal education and usually found employment as unskilled laborers or as self-employed peddlers or grocery store owners. Today Arab Americans are found in virtually every profession in America. Arab American culture has a strong propensity toward education and entrepreneurship; compared to the general population, Arab Americans are highly educated and are frequently business owners. Business interests range from small businesses to nationwide firms and multinational corporations. In places with significant Arab American populations such as southeastern Michigan, the professional lives of Arab Americans have a positive effect on the local economy, creating jobs and increasing consumer spending.

Chapter 7, "Public and Political Life," is a retrospective on Arab American participation in politics, both as individual citizens and advocates and as collective groups seeking to influence public policy related to Arab Americans and the Arab world. The chapter traces the development of the Arab American voice in public affairs, including those Arab Americans who hold public office at a variety of levels, local, state, and national, or who serve in the U.S. military. Arab American political organizations have been a key factor in galvanizing the political aspirations of Arab Americans, providing an avenue for political action on a wide range of issues, but particularly with regard to conflict in their Arab home countries and countering anti-Arab discrimination in America. Arab Americans are a diverse group in terms of political affiliation, and the scope of their involvement in the political and public spheres indicates a deep investment in the American political system.

Chapter 8, "The Arts," defines Arab American art and explains how an actual art movement came together around the shared interest of artists in defining for themselves and for their audiences what it means to be Arab American. Arab American artists create work in a wide range of artistic mediums, but a number of recurrent themes that reflect Arab American life can be identified: family, migration, cross-cultural identity, and homeland, as well as American values, ideals, and concerns. Some artists have even used their art as a form of activism in response to the political landscape. Arab American art has moved into the mainstream and has become a conduit for understanding the Arab world and Arab American life, connecting the artists that create it, the audience that participates in it, and the subject of the art created.

The 21st century has been a dynamic time for Arab Americans. During this period, they mourned as the lives of their fellow Americans, family members, or friends were destroyed in the 9/11 attacks. Arab Americans watched with despair as political instability and violent conflict destroyed the lives of Iraqis, Lebanese, and Palestinians, and as many other Arab countries were impacted by the U.S.-led War on Terror. Not unlike other minority or immigrant groups, Arab Americans have historically faced some prejudice and discrimination in America, but the terrorism on 9/11 caused unprecedented fear and backlash. While much of this book speaks to the challenges that Arab Americans have faced in many facets of their lives amid the political landscape of the 9/11 aftermath, it also shows that Arab American individuals, leaders, and organizations have met these obstacles with a positive response by working toward combating stereotypes. In this effort, they were helped along by non-Arab individuals, organizations, and sometimes government offices that worked in cooperation to protect the civil liberties of Arab Americans.

Today, Arab Americans continue to be a vibrant part of American life and culture. Arab Americans persist in immigrating to the United States to seek the American Dream. They support institutions that combat discrimination and believe in their right to enjoy the freedoms and rights of American citizenship. They maintain strong family bonds and connections and live a hybrid family culture forged through combining traditions from their Arab home countries and newfound American ways. They practice their religion and build social networks with fellow worshipers. They devote themselves to obtaining a good education. They work hard, often in family businesses when they first arrive, and then grow their businesses or their professional careers, contributing to the American economy. They participate in public and political life by voting, being politically active, running for office, or joining the military. They create and patronize art that reflects who they truly are. Despite the obstacles, Arab American life and culture today is flourishing and remains a rich component of the American mosaic.

NOTE

1. Joanne Kadi, *Food for Our Grandmothers: Writings by Arab-American and Arab-Canadian Feminists* (Boston: South End Press, 1999), xviii.

CHRONOLOGY

1528	The first recorded arrival of an Arab on the North American continent, a slave from Morocco.
1875	Arab immigration to the United States in significant numbers begins.
1880s	The "Age of Peddling," through which many Arab immigrants make a living, begins.
1890s	The first Arab Christian churches are built in New York City.
1892	The first Arabic-language newspaper in the United States, *Kawkab Amrika* (*Star of America*), begins publication.
1899	The U.S. Bureau of Immigration acknowledges that most of the increasing flow of "Turks from Asia" are actually Arabs from Syria and adds the classification "Syrian" to its records.
1911	Ameen Rihani publishes *The Book of Khalid*, the first Arab American novel.
1920	An Arab American writers group called the Pen League is founded in New York City.
1920s	Rudolph Valentino's role in *The Sheik* is the first major Hollywood portrayal of an Arab character; the movie promotes stereotypes by distorting Arab culture.

1923	The first Arab mosque is built in Highland Park, Michigan.
1924	The Johnson-Reed Quota Act is passed, setting a limit on the numbers of immigrants entering the United States from certain countries. Each Arab country received a maximum quota of 100 new immigrants per year.
1931	The Southern Syrian and Lebanese American Clubs are founded.
1936	Palestinians hold a six-month strike in Palestine protesting British support of the creation of a Jewish state in what they considered their own country. For the first time the number of Palestinian immigrants to the United States exceeds the number of Syrians and Lebanese.
1937	*History of the Arabs* by Philip Hitti is published.
1948	The state of Israel is established in part of historic Palestine, resulting in a large number of Palestinian refugees immigrating to the United States.
1952	The first Federation of Islamic Associations is founded and calls on Muslim communities in North America to organize themselves into local associations to administer to their members' religious needs.
1953	The U.S. Congress passes a special law allowing more Palestinian refugees to settle in the United States.
1950s–1960s	Significant numbers of highly educated Arab immigrants arrive in the United States, causing a brain drain in the Arab world; this migration phenomenon occurs when the most educated leave their developing countries of origin and move to more affluent countries.
1957	American Lebanese Syrian Associated Charities (ALSAC) is formed, becoming the exclusive fundraising organization of St. Jude Children's Hospital; ALSAC is currently the third-largest health care–related charity in the United States.
1965	The Hart-Cellar Act, also known as the Immigration Act of 1965, is passed, removing immigration quotas based on country of origin, revitalizing Arab immigration.
1967	War erupts between Israel and the surrounding Arab countries, resulting in the Israeli occupation of the Palestinian territories of East Jerusalem, the West Bank, and the Gaza

Strip. This prompts another wave of Palestinian immigration to the United States.

The Association of Arab-American University Graduates (AAUG) is formed to foster better understanding between the Arab and American peoples.

1972   The Arab Community Center for Economic and Social Services (ACCESS) is founded in Dearborn, Michigan, in order to help the newly arrived Arab immigrants adjust to their new life in the United States.

1973   Nagi Diafullah, a young Yemeni American, is killed while participating in a United Farm Workers (UFW) protest.

The National Association of Arab Americans (NAAA) is formed to encourage Arab Americans to participate in political life.

1975   Civil war breaks out in Lebanon, greatly increasing the number of Lebanese immigrants to the United States.

1980   The American-Arab Anti-Discrimination Committee (ADC) is founded by U.S. Senator James Abourezk to fight discrimination against Arab Americans.

1985   Alexander Michel Odeh, the Western Regional Director of the American-Arab Anti-Discrimination Committee (ADC), is killed in his office in California after a bomb explodes.

The Arab American Institute (AAI) is formed to encourage the participation of Arab Americans in electoral politics.

1987   In *St. Francis College v. Al-Khazraji*, 481 U.S. 604, Arab Americans win acknowledgment from the Supreme Court that they are protected, under existing U.S. civil rights legislation, from discrimination based on ethnicity.

The American Task Force for Lebanon (ATFL) emerges as part of the National Association of Arab Americans.

1988   The Arab Network of America (ANA) begins operation as a national radio broadcast.

1991   The U.S.-led military coalition launches the Gulf War to remove the invading Iraqi army from Kuwait and swiftly defeats the Iraqi forces. A crackdown by Saddam Hussein against Shi'a rebels in Iraq and the eviction of Palestinians by the restored Kuwaiti government prompts a new wave of Iraqi and Palestinian immigrants to the United States.

Arab Network of America (ANA) TV is launched.

1992 American Arab Chamber of Commerce is formed to better serve the Arab American business communities.

1995 Bill Clinton sends an Arab American, former U.S. Senator George Mitchell, to act as a special envoy to facilitate peace talks in Ireland. Mitchell acts as a mediator between the involved parties and succeeds in reaching a peace treaty that brings a long war to a conclusion. Mitchell receives the Presidential Medal of Freedom, the highest civilian honor in the United States.

1996 Ralph Nader, an Arab American, runs for president in the first of his four presidential campaigns.

The U. S. Congress passes the Illegal Immigration Reform and Immigrant Responsibility Act of 1996 and the Antiterrorism and Effective Death Penalty Act of 1996. These laws, implemented almost exclusively against Arabs and Arab Americans, allow secret evidence to be used against immigrants and foreign visitors for purposes of deportation.

The Federal Aviation Administration (FAA) institutes a profiling system that describes Arabs and Arab Americans as persons likely to commit acts of terrorism.

2001 On September 11, 19 terrorists from Arab countries hijack American commercial jetliners and attack the World Trade Center and the Pentagon, killing almost 3,000 victims and prompting the U.S.-led War on Terror.

The USA PATRIOT Act is passed and the U.S. Transportation Security Administration (TSA) is established to identify passengers on public transportation systems who may be a threat to national security.

The Association of Patriotic Arab Americans in the Military (APAAM) is formed to recognize the thousands of Americans of Arab descent who have served in the U.S. military.

2001–2002 By order of Attorney General John Ashcroft, 2,000 Arabs and/or Muslims are arrested by the Federal Bureau of Investigation and Immigration and Naturalization Service and detained in state and county jails. A later review by the Justice Department's Office of the Inspector General verifies the abuses suffered during these detentions. Not one person was found to have anything to do with terrorism or 9/11.

2002   National Security Entry/Exit Registration System (NSEERS) is implemented to monitor aliens from 26 Muslim and Arab countries and the non-Muslim country of North Korea upon arrival in and departure from the United States.

2004   The National Network for Arab American Communities (NNAAC) is founded to enhance the effectiveness of local organizations, many formed since 2001, that serve Arab immigrants.

2005   The Arab American National Museum, the only museum in the United States dedicated to documenting, preserving, and presenting to the public the history, culture, and contributions of Arab Americans, is established in Dearborn, Michigan.

2006   The Center for Arab American Philanthropy (CAAP) is formed to harness the collective power of Arab American giving and strengthen the voice of the community in American civil society.

2009   Two Arab Americans are appointed to the Obama administration, George Mitchell, as Special Envoy to the Middle East, and Ray LaHood, as Secretary of Transportation.

2010   Public controversy erupts over the so-called Ground Zero Mosque, a plan to construct a Muslim community center two blocks from the former site of the World Trade Center in Lower Manhattan. The site is also historically known as Little Syria; a vibrant neighborhood where Syrian and Lebanese immigrants settled in the early 1900s.

Lebanese American Rima Fakih of Dearborn, Michigan, wins the title of Miss USA during an international TV broadcast. She is both the first Muslim and the first woman of Arab American descent to wear that crown.

2011   U.S. representative Peter T. King (R-NY), chairman of the House Homeland Security Committee, holds public hearings on the national security threat he claims is posed by the radicalization of young Muslim Americans. Many Americans, Muslim and non-Muslims alike, protest the hearing as an unjust witch-hunt, infringing on the civil rights of all Americans.

The New York State Supreme Court dismisses a lawsuit filed by the American Center for Law and Justice in an effort to prevent the construction of the so-called Ground Zero Mosque.

The centennial of the Arab American novel—*The Book of Khalid* by Ameen Rihani—is celebrated by www.project khalid.org and the Arab American National Museum. The 10th anniversary of the September 11, 2001, attacks is observed.

1

ARAB AMERICAN IMMIGRATION

Anan Ameri

The United States is a country of immigrants, and that is what makes it unique, innovative, prosperous, and in constant renewal. With the exception of the Native Americans who inhabited the land before the arrival of Europeans and the African Americans who came as slaves, all Americans or their ancestors chose to immigrate. Immigration is an extremely difficult process. People leave their country, where they are familiar with the language and culture and have an extended circle of family and friends, and arrive in a new, very different place. They have to learn a new language, adjust to a new culture and physical environment, and live in isolation until they find employment and start making friends. They may face economic hardship or encounter prejudice and discrimination. Why, then, have millions upon millions of people migrated throughout history to face the difficulties of beginning a new life?

Two factors prompt people to relocate, whether transnationally or by moving within their own country, for example, from rural to urban areas: the pull factor is whatever attracts people to the country to which they immigrate and the push factor is the situation in the immigrants' hometown or country of origin that inspires them to leave. Examples of pull factors are the availability of better jobs, better pay, education, health services, freedom, and democracy.

Examples of push factors are poverty, war, discrimination, and lack of public services. Throughout history, immigrants have been pushed away from their countries by war, famine, or discrimination and pulled toward other countries, including the United States, by economic opportunity, political stability, and the promise of a better life. These dynamics have certainly been the impetus for Arab American immigrants to leave their Arab homeland and come to America.

Despite the promise of a better future, immigrants to the United States face many challenges beyond making a new life in a new land. Typically, whenever the U.S. economy suffers from a recession or depression, there is a rise in anti-immigrant rhetoric and an increase in popular demands for immigration reform or for banning immigration altogether. Anti-immigrant sentiment peaked after World War II (1914–1918) and during the Great Depression of the 1930s, and made a resurgence during the most recent economic recession (2007–2010). The tragic events of September 11, 2001, also increased anti-immigrant attitudes, especially toward Arab and Muslim immigrants.

Arab Americans trace their roots to one of the 22 countries, half in Africa and half in west Asia, that make up the Arab world. Like people from other parts of the world, Arab immigrants came to the United States to pursue a better life for themselves and their families. Some came with the intention of making the United States their permanent home country; others planned to stay for only a short period, either to make money or get a higher education before returning home, but later decided to become residents. Today it is estimated that there are 4.2 million Arab Americans in the United States. They live in every state, and while some reside in small towns, the majority live in major metropolitan areas such as Chicago, Detroit, Houston, Los Angeles, New York, and Washington, D.C.

What makes Arab immigration interesting and distinct from other ethnic groups is that Arab Americans do not trace their ancestry to one nation, as do Italian Americans or Irish Americans. Another distinction is that Arab immigration to the United States has occurred in many waves rather than within a single, short period of time, as, for example, in the decades following the revolutions of 1848, when Western Europeans fled to the United States to escape the turmoil, or as the result of one distinct event, such as the Irish potato famine. There have been three distinct waves of Arab immigration: the first during the period known as the Great Migration

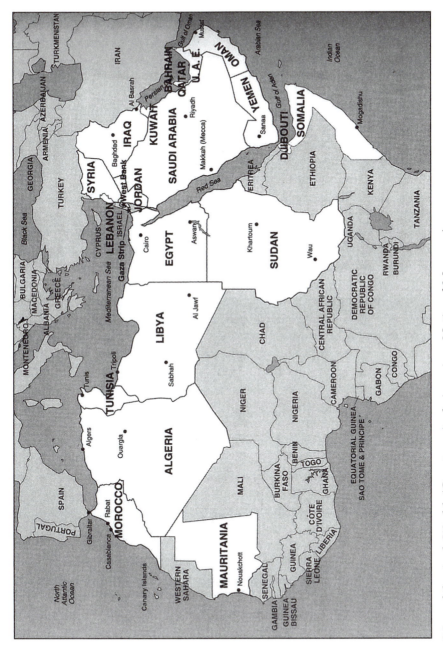

Map of the Arab World. (Courtesy Arab American National Museum)

(1880–1924), the second wave during the 1950s and 1960s, and the third or current wave, which started in the 1970s and continues today.

THE EARLY ARRIVALS

Contrary to the widely held perception that they are mostly new immigrants, Arab Americans have been part of the fabric of American society since its inception. However, until the Great Migration, their numbers were relatively small, and they arrived sporadically. Some early Arab immigrants came voluntarily while others were brought to America as slaves.

It is hard to estimate the number of slaves who came from Arab countries, but records indicate that there were some who traced their ancestry to Arab countries. At least one document refers to the arrival in 1717 of Arabic-speaking Muslim slaves who would not eat pork.[1] But since all slaves were given new names by their captors or owners, it is very difficult to trace these slaves to their original families or hometowns.

The first documented Arab to come to North America arrived in 1528 as a slave and is known both by his Arabic name, Al-Zammouri, a reference to Zammour, his hometown in the North African country of Morocco, and as Estebanico, the Spanish name given to him by his Portuguese captors. (Since Morocco is both an Arab and an African nation, African Americans also claim Zammouri as the first African to arrive in the United States.) Zammouri's ship was wrecked in the Gulf of Mexico, and he managed to flee with a few other slaves. Between 1528 and 1536, Zammouri traveled more than 6,000 miles on the North American continent and is recognized by historians for his contributions to the exploration of the Southwest. The city of El Paso commissioned artist John Houser to create a statue honoring him.[2] Another Arabic-speaking slave, who was trained to read the Qur'an in Arabic before he arrived in the United States, was Omar Ibn Said. Ibn Said was owned by John Owen, an early governor of North Carolina who later decided to free him.[3] After he died, Ibn Said was buried in the Owen family plot. The existence of another slave, Ben Ali, is also well documented. Under circumstances that are unclear, he became a scout for the famous general Thomas Sumter during the Revolutionary War. Ben Ali changed his family name to Benenhaly and his sons later fought with the Confederate Army in the Civil War.[4]

During the late 1700s the South Carolina House of Representatives ruled that Moroccan Arabs should be treated according to the same laws governing whites.[5] This acknowledgment of the presence of Moroccan Arabs in a court document clearly indicates that there were enough Arabs in South Carolina at the time to warrant such a decision.

TRADE AND RELIGION

The invention of the steamship in the 1800s led to dramatically increased interaction between the Arab world and the United States, as it became much easier for tourists to visit the Christian "Holy Land" and for Christian missionaries, following in the footsteps of their European predecessors, to travel to, and settle in, the Arab world, where they opened their own churches and church-affiliated schools. The American University of Beirut, founded in 1866, and the Friends School in Ramallah, Palestine, founded by the Quakers in 1918, are among the most important schools that U.S. missionaries established in the Arab world. Many Arabs, especially those who were Christians, first learned about the United States from these missionaries, and soon the flow of travel moved in the other direction as Arabs began to visit the United States and then to emigrate.[6]

Another factor that prompted Arabs to migrate to the United States was the desire to pursue business and trade. The famous 1876 Philadelphia Centennial Exposition and the 1893 Chicago Exposition invited countries from around the world to exhibit their products and attracted a number of Arab merchants and entrepreneurs from Egypt, Syria, Lebanon, Morocco, Tunisia, and Algeria. Recognizing a great opportunity to break into the new and rich U.S. market, Arabs enthusiastically participated in these world fairs. They brought their best products and luxury items and many of them ended up settling in the United States.[7]

THE GREAT MIGRATION (1880–1924)

During the Great Migration period, an estimated 20 million immigrants from around the globe came to the United States seeking the American Dream. Over the course of these four decades, as the United States sought to industrialize its agrarian economy, America's need for labor sharply increased. Workers were needed to build the infrastructure—bridges, roads, and railroads—to support this transformation and to work in coal mines, steel mills, and other rapidly expanding U.S. industries. The U.S. government was also looking for people to homestead the vast terrain of the West, where such isolated areas as the Dakotas had rich agricultural land but severe weather and scarce population.

It is estimated that during the Great Migration, some 95,000 to 100,000 Arab immigrants arrived in the United States, the majority of whom came through New York or Boston.[8] Prior to 1924, the United States had a relatively open-door immigration policy. Immigrants did not need to make an application or have an immigrant visa before they came to the United States, and, provided that on arrival they were healthy, they would be allowed to enter. Depending on the severity of their situation, individuals with health-related problems would either be placed temporarily in a medical facility that was part of the immigration center or would be sent back to their country of origin. Those who were not allowed entry were devastated. They had traveled for a long time over great distances, and many had no doubt incurred some debt in their country of origin by borrowing money to help them travel and start a new life.

Some Arab immigrants who were sent back home ended up going to countries in Central and South America that had much less restrictive immigration laws. While some of these immigrants settled permanently in Latin America, others ultimately found their way to the United States. By the early 1900s, many Arabs were coming to Texas via Mexico. The El Paso city directories at that time listed many individuals with Spanish first names and Arabic last names. The number of Arab immigrants prompted the El Paso Immigration Service to hire two Syrian interpreters, Salim Mattar and Esau Malooly.[9]

The last years of the 19th century and the early years of the 20th were years of hardship in the Arab world. The majority of Arabs were then subjects of the Ottoman Empire, which practiced political repression and was characterized by economic instability. A major player in World War I, the empire suffered widespread famine and poverty in the aftermath. Additionally, around the turn of the century, the silk and vineyard industries in what is now Lebanon began to collapse. All of these factors contributed to a surge in Arab migration to the United States.[10]

During the Great Migration period, the majority of Arab immigrants came from what was known at the time as Greater Syria, which included present-day Syria, Lebanon, Jordan, Palestine, and

Bachara Kalil (B.K.) Forzley and family, immigrants from Karhoun, Lebanon. Relatives already living in the United States helped Forzley when he came to America to find work to support his family back home; in turn he did the same for newcomers. This phenomenon is called "chain migration." (Courtesy Arab American National Museum)

Israel. The immigrants were mostly peasants, Christian men with very little formal education.[11] They came with the intention of working for a few years, making money, and returning to their home country. They settled in New York, Boston, and Detroit, where the textile and automotive industries promised employment. Some settled in Chicago and Pennsylvania to work in the meatpacking or steel industries, and others homesteaded in South Dakota. Many Arab immigrants also worked as peddlers, moving from town to town and to remote farms, selling their products in areas that were not served by stores. As these peddlers made more money, many of them brought their families to join them; some went back to their country of origin to marry and returned with their wives.

There were, of course, immigrants who arrived from other areas. By 1890, a small number of Yemeni immigrants had settled in the

United States; a few of them even served in the U.S. Army during World War I.[12] A small number of Iraqi Chaldeans immigrated to the United States as early as 1910. The Chaldeans followed in the footsteps of Syrian and Lebanese immigrants, becoming peddlers and opening stores in cities like Detroit and San Diego. Today, both metropolitan areas are home to sizable Chaldean communities. A few immigrants also arrived from Sudan during this period.[13]

While early Arab immigrants were mostly men, of Arab immigrants who arrived before 1899, 27 percent were women, and by the end of the Great Migration, the number was almost 50 percent,[14] a much higher percentage than other ethnic groups arriving at the time. Some women came to the United States to join their husbands. Some came alone to join a relative after hearing about the availability of jobs for both men and women. Most of the women who came knew a relative or a friend who could help them upon arrival.[15]

The majority of Arab immigrants who came during the Great Migration had little formal education. A few, however, had already acquired a high level of education before arriving in the United States. Among the very early Arab immigrants to arrive with the intention of staying to become U.S. citizens were the Arbeelys, who came from Damascus, Syria. Dr. Joseph Arbeely immigrated to New York in 1878 with his wife, six sons, and niece.[16] Because of his higher education and the status associated with medical doctors, the family was welcomed in America, and their pictures and an announcement of their arrival appeared in a New York paper. One son, Najeeb Arbeely, was later hired as a facilitator and interpreter for the growing number of Arab immigrants who were arriving at Ellis Island. Najeeb, along with his brother Ibrahim, established the first Arabic newspaper in America, the *Star of America,* in 1892.[17] By 1907, the number of Arab American newspapers had reached 21, and by 1930 the number had increased to 50. As early as 1911, writer Ameen Rihani published the first Arab Amer-

---

THE *TITANIC*

When the *Titanic* struck an iceberg while crossing the Atlantic in 1912, there were 154 Arabs on board. Of this number 4 men, 5 children, and 20 women survived the wreck. More than half of the crew and passengers died.

ican novel, *The Book of Khalid*. By 1920, there was a relatively large community of Arab American writers, poets, and scholars in New York City, a group of whom established the Pen League.[18] Among the founding members of the Pen League was Kahlil Gibran; his famous book *The Prophet* was published in 1923.

NUMBER OF ARAB IMMIGRANTS

Although it is impossible to know their exact number because of lack of records, it is estimated that by the end of the Great Migration 200,000 Arab immigrants had settled in the United States.[19] The original New York point of entry for immigrants was Castle Garden. Between the time Castle Garden opened in 1855 and when it closed in 1890 more than 8 million immigrants were processed there. All Castle Garden records were destroyed by fire, including those of Arab immigrants. Only a few immigrant arrivals from that period are documented, either in stories that were passed down and recorded by family members, articles that appeared in newspapers such as the one about the Arbeely family mentioned earlier, or in other public records.

Because of the classification system used by U.S. Customs officers, accurate records of the number of Arab immigrants are hard to find even for the period after Ellis Island was established in 1892. Since most Arab immigrants came from Syrian and Lebanon, which are located in the furthest-west part of Asia, they were often classified as Asian. In other cases, because they came from regions that were at the time ruled by the Ottoman Empire, many Arab immigrants were classified as Ottomans, a group that also included Turks and other non-Arabs. Further complicating matters is the fact that Arab physical features did not fit any of the race categories then in use (white, black, or yellow). As a consequence, their classification was often arbitrarily, and confusingly, decided by the immigration officers at their point of entry and many Arab immigrants who came to the United States via Mexico were classified as either Spanish or Mexican.[20]

THE END OF THE OPEN IMMIGRATION ERA

The large number of immigrants who came to the United States during the Great Migration, coupled with a slowdown of the economy during World War I (1914–1918), generated an increase in anti-immigrant sentiments. Immigrants were portrayed as having inferior cultures and blamed for taking jobs from "real Americans." This anti-immigrant rhetoric and the political pressure exerted mostly by European Americans, who had arrived earlier and were much more established and influential, led the government to pass a number of laws between 1917 and 1924 that restricted immigration from most parts of the world other than northern and western European countries.[21]

THE SECOND WAVE (1950s–1960s)

Between the end of the Great Migration in 1924, and the end of World War II in 1945, the restrictive immigration laws allowed non-European immigrants to come to the United States only in very limited numbers. This drastic slowdown of immigration ended after World War II (1939–1945), when the destruction in European countries that had previously dominated the world, such as England, France, and Germany, seriously diminished their economic and political power. While the United States played a major role, through its Marshall Plan, in rebuilding Europe, it also moved quickly to take advantage of its historic opportunity to replace the Europeans and emerge as the new superpower. In order to take advantage of the expanding international market, the United States needed to quickly transform its economy from one of wartime production to one of industrial growth by drastically increasing the production of consumer goods.

The transformation of the U.S. economy required certain skills that were not readily available. Without officially changing any of the restrictive immigration laws, the government, along with major industrial companies, began to actively recruit highly educated professionals from around the world, including scientists and engineers, to help rebuild and expand the U.S. economy.

THE BRAIN DRAIN

The phenomenon that occurs when the most educated and talented people, attracted by a higher standard of living, leave their countries of origin to work in Europe or the United States is known as the "brain drain."

Between 1950 and 1960, immigration from Arab countries resumed, but the new immigrants were very different from those
who came during the Great Migration. Earlier immigrants were
mostly from Christian Lebanese and Syrian villages and had little
formal education, but the new wave included professionals who
had already acquired a high level of education in the Arab world
and students who came to study in U.S. universities. These new
immigrants were both Muslim and Christian and came from a
wider range of Arab countries that included not only Syria, Lebanon, and Palestine but also Egypt and Iraq. These immigrants were
from upper- and upper-middle-class backgrounds and came from
large cosmopolitan urban centers, such as Damascus, Beirut, and
Cairo; almost all of them spoke fluent English and some also spoke
fluent French. Many Arab countries started to send their students
to study at U.S. universities. Most of these students came from
Syria, Palestine, Jordan, Egypt, Iraq, and Lebanon. A large number,
especially those in scientific fields, were later recruited by American companies, were offered high-paying jobs, and ended up staying in the United States and acquiring citizenship. Additionally,
since the 1950s a contingent of Arab students who come to study at
United States universities, particularly from the oil-rich countries
of Saudi Arabia, Bahrain, Qatar, Oman, and the United Arab Emirates, return to their countries to work and live. Attracted by the
high standards of living in Saudi Arabia and the Gulf States, these
students prefer to return to their home countries, where they can
easily find high-paying jobs.

Most Arab immigrants who came during the Great Migration
initially lived in poor housing located in neighborhoods populated
by other immigrants like themselves, which are also known as ethnic enclaves. However, most of the professional Arab immigrants
who arrived in the 1950s and 1960s settled in affluent suburban
neighborhoods where they assimilated easily. Another difference
is that unlike the earlier wave of immigrants, who identified most
strongly with the village or the country they came from, this later
group had a much stronger Arab identity. They arrived in the United
States at a time when most Arab countries had recently gained their
independence from Britain and France, and Arab nationalism and
the growing drive for Arab unity were dominant forces. While it
was much easier for this group to assimilate, they nevertheless
played a very significant role in reviving the Arab ethnic identity of
the immigrants who had arrived before them. They played important roles in mobilizing Arab Americans to become more politically

active, both domestically and in the arena of international politics. This wave of immigrants was instrumental in establishing a number of Arab American organizations. In 1967, they established the Association of Arab-American University Graduates, the first "hyphenated" Arab American organization; many more such organizations were established in the 1970s and 1980s.

Palestinian immigration to the United States has been historically tied to the Palestinian-Israeli conflict. After World War I, Palestine was colonized by the British, who had promised to help the Jews create a homeland in the region. This promise increased Jewish migration to Palestine and gave rise to increased conflict between Palestinians, British occupying forces, and the Jewish immigrants. During the 1930s, when conflict reached its peak, and especially during the six-month Palestinian strike in 1936, the number of Palestinian immigrants to the United States exceeded those coming from Syria and Lebanon.[22] The creation of the state of Israel in 1948 resulted in the displacement of a large number of Palestinians, estimated by the United Nations at between 726,000 and 914,000. The majority of these refugees settled in the neighboring countries of Lebanon, Syria, and Jordan. Some immigrated to European countries, Australia, and Canada, while others came to the United States to join relatives who had immigrated before them. Two things gave further impetus to Palestinian immigration. First, Palestinians who had a high level of education were sometimes recruited by the U.S. government or corporations, and second, in 1953, prompted by the Palestinian refugee crisis, the U.S. Congress passed the Refugee Relief Act. This act allowed 2,000 Palestinian families to immigrate immediately, with another 985 families allowed entry between 1958 and 1963.[23] Many extended family members of these refugees followed in their footsteps.

Another major influence on the course of Arab immigration to the United States during this period was a by-product of the American civil rights movement. The U.S. immigration laws that drastically limited the number of non-European immigrants were viewed as discriminatory because they favored white Europeans over people of color. Pressure from civil rights activists, led by Dr. Martin Luther King Jr., resulted in the abolition of immigration laws based on race or ethnicity. More specifically, the Immigration Act of 1965, also known as the Hart-Cellar Act,[24] ended all immigration limitations based on national origin. This law opened the door to millions of people from around the world, including Arab immigrants.

THE THIRD AND LATEST WAVE
(1970s TO THE PRESENT)

Immigration from Arab countries, which began to increase rapidly in the early 1970s, continues to the present day. As a group, immigrants during this period show a high level of diversity in terms of national origin, religious affiliation, and educational and professional backgrounds, making it difficult to discuss them as a single entity. Some come from countries like Syria, Lebanon, Yemen, and Palestine, following in the footsteps of earlier Arab immigrants, others from countries whose people have not in the past immigrated to the United States in any significant numbers, such as Morocco, Tunisia, Sudan, and Somalia. What distinguishes this particular wave of immigration is the high percentage of people who came from areas devastated by war—Iraq, Palestine, Lebanon, Yemen, Somalia, and Sudan. Unlike earlier immigrants who came from rural backgrounds and had limited formal education, many of the newly arrived immigrants come from urban areas, are highly educated, and possess entrepreneurial skills.[25] A significant number of these highly educated professionals have emigrated from Syria and Egypt, and many of them are in the medical field. The National Arab American Medical Association (NAMA), headquartered in Michigan, has 24 chapters and thousands of members,[26] many of whom have arrived here since the mid-1960s.

The number of Yemeni immigrants increased rapidly after the abolishment of the quota system in 1965. Many Yemenis have worked on farms in California, in automobile factories in Detroit, and in steel plants in Buffalo, New York. Others have opened small businesses. The number of younger-generation Yemeni professionals is increasing rapidly.[27] Interestingly enough, in the years right after World War II, many Yemenis came to the United States from Vietnam, where they worked in a variety of jobs. At the time, it was much easier to get an immigrant visa to allow entry to the United States in Vietnam than in Yemen.

War Refugees

In 1967, tensions between Israel and neighboring Arab countries culminated in a war that resulted in the Israeli occupation of the Palestinian territories of East Jerusalem, the West Bank, and the Gaza Strip as well as the Golan Heights in Syria and the Sinai Peninsula in Egypt. The 1967 War generated 300,000 Palestinian refugees, most of whom settled in Jordan and other Arab countries, although several thousand immigrated to the United States. The continued occupation of Palestinian territories and the lack of a peaceful resolution to the Palestinian-Israeli conflict has created an uninterrupted flow of Palestinian immigration. Today, large Palestinian communities are found in the New York (Brooklyn), Chicago, Detroit, Los Angeles, and San Francisco metropolitan areas. The largest single Palestinian group comes from the West Bank city of Ramallah; thousands of former residents inhabit almost every major U.S. city.

Lebanon is another Arab country that has had its share of civil strife, war, and political unrest. A 17-year-long civil war erupted in 1975 and was followed by the 1982 Israeli invasion, which resulted in the occupation of the southern part of the country until 1997. During these years, many Lebanese families left to seek a more secure and safe life in Europe, Australia, Canada, and the United States. While most earlier Lebanese immigrants were Christians, this time the majority, especially those who came from areas occupied by Israel, are Muslim.[28] Many of these immigrants, like the Palestinians, come from urban, middle-class areas, and a high percentage are entrepreneurs or trained professionals. Some of the Lebanese university students who were in the United States during the war decided to stay. Today, a large number of Lebanese immigrants are found in most major urban centers; many come from the same extended families and villages and form their own clubs and associations. For example, in Dearborn, Michigan, thousands of people came from the southern town of Bint Jbeil. Other local families like the Bazzis and the Berrys include hundreds of members, of whom some are newly arrived immigrants, while others came during the Great Migration.

Iraqi Refugees

Iraq, long known as the Cradle of Civilization, is a rich country. Throughout history, its people have enjoyed a relatively high standard of living and therefore did not migrate in any significant number to the United States or to any other part of the world. Before the first U.S.-led Gulf War in 1991, the size of the Iraqi community in the United States was rather small.

But over the last few decades, Iraqis have been subjected to extremely destructive wars and political repression. The long period of Saddam Hussein's regime; a 10-year war between Iraq and Iran in the 1980s; the 1991 Gulf War followed by 12 years of international economic sanctions against Iraq; and the 2003 U.S.-led Iraq War have had a devastating effect on Iraqi civilians. Millions of Iraqis have left the country; the majority of them have resettled in neighboring Arab countries, others went to Europe, and a smaller number have come to the United States. As the impact of these wars continues, so does the daily arrival of new Iraqi refugees. Sizeable Iraqi communities have emerged in major metropolitan areas such as Detroit, New York, and Phoenix.

New Communities

In the past, very few immigrants from Sudan or Somalia came to the United States. However, since the early 1990s, as a result of the civil wars that have devastated these countries, immigrants from these regions have started to arrive. Today small Sudanese communities have been established in New York and Washington, D.C., and Somali communities are emerging in the Midwest, especially in the twin cities of Minneapolis and St. Paul, Minnesota. A few Somalis have settled in Washington, New York, and Boston.

Immigration to the United States from the North African Arab countries of Tunisia, Algeria, and Morocco is also relatively new. Previously, people from these countries have most often migrated to Europe, especially France, given that country's relative geographical proximity as well as the historic ties to this region through French colonization, which resulted in familiarity of the North African population with the French language. By the late 1960s, however, immigrants from North Africa, especially from Morocco, started to arrive in the United States. Some came as students, found jobs, and decided to stay; others came as immigrants and settled in major cities like New York, Washington, D.C., Los Angeles, and Boston. Immigrants from North Africa's Sudan and Somalia tend to be diverse in their socioeconomic backgrounds; some are professionals, while others lack higher education and are of a working-class background.

ETHNIC ENCLAVES

Ethnic enclaves play an important role in the lives of new immigrants, helping them adjust easily to life in a country whose culture and language is different from their own, providing employment in businesses usually owned by someone from their extended family, hometown, or country of origin, and providing certain bilingual services, such as job training and translation, that are not usually available outside the neighborhood.

While most ethnic enclaves are based on national background, as are Polish, Italian, or Greek neighborhoods, some, like Jewish neighborhoods, are based on religion and cultural heritage. In some cases these neighborhoods might include immigrants from a number of countries that have a shared language or culture, such as Latin Americans or Arab Americans. Ethnic enclaves have historically been an integral part of the social fabric of the United States, especially in major metropolitan areas, easing the transition for new immigrants who feel the need to live with people who share their language and culture. During the early immigration periods, especially the Great Migration, a large number of ethnic enclaves were established in the inner cities of the immigrants' port of entry. Many of these, like Little Italy in Boston, Chinatown in San Francisco, and Greektown in Detroit, still exist. Ethnic enclaves for more recent immigrants are found mostly in major metropolitan areas, but some are also being established in the suburbs.

Over time, as immigrants' children and grandchildren become assimilated and affluent, and start to marry outside their own group, they do not feel the same need to live with people from their own ethnic background. The original ethnic neighborhoods then become home to new groups of immigrants. This process has occurred throughout the United States, as immigrant neighborhoods gradually lose their distinct ethnic flavor and become home to a more diverse population.

For new immigrants ethnic enclaves are more than just a place of residence; they also provide security, comfort, and a sense of belonging. An important aspect of the U.S. mosaic, these neighborhoods are often self-sustaining and form an important part of the economy. They provide opportunities for immigrants to establish new businesses and offer employment to new immigrants who do not speak the language or have access to transportation. Ethnic enclaves encompass many things such as stores that have immigrants' familiar ethnic food and clothing, places of worship, bilingual social services, medical clinics, pharmacies, law offices, coffee shops, youth clubs, and English-language classes. Bilingual media, including radio, television, and newspapers, are also found in these enclaves, providing new immigrants with local, national, and international news about their countries of origin and connecting them with other Arab American communities in various U.S. cities. However, with the growth of satellite television and radio and the

Internet, local ethnic media sources are becoming less relevant. Ethnic enclaves are also important assets that are often promoted by city or state governments as tourist attractions. Many second- and third-generation immigrants return to these neighborhoods to buy authentic ethnic food, as well as music, books, and films not found in mainstream stores, or to dine in the neighborhood's restaurants.

Ethnic enclaves are often created by and sustained through chain migration, the process by which a family member immigrates to a specific location and is soon followed by other immediate family members: first, brothers, sisters, parents, and children, then in-laws, and finally the relatives of in-laws. In a typical scenario, when new immigrants arrive they live temporarily with their relatives and often work in a relative's store. Once they have a steady income, they move into their own home and possibly establish their own store. The process of chain migration has contributed greatly to supporting new immigrants, as well as to establishing ethnic neighborhoods.

While most ethnic enclaves today are formed by newly arrived immigrants who voluntarily decide to live there, historically some were formed in response to discrimination. For example, in San Francisco, Chinese immigrants were not allowed to live outside Chinatown, and in Dearborn, Arab immigrants were allowed to live only in the South End. Many recent immigrants still feel unwelcome in some neighborhoods.

Arab American Ethnic Enclaves

Many of the Syrian Lebanese Christians who immigrated during the Great Migration came with an address or the name of a family member or a fellow villager who had already come to the United States and who could help them adjust to life in America. Like other immigrants at the time, Arab immigrants arrived with very little money and often lived with relatives or friends in crowded apartments. Once they managed to find their own jobs and felt more secure, they would rent their own place, usually in the same apartment building or on the same street, so gradually Syrian and Lebanese neighborhoods started to emerge in major urban centers. Among the oldest Arab American neighborhoods are the ones in Boston and New York, cities which were both points of entry for many Arab immigrants. Other immigrants resettled where they could find work, in places like Detroit, Chicago, and Cleveland,

and later sent for their family members, friends, and fellow villagers. Some started to import food and clothing from their country of origin, while others opened restaurants and coffee shops. Arab-language newspapers and institutions soon followed.

Between 1924 and the early 1970s, immigration for Arab countries to the United States was rather limited. Arab ethnic enclaves established by immigrants who came during the Great Migration started to disappear or get smaller, as their children moved to the suburbs or more affluent neighborhoods. Only a few bakeries, grocery stores, restaurants, and video or music stores survived, dependent on those who would come back to the old neighborhood to visit elderly relatives, shop, or go to a restaurant, church, or mosque.

The new wave of Arab immigration brought with it the revival and expansion of some of the older ethnic enclaves as well as the establishment of new ones. The largest and most well known is the Arab American neighborhood of Dearborn, Michigan, which is also home to the Ford Motor Company. In the early 1900s, Arab immigrants, mostly Syrian and Lebanese, started to settle in Detroit, where the rapidly growing auto industry was attracting large numbers of both Arab and non-Arab immigrants. The first Arab American enclave in Michigan was created in Highland Park, a small city bordering Detroit, when Henry Ford opened a plant there to produce the Model T. Ford's eight-hour, five-dollar workday was revolutionary at the time and enticed many Arab immigrants to move to the area. In 1917, Ford Motor Company opened its Rouge Plant, the largest industrial complex in the world, in Dearborn. Following the new plant, Arab workers and their families started to move from Highland Park to southeast Dearborn, a neighborhood close to the Ford plant, known as the South End. Initially, the neighborhood was also home to other immigrants who came to work for Ford. Gradually, Arab immigrants built their own shops, restaurants, and other businesses and services and slowly but surely established an enclave in the shadow of the Rouge Plant.

As the children of the original immigrants received a better education and moved to more affluent neighborhoods, new immigrants arrived to live in the South End enclave. Beginning in the 1960s, as even more Arab immigrants arrived, a new and larger ethnic enclave emerged in East Dearborn and over the next few decades transformed that part of Dearborn into what is locally called Arab Town. New immigrants took over abandoned buildings and renovated them, but also constructed new ones. New grocery stores,

A traditional American strip mall in Dearborn, Michigan, populated by businesses appealing to both Arabs and non-Arabs. Family-run small businesses owned by Arab Americans often provide employment opportunities for those newly arrived from the Arab World. (Marvin Asuncion II / Arab American National Museum)

bakeries, restaurants, and clothing stores opened, whose diverse ownership included Yemenis, Lebanese, Palestinians, and Iraqis. Arab American lawyers, doctors, and pharmacists began to serve clients in the area and established thriving practices. Today Arabic-language signs are found on every street, while most Dearborn schools offer bilingual education and observe Muslim holidays.

With its religious, educational, social service, and cultural institutions, Dearborn became the de facto capital of Arab Americans, attracting many new immigrants on that basis alone to this substantial and well-established community.

Arab American enclaves were also established in other major U.S. cities. Among the largest and oldest is found in New York City and was once home to Kahlil Gibran and his literary circle, who

along with other Arab American intellectuals and successful entre-
preneurs made New York a center for Arab American culture and
business. The Bay Ridge section of Brooklyn is also home to an
Arab American ethnic enclave. Like Dearborn, this neighborhood
has been passed on from earlier to more recent immigrants. Other
Arab American ethnic enclaves can be found in California's Orange
County and Los Angeles, in Chicago's South Side, and in Jersey
City, New Jersey.

Impact of 9/11

Because most of the people who live in Arab American ethnic
neighborhoods are recent immigrants and Muslims, they became
easy targets for law enforcement agencies after the tragic events
of September 11. Insecurity and fear were rampant in these communities as visits from the FBI, the Border Patrol, and Immigration
and Naturalization Service (INS) officials increased dramatically.
Media outlets from around the country flocked to these neighborhoods looking for sensational stories, which, rushed into print or
broadcast without adequate research, often destroyed innocent
people's reputations and livelihood. Writers, researchers, college
students, and filmmakers came in large numbers, eager to meet,
film, and write about Arab and Muslim Americans. Arab American
students and workers were sometimes harassed in their schools,
on the streets, or at their place of work. In this climate Arab American businesses, institutions, and places of worship came to feel
that their visibility made them easy potential targets for angry individuals who misguidedly sought revenge for the tragedy.

Immediately after 9/11 there was fear within the Arab American
community of a repeat of the Japanese internment camps. Later,
the expression "virtual camps" was coined to describe life in these
Arab ethnic neighborhoods, as intimidation, fear of the unexpected,
and self-imposed censorship became part of the everyday lives of
Arab Americans. At the same time, many non-Arabs, recognizing
the extent of the pain and fear Arab Americans were experiencing, extended their hands and expressed their solidarity with their
Arab American colleagues, friends, and neighbors. Many mayors
in cities with Arab American enclaves and other politicians were
vocal in support of their Arab American constituents. At the same
time, Arab American community leaders in these neighborhoods,
along with their educational, religious, and cultural institutions,

reached out to other Americans to provide them with opportunities to learn more about Arab American history, culture, and contributions.

9/11 and Immigration Laws

In an address to a joint session of the U.S. Congress immediately following the tragic events of 9/11, President George W. Bush stated that America was at war against the terrorists and not against a particular ethnicity or religion. These words provided a great level of comfort to the Arab American community. Unfortunately, a number of the laws passed in response to the 9/11 attacks and the government's official actions were not consistent with this message. The most of famous of these laws is the USA PATRIOT Act, which has been the focus of much discussion and concern among civil libertarians and the media. The Patriot Act was a massive expansion of government authority and power to conduct searches, use electronic surveillance, and detain suspected terrorists. Of major concern to the community and civil libertarians was the act's attempt to limit the role of the federal court in supervising the use of these new powers.

The impact of the Patriot Act is discussed in more detail in the next chapter, so the focus here is on a number of additional laws and changes in the immigration regulations and policies that significantly impacted Arab and Muslim American immigrants, who are either citizens of the United States or permanent residents, meaning they are legally in the United States waiting to become citizens. These laws additionally had a very negative impact on Arab and Muslim nonimmigrants, also called aliens, a group that includes individuals who are in the United States legally but not seeking citizenship, such as students, temporary workers, and business people, as well as undocumented immigrants.

These laws, most of which are still in effect today, allow for mass arrests, secret detentions, closed-door hearings, mandatory deportation interviews, background checks, detention at borders, and no-fly lists. Taken together they created a very strong anti-immigrant climate. They also amplified insecurity and fear in Arab American immigrant communities, especially among those who had arrived recently, whether because they felt under scrutiny themselves or because they had friends and relatives who were wrongly victimized by these new laws.

Mass Arrests and Secret Detention

Within a week of September 11, the Department of Justice (DOJ) began arresting Arab and Muslim males for questioning. The details and basis for these detentions has never been explained, the sole reason seeming to be that the individuals detained were immigrants. Approximately 1,200 men were taken from their homes, jobs, and schools and placed in local jails and prisons, with orders from the DOJ that they were to be held in secret. During their detention these individuals were routinely denied their basic constitutional right to communicate with legal counsel or family. While not officially charged, they were also subjected to both physical and emotional abuse and harassment.[29] Additionally, the DOJ issued a new regulation allowing for detention without charges for 48 hours plus an additional reasonable period of time in the event of an emergency or other extraordinary circumstance. Under this regulation, the detainees were held for weeks before being brought before an immigration judge. While the Justice Department claimed these arrests were terrorism related, most detainees were deported on minor immigration violations and none were charged with any offense related to terrorism. The majority of noncitizens detained by the government were long-term residents, business owners and taxpayers, many of whom were married to U.S. citizens and/or had American children.[30] Of the 1,200 men who were placed in deportation proceedings, many agreed to leave the country, but those who contested the detention had their rights further curtailed. In bond determination hearings in the Immigration Courts, the Immigration and Naturalization Service opposed bond in these cases. Furthermore, the DOJ issued another regulation that provided expanded detention power to the INS and allowed it to "suspend an immigration judge's decision that a detainee should be released on bond."[31]

Closed-Door Hearings

On September 21, 2001, the attorney general of the United States implemented additional security procedures for certain cases in the immigration courts requesting judges to close the hearings to the public.[32] This policy barred spouses, other family members, and the press. In the midst of these mass secret deportations hearings, the American Civil Liberties Union, U.S. congressman John Conyers Jr. (D-MI), and four Michigan newspapers brought suit to challenge the attorney general's closed-hearing policy as unconstitutional. Both the Federal District Court and the Court of Appeals ruled that the attempt by Attorney General John Ashcroft and the Justice Department to close deportation hearings was unlawful. Judge Damon Keith, in the appeals court decision, famously concluded, "Democracy dies behind closed doors."[33]

Mandatory Interviews

On November 9, 2001, Attorney General Ashcroft issued a memo requesting that 5,000 nonimmigrant Arab men, such as students, visitors, and business people, ages 18 to 33, who had entered the United States since January 2000 and who came from countries where Al Qaeda has "terrorist presence or activity," be interviewed. The interviews were said to be voluntary, but in many cases federal agents simply appeared in the early morning at people's homes or at their school and work sites and took them to the "voluntary" interview. On February 26, 2002, the DOJ issued a final report on the interviewing project. The report stated that approximately one-half of those on the list were actually interviewed and that fewer than 20 were taken into custody. Of those, most were charged with visa violations; only 3 were arrested on criminal charges, and none of these were in any way related to terrorism.[34] Despite the lack of any useful information from this program, on March 19, 2002, the DOJ announced another round of interviews of 3,000 more Arabs and Muslims who were in the United States as visitors or students.

Background Checks

On May 10, 2002, the INS issued a memo requiring INS district offices and service centers to run security checks on all those who made immigration applications and petitions, including those for naturalization. The memo requires that approval of any application should be withheld until an FBI clearance is received. The problem that arose was with the phonetic similarity of many Arabic names. For example, Muhammad is also spelled as Mohammad, Hussein as Husain, Nissreen as Nissrine. This meant that the records of one individual were often incorrectly associated with a completely different individual. Over the past eight years, thousands of applications have been put on hold, with many applicants waiting in excess of two years for resolution.

Reporting Requirements (NSEERS)

On June 13, 2002, the attorney general proposed a new requirement for all male nonimmigrants arriving from certain specified
countries. According to this proposal, individuals from these countries were deemed a potential national security risk; they were to be
interviewed and required to submit fingerprints and photographs
upon arrival in the United States. These individuals were furthermore required to report to the INS at regular intervals and notify
an INS agent of their departure from the country. On August 12,
2002, the attorney general announced the formal implementation of
this program, the National Security Entry-Exit Registration System
(NSEERS), which applies to all arriving aliens from 26 Arab and
Muslim countries, as well as North Korea.

Detention at the Border and No-Fly Lists

Following 9/11, the U.S. government developed two lists, the
no-fly list with about one thousand names and a second list that
subjects people to increased security every time they fly. Being on
the lists could result in a person being denied boarding. Even more
seriously, persons on either list, even if they are U.S. citizens, have
been arrested, handcuffed, and questioned for hours at international ports of entry. The government admits that many names
should not be on either list, but to date there is no method for re-
moving the name of an individual who poses no threat.

Operation Frontline

In 2008, the American Arab Anti-Discrimination Committee
(ADC) and Yale Law School's National Litigation Project revealed
that the office of Immigration and Customs Enforcement (ICE)
ran Operation Front Line, a secret program that began prior to
the 2004 presidential election and ran until after the inauguration
in January 2005. The program targeted immigrants from Muslim-
majority countries, which for practical purposes included immigrants from all Arab countries. In theory, Operation Front Line was
designed to "detect, deter, and disrupt terrorist operations." However, ICE records, which were released to the Yale Law School's
Lowenstein Human Rights Clinic National Litigation Project, confirmed that under Operation Front Line, ICE investigated and ar-

rested hundreds of immigrants from Muslim-majority countries from May 2004 to February 2005. Of the hundreds arrested on minor visa violations, not a single person was charged with a terrorism-related crime.

The Impact on Arab Americans

While immigration from Arab countries to the United States has not decreased since 9/11, the cumulative effect of the above programs has been to invoke a feeling of a state of siege among Arab Americans, whether they are U.S. citizens, lawful residents, or non-immigrant residents and visitors. Most people who were subjected to these laws, although not citizens themselves, were the relative—a husband, a wife, a parent—of an American citizen. Additionally, these laws created a climate that has led to a substantial increase in reported hate crimes against Arabs and Muslims and a 2,000 percent increase in complaints of anti-Arab and anti-Muslim discrimination in the years following 9/11.

CONCLUSION

The United States of America is a country of immigrants. Regardless of their time of arrival, immigrants came seeking a better life for themselves and a brighter future for their children. Arab immigrants are no exception. Arab Americans have been an integral part of the United States since its inception. A small number came to American shores before 1880, from either the Arab North African countries as slaves or (like other immigrants) to seek America's promise of freedom and prosperity.

Arab immigrants arrived in significant numbers during the Great Migration (1880–1924), a period when almost 20 million immigrants came to America from around the globe. It was a period when the United States had an open immigration policy and was in need for labor to build the infrastructure that could transform its agrarian economy to an industrial one. By the end of the Great Migration period an estimated 200,000 Arab immigrants arrived; the majority of them came from Syria and Lebanon and a smaller number came from Palestine. At the time, Arab immigrants were mostly Christian men who came from rural backgrounds and had had little formal education; a few came from urban areas and were more educated.

The arrival of a large number of immigrants who were perceived as having inferior cultures, coupled with World War I and the economic recession that followed, generated strong public anti-immigrant fervor. Between 1917 and 1924, the U.S. Congress passed a number of immigration laws that restricted immigration to the United States except for immigrants from Northern Europe. These laws brought an end to the open immigration policy and closed the doors to immigrants from Asian and African countries, including Arab counties.

Arab immigration to the United States resumed after World War II. The war resulted in the destruction of most European cities as well as the weakening of European political and economic dominance, presenting a historic opportunity to the United States to emerge as the new superpower. This, however, required a speedy transformation of the U.S. economy from a war economy into a consumer one. Without changing much about its restrictive immigration laws passed between 1917 and 1924, the U.S. government, in collaboration with major industrial corporations, recruited professionals from around the world, including from Arab countries. Arab immigrants who arrived during that period came from middle and upper urban classes, and were both Muslims and Christians; the majority of them came from Syria, Lebanon, Palestine, Jordan, and Egypt. With their high level of education this wave of immigrants found economic prosperity and assimilation more easily.

The last and third wave of Arab immigrants came after the 1965 ease of the U.S. immigration laws. Arab immigrants who came since then were extremely diverse in terms of their national backgrounds, religious affiliation, and educational level. Many of them came from war-devastated areas of Iraq, Palestine, and Lebanon. Arab immigrants started to arrive from countries such as Morocco, Tunisia, Sudan, and Somalia, countries whose people had not traditionally immigrated to the United States.

While the tragic events of September 11 did not directly impact the number of Arab immigrants arriving to the United States, it reshaped the Arab American experience because the government passed a number of laws targeting the community that are still in effect today. These laws created a great level of insecurity and fear among Arab Americans, especially recent immigrants. At the same time, many non-Arabs, as individuals or as institutions, joined Arab and Muslim Americans in protesting these discriminatory laws. They also reached out to their fellow Arab and Muslim Americans neighbors and friends to express their support and create solidarity among a nation of immigrants and their descendants who represent the richly diverse fabric of American society.

NOTES

1. Arab American National Museum, *Telling Our Story* (Dearborn, MI: Arab American National Museum, 2007), 26.

2. Kitty Morse, "Esteban of Azemmour and His New World Adventures," *Saudi Aramco World* (March–April 2002): 2–9.

3. American Historical Association, "Autobiography of Omar ibn Said, Slave in North Carolina, 1831," *American Historical Review* 30 (July 1925): 787–95.

4. Arab American National Museum, *Telling Our Story*, 26.

5. Arab American National Museum, *Telling Our Story*, 26.

6. Janice J. Terry, "Modern History," in *Arab American Encyclopedia*, ed. Anan Ameri and Dawn Ramey (Woodbridge, CT: U.X.L, 2000), 23.

7. Elizabeth Boosahda, *Arab-American Faces and Voices: The Origin of an Immigrant Community* (Austin: University of Texas Press, 2003), 6–7.

8. Alixa Naff, *Becoming American: The Early Arab Immigrant Experience* (Carbondale: Southern Illinois University Press, 1985), 108.

9. Sarah E. John, "Arabic-Speaking Immigrants to El Paso," in *Crossing the Waters: Arabic Speaking Immigrants to the United States before 1940*, ed. Eric J. Hooglund (Washington, DC: Smithsonian Institution Press, 1987), 105.

10. Samir Khalaf, "The Background and Causes of Lebanese/Syrian Immigration to the United States before World War I," in Hooglund, *Crossing the Waters*, 22.

11. Khalaf, "Background and Causes of Lebanese/ Syrian Immigration," 22.

12. Arab American National Museum, *Telling Our Story*, 56.

13. Louise Cainkar, "Immigration to the United States," in Ameri and Ramey, *Arab American Encyclopedia*, 41–42.

14. Naff, *Becoming American*, 115–16.

15. Naff, Becoming American, 115–16.

16. Jonathon Friedlander, "Rare Sights: Images of Early Arab Immigration to New York City," in *A Community of Many Worlds: Arab Americans in New York City*, ed. Kathleen Benson and Philip Kayal (New York: Museum of the City of New York; Syracuse: Syracuse University Press, 2002), 46.

17. Boosahda, *Arab-American Faces and Voices*, 86.

18. Michael Suleiman, "Impression of New York City by Early Arab Immigrants," in Benson and Kayal, *A Community of Many Worlds*, 36–38.

19. Naff, *Becoming American*, 108.

20. Naff, *Becoming American*, 108–9.

21. Randa A. Kayyali, *The Arab Americans* (Westport, CT: Greenwood Press, 2006), 23–24.

22. Naff, *Becoming American*, 111–12.

23. Cainkar, "Immigration to the United States," 43.

24. Kayyali, *The Arab Americans*, 24.

25. Kayyali, *The Arab Americans*, 33–35.

26. NAAMA Chapters, ed. National Arab American Medical Association, http://www.naama.com/naama-chapters.php.

27. Cainkar, "Immigration to the United States," 41.

28. Cainkar, "Immigration to the United States," 53.

29. U.S. Department of Justice, "The September 11 Detainees: A Review of the Treatment of Aliens Held on Immigration Charges in Connection with the Investigation of the September 11 Attacks," Office of the Inspector General, June 2003, http://www.justice.gov/oig/special/0306/index.htm.

30. "A Year of Loss: Reexamining Civil Liberties since September 11," Lawyers Committee for Human Rights, New York, 2002, http://www.humanrightsfirst.org/pubs/descriptions/loss_report.pdf.

31. "A Year of Loss: Reexamining Civil Liberties since September 11," Lawyers Committee for Human Rights, New York, 2002, http://www.humanrightsfirst.org/pubs/descriptions/loss_report.pdf.

32. Chief immigration judge Michael Creppy issued a memo stating, "The Attorney General has implemented additional security procedures for certain cases in the Immigration Court." Creppy further stated that these procedures "require" IJs to "close the hearing to the public." *Creppy Memo*, September 21, 2001.

33. *Detroit Free Press v. Ashcroft*, 303 F.3d 681 (6th Cir. 2002).

34. Report from U.S. Department of Justice, Executive Office for U.S. Attorneys, Memorandum for the Attorney General, from Kenneth L. Wainstein, Director, entitled "Final Report on Interview Project," dated February 26, 2002, http://www.ailf.org/lac/lac_otherresources_execbranchactions.asp.

2

THE IMPACT OF 9/11, MIDDLE EAST CONFLICTS, AND ANTI-ARAB DISCRIMINATION

Marvin Wingfield

ARAB AMERICANS ON 9/11: HEROES AND VICTIMS

Peter Hashem was a soccer dad. That is why he was a passenger on Flight 11 out of Boston that morning. He died with 91 others when the plane crashed into the North Tower of the World Trade Center. Originally, he had planned to take a flight the day before but rescheduled so that he could attend his son's game. Hashem had arrived in the Lawrence, Massachusetts, area as a boy, when his family came from Lebanon in 1970. He was born in Akoura in the heart of the Maronite Catholic community. He graduated from the University of Massachusetts at Amherst, then from the Greater Lawrence Technical School in Andover. At 40 years old he was working as a senior software engineering manager at a high-tech electronics testing and semiconductor company. His family remembers him as a devoted husband to Rita and father to Christopher, age 11, and Patrick, age 9. The couple and their children were faithful parishioners at St. Anthony's Maronite Catholic Church.[1]

When Flight 11 crashed into the North Tower, Jude Safi was at work on the 104th floor. An ambitious equity trader, he was one of 658 employees of a financial services company who died that day. He had worked there for only four months. His family was originally from Lebanon, but he had lived with his parents all his life on 74th Street in Dyker Heights, Brooklyn. A friend he had known since kindergarten, Robert Tipaldi, got him the job; another close childhood friend, Richard Caggiano, also worked at the same company. Before graduating from Staten Island College in business finance, he had attended the all-male Xavierian High School, run by the Xavierian Fathers. The school lost 23 alumni on September 11. Safi rooted for the Yankees and the Knicks and was a big fan of Sinatra and Elvis. He knew the lyrics to all their songs and watched all their films. The 1950s attracted him—the music, the clothing styles, the cars. He had bought and restored a 1957 Chevy pickup truck. The Community Board and Dyker Heights City Council renamed 74th Street in his honor; other streets were also renamed in honor of Tipaldi, Caggiano, and firefighter Dennis Patrick O'Berg.[2]

Ahmed Nasser was among the heroes of 9/11. He had emigrated to the United States from the town of Ryachia in Yemen 15 years earlier, determined to get an education and make a better life for himself. He got jobs as a waiter and maintenance man and worked full time while going to college full time. He married a Brooklyn-born Yemeni American woman. They had two sons. His brother-in-law Adil Almontaser was on the New York City police force and persuaded him to join in 2000. He says that his greatest moment in the military was going to Iwo Jima and climbing Mount Surabachi.

Nasser was having his morning coffee when the first plane hit. He was immediately ordered to the World Trade Center by his precinct captain. The South Tower collapsed just as he arrived: "I couldn't see anything, the dust and debris that really was as thick as soup. I just heard the screams all around me, and I couldn't see where they were coming from. It was awful, and something I will never forget." He worked continually for 2 days, while his family "didn't know if [he] was dead or alive." He spent 10 days total at Ground Zero. Nasser, Almontaser, and fellow officers Rafet Awad and Faisal Khan shared the rescue-effort ordeal. Later, all of them were honored for what they had done. U.S. Assistant Attorney General Ralph Boyd came to "give them great thanks and to claim them as America's own." President Bush sent a message, identifying them as "among our nation's greatest heroes."[3]

Whether a passenger on one of the doomed planes, a worker in one of the World Trade Center towers, or a heroic rescuer, these men all shared in the typical pattern of Arab American life—immigrant success, integration into their neighborhoods, and closeness to family—characteristics that should be kept in mind when exploring the anti-Arab discrimination that followed 9/11.

Across the country on 9/11 Arab Americans and Muslims watched events unfold with the same shock and horror as their fellow citizens. They donated blood, held candlelight vigils, conducted prayer services, and offered their skills as translators. In four days Arab Americans in Orlando, Florida, raised $50,000 for the Red Cross. Restaurant owners donated profits to relief funds and the families of those who died. Arab American and Muslim organizations issued public statements condemning the attacks as a "barbaric act of terrorism" and called on their communities to cooperate with law enforcement authorities in apprehending those who were responsible and in preventing any future attacks. In a poll, 80 percent of Arab Americans reported that they had contributed to a victims' fund, donated blood, or displayed an American flag.[4]

The whole world knows that the 19 men who hijacked airliners and killed nearly three thousand people on 9/11 were Arabs who were motivated by an extreme, politicized version of Islam. Everyone knows of the heroic rescue efforts of police, firefighters, and medical personnel. But an underreported tragedy of 9/11 is that Arab Americans, Arab nationals, and Muslims were also among the victims, though they served as rescuers as well.

In addition, some of the public immediately blamed Arabs and Muslims for the attacks because they shared either ethnicity or religion with the perpetrators. Innocent people were physically assaulted and murdered. Mosques and Islamic centers were vandalized and became the target of death threats. Individuals lost their jobs or were refused service in stores. Children were harassed and beaten by their classmates. Often Arabs and Muslims were vilified by some media and in some cases by elected officials. Also some law enforcement and security agencies disregarded constitutional limitations on their power, and the rights of thousands of people were disregarded. Arab Americans, Arab nationals, and Muslims were truly both primary and secondary victims of the tragedy.

THE IMMEDIATE AFTERMATH OF 9/11

It did not take long for the backlash to begin.[5] A Sikh man wearing a religiously mandated turban saw the second plane hit the World Trade Center. He fled the debris crashing down, along with hundreds of others. He was neither Arab nor Muslim, but two young men saw the turban, shouted obscenities at him, and called him a terrorist. The Sikh man had to flee again, as they chased him down the street. He escaped into a subway.

While police officer Ahmad Nasser risked his life at Ground Zero, his wife, Hadjirah, who wears a hijab, was picking up their children to take them home early from school. On the way back, someone told them, "Go back where you came from, you terrorists." Neighbors threw eggs at her sister's home in Brooklyn.[6]

The Sikh and South Asian community was hard hit. The first person murdered was Indian Sikh Balbir Singh Sodhi, a gas station owner in Mesa, Arizona. On September 15, 42-year-old Frank Roque went on a rampage. Drinking heavily, he told a bartender and others that he was going to "kill some ragheads." He drove his Chevy pickup to Singh Sodhi's gas station, shot him, then went to another gas station and fired on a Lebanese American clerk. His final act before being arrested was to fire on the home of an Afghan American family. He received a death sentence, but the state Supreme Court changed it to life imprisonment without parole, on the grounds of mental illness.

Within a week, there were 11 confirmed or suspected hate-crime murders and many brutal assaults linked to 9/11. An Egyptian American grocery store owner was shot in San Gabriel, California. A Palestinian American clothing salesman was killed in Los Angeles. A man in the Dallas area shot a Pakistani grocer in the face, killed an Indian gas station owner, and shot a Bangladeshi man. An Egyptian American honor student in Queens was chased and attacked by a gang. He was held down while his eye was gouged out with a broomstick. Teenagers beat a pregnant Yemeni woman wearing a hijab, who had to be hospitalized. The baby was delivered unharmed. A Muslim mother at home with two children was attacked by a "mob of vandals" yelling slurs and vulgarities. The family's door was kicked in and their cars firebombed and tires slashed.

In Bridgeview, Illinois, a "pro-American" demonstration on September 11 turned into an angry march to the local mosque. It took more than 100 police to control the crowd of 300–500 people surrounding the mosque. Some people shouted, "Kill the Arabs"; some had weapons. A teenage participant said, "I'm proud to be an American and I hate Arabs and I always have." There were 15 arrests. On police advice, leaders of the mosque closed their schools for a week.

Muslims wearing distinctive dress and Arab Americans with accents or obviously Arab names were the most visible and vulnerable targets. In the United States the traditional Arab kaffiyeh had become a symbol of Arab identity, but now it was treated as a sign of terrorist sympathies. Many women had their hijabs forcefully pulled off their heads. Anyone mistaken for Arab or Muslim was also in danger. Sikhs and other Indians, Hispanics, Brazilians, Ethiopians, Filipinos, and Greeks were all targets of blind anger. Middle Eastern restaurants lost customers. Some were picketed and boycotted or were the targets of vandalism, arson attacks, and gunfire.

The American-Arab Anti-Discrimination Committee documented more than 700 hate crimes during the nine-week period after the attacks—deaths, beatings, stabbings, firebombs, and death threats. Many more incidents went unreported.

Normal life was impossible. Any public place could be dangerous, so people took precautions. A great many simply stayed home and did not go to work or out shopping, especially women who wore a hijab. Some women temporarily stopped wearing a head covering, so as not to call attention to themselves. Parents kept their children home from school and would not let them go out to play. Arab American Christians began wearing a crucifix more prominently on the outside of their clothing. Harassment and discrimination in the workplace was common and sometimes blatant. People lost their jobs because of their ethnicity or religion.

Government and Public Support

At the same time that Arab Americans were going through the most difficult moment in their history, they were gaining unprecedented public recognition and acceptance. Fortunately, American leaders from grassroots and local levels to the White House spoke out against hate crimes, as did ordinary citizens who came to the defense of their neighbors. Churches and synagogues and civil rights and ethnic organizations urged their fellow citizens not to seek scapegoats or blame the innocent. Arab American and Muslim organizations reached out to policy makers and educated the public about the Arab and Muslim worlds. They forged strong new relationships with government agencies and assisted the government in making its War on Terror more effective in identifying real threats and avoiding harm to innocent people.

The hate crimes would likely have been worse had not public officials spoken up so strongly against blaming the innocent.

President Bush made a highly publicized visit to the Washington Islamic Center. He called Islam a religion of peace and said, "The face of terror is not the true face of Islam." Secretary of State Colin Powell spoke out, and the U.S. Congress passed a unanimous resolution condemning hate crimes. Secretary of Education Rod Paige warned universities and school districts to be aware of the possibility of hate crimes and reminded them that a pattern of discrimination would put their federal funding at risk. These sentiments were echoed by government, police, and education officials in states and cities across the country.

In Dearborn, Michigan, the home of the largest Arab American community in the country, Arab community leaders had strong ties to local authorities. They were able to mobilize officials and police immediately. Imad Hamad, Midwestern director of the American-Arab Anti-Discrimination Committee commented, "We were able to call the mayor's office on the morning of September 11 about our concerns. . . . By 11:30 A.M. we were meeting with the mayor and chief of police about a possible backlash against our community. By 1:00 P.M. the mayor was on the local cable public access channel warning people against committing hate crimes against Arabs . . . and the police cars were patrolling our shopping areas and neighborhoods."[7]

Many ordinary Americans rallied to the support of their Arab and Muslim neighbors. A couple in Silver Spring, Maryland, offered their home as a refuge, if there was an Arab family whose own home had become unsafe. In Reston, Virginia, St. Anne's Episcopal Church organized volunteers to escort Muslim women for grocery shopping and visits to the doctor.[8] Neighbors stopped by to bring sweets and messages of welcome. Non-Muslim women on college campuses wore the hijab in solidarity with their Muslim friends.

Support messages arrived at Arab American organizations as immediately as hate messages. Three hundred regular customers showed their support and packed an Afghani restaurant in San Carlos, California, on the Friday after the attacks. Groups raised money to assist mosques and individuals who had been attacked. In Salt Lake City Jewish, Catholic, and Mormon representatives brought flowers and signs, "We love our Muslim neighbors."[9] The Utah governor visited and announced that hate crimes would not be tolerated.[10] The Qur'an and books on the Middle East became best sellers, as Americans sought to better understand Islam and the history and culture of their Arab American and Muslim neighbors.

All these efforts helped Arab Americans and Muslims feel less isolated. American traditions and laws rooted in democratic, religious, and humanistic values had come into play, and ethnic and religious bigotry, nativism, and antiforeign hostility were publicly condemned. They did not, however, go away. Negative sentiments toward Arabs and Muslims are deeply rooted in popular American culture and have been fueled by U.S. involvement, both past and present, in various theaters of war and conflict in the Middle East.

A BRIEF HISTORY OF MIDDLE EAST CONFLICT

Cooperation and positive relationship had dominated the relationship between the United States and most Arab countries for the last 200 years. In fact, Morocco was the first country to recognize the United States as an independent country after the successful revolutionary war in 1776. Even today, the United States considers most of the Arab countries its allies, including Jordan, Saudi Arabia, Egypt, and Morocco, to mention only a few. However, in the last few decades political tensions between the United States and some Arab and Muslim countries, such as Iraq and Iran, emerged. This conflict has resulted in a widespread hostility toward Arabs and Muslims that has had personal consequences for Arab Americans, including media stereotyping, defamation and discrimination, and increased government scrutiny.

Iran

From the end of World War II until the Iranian Revolution in 1979, the United States considered Iran, which bordered the Soviet Union, to be essential to its strategy of containing the expansion of Soviet power during the Cold War. In 1953 the CIA sponsored a coup d'état that overthrew a democratically elected government and installed the anticommunist Shah Pahlavi. The shah became unpopular with the Iranian people and was overthrown in 1979. He was replaced by an Islamist government under the anti-American spiritual leader Ayatollah Khomeini. U.S.-Iranian antagonism worsened when Iran held 53 U.S. diplomats hostage for 444 days. The hostage crisis was daily news in the United States and became the basis for a great deal of hostility toward Muslims. Tensions between the United States and Iran increased again following 9/11, when President George Bush named Iran part of an Axis of Evil, and tension arose over Iran's nuclear ambitions under the leadership of President Mahmoud Ahmadinejad.

Arab-Israeli Conflict

The establishment of the state of Israel in 1948 in part of what had been historic Palestine caused significant war and strife in the region. According to the United Nations, more than 700,000 Palestinians were displaced, the majority of whom found refuge in other parts of Palestine—the West Bank, the Gaza Strip, and East Jerusalem—as well as in the surrounding Arab countries of Jordan, Syria, and Lebanon. This displacement and the resulting statelessness of a large number of Palestinians created a significant refugee problem. In 1967, war erupted again between several Arab counties and Israel, which resulted in Israel occupying the rest of historic Palestine, the Syrian Golan Heights, and the Egyptian Sinai, causing further displacement of Palestinians, who again took refuge in the surrounding Arab countries.

The unresolved 1967 occupation of the West Bank, Gaza, and Jerusalem led to continuous conflict in the region and to the Palestinian uprisings against Israel in 1987 and 2000. The United States is a strong financial and military supporter of Israel and has helped broker two significant peace agreements between Israel and the Arabs. The Camp David Peace Accord in 1978, signed under the auspices of President Jimmy Carter, led to Israeli withdrawal from the Egyptian Sinai and a lasting peace between Egypt and Israel. The Oslo Peace Accords in 1993, overseen by President Bill Clinton, consisted of a land-for-peace deal that was supposed to provide for the cessation of violence between Israel and the Palestinians, Palestinian recognition of the state of Israel, and Israeli withdrawal from Palestinian areas to allow for autonomy, but the agreement was only partially implemented.

While the U.S government, as well as the international community, officially recognizes that the only realistic solution to this conflict is a two-state solution, with Israel and Palestine living side by side, this solution has not been easy to accomplish. The Arab-Israeli conflict is important not only because the United States has geopolitical interests in the region but also because many Americans, including American Jews and Christian Zionists, consider Israel a strong ally and they advocate for strong ties and unconditional support for Israeli policies. On the other hand, many Americans, par-

ADC founder and former senator James Abourezk (*right*) at the 2003 ADC convention, introducing keynote speaker Secretary of State Colin Powell. After September 11, 2001, Arab American organizations and top U.S. officials built new bridges of cooperation and common purpose. (Courtesy of American-Arab Anti-Discrimination Committee [ADC])

ticularly those of Arab and Palestinian origin, are concerned with Palestinian rights and the conditions of those living as refugees and under sustained military occupation. The conflict, particularly when it has turned violent, has been covered widely in the U.S. media and has greatly contributed to the negative perception of Arabs that has spilled over to include Arab Americans. Under the administration of Barack Obama, there have been renewed efforts to resolve the conflict and a call for Palestinian statehood.

Iraq

When Iraq invaded Kuwait in 1990, the United States, along with a broad coalition of allies, decisively defeated Saddam Hussein, and then in concert with the United Nations imposed very severe economic sanctions on Iraq. The Iraqi economy was devastated. As a result there was widespread malnutrition, disease, and death, although these hardships did little to loosen Saddam Hussein's hold on power. After 9/11 the U.S. government accused Saddam

Hussein of having weapons of mass destruction and U.S. led coalition forces subsequently invaded Iraq in 2003. While the invasion resulted in the overthrow of Hussein, it also resulted in the destruction of many cities and towns in Iraq, the death of hundreds of thousands of Iraqi civilians, and close to 4 million Iraqi refugees. No weapons of mass destruction were actually found.

Afghanistan

In another Cold War effort, the United States sought to counter the Soviet presence in Afghanistan, by working through a Pakistani intelligence agency. This agency trained and provided funding and weapons for tens of thousands of Afghani, Pakistani, and Arab "mujahedeen" to engage in guerrilla war against the Russians. U.S. support for these insurgents had unanticipated consequences. Many of the fighters, among whom was Osama bin Laden, were motivated by a militant Islamist ideology and a desire to resist Soviet domination of a Muslim country. During the 1990s the extreme fundamentalist Muslim group known as the Taliban allied itself with bin Laden's Al Qaeda ("the base") organization and seized control in Afghanistan. The irony is that U.S. money and arms may have made possible the rise of the Taliban and bin Laden, who in addition to being involved in the events of 9/11 is widely acknowledged to have encouraged his adherents to attack the American military at Khobar Towers in Saudi Arabia in 1996 and the USS *Cole* in the Yemeni port of Aden in 2000.

Lebanon

Ever since Lebanon gained independence from France in 1943, its national identity has been factious, with 17 different ethnoreligious groups sharing one country. The United States has aligned itself with several of the Christian-led governments, most notably under President Dwight Eisenhower in the 1950s and during the Lebanese civil war (1975–1989). There was outside interference in the Lebanese civil war from many countries, including Syria and Israel, during these years, and the United States was inevitably drawn into the conflict. The Reagan administration sent a U.S. Marine peacekeeping force to Beirut, and in 1983 their barracks were blown up by Lebanese militants. Several other Americans were kidnapped or killed, including the president of the American University of Beirut. Once again the actions of a violent faction had a negative impact on

American perceptions of the Arab world and subsequently there was a backlash against Arab Americans.

A New Beginning

In his historic address to the Arab and Muslim worlds in Cairo on June 4, 2009, President Barack Obama's appeal for a "new beginning" of cooperation between the United States and the Muslim world was welcomed in the Middle East as a sign of hope that more balanced and far-sighted U.S. policies based on "mutual interest and mutual respect" would be forthcoming. President Obama also expressed the hope that the extremist movements would lose support and become marginalized, acknowledged the achievements of Islamic civilization and the 60 years of Palestinian suffering and dispossession, and strongly criticized Israel's settlement program. Obama further affirmed the U.S. commitment to resolving the Palestinian-Israeli conflict, including the creation of a Palestinian state. One of the early steps he took after taking office was the appointment of former senator George Mitchell, an Arab American, as a special envoy to the Middle East.

ANTI-ARAB DISCRIMINATION PRIOR TO 9/11

The backlash that followed September 11 was not the first time Arab and Muslim Americans have been the targets of hate crimes, discrimination, and defamation.[11] War generates racism and bigotry. During World War I, German Americans were persecuted. In World War II, hundreds of thousands of Japanese Americans were forcibly placed in internment camps. The Korean and Vietnam wars generated references to Asians as "gooks" and "slopes." During the U.S.-Iraq War, which started in 2003, Iraqi citizens were often referred to by some U.S. media as "hajjis," a contemptuous use of the term referring to Muslims who have made the pilgrimage to Mecca. As the United States became more involved in the Middle East after the 1967 Arab-Israeli war, Arabs and Muslims in America experienced increased public hostility and media stereotyping.

Arabs in the Media

Negative stereotypes of Arabs and the Arab world, portraying them only in terms of deserts, sheikhs, camels, and harem girls, have long been a part of popular American culture. Events of the

1970s and 1980s produced harsher images with a political character. The U.S. support for the Israeli military in the 1973 Arab-Israeli conflict led to an oil boycott against the United States. There were shortages of gas and rising prices. One consequence was the appearance in major films like *Network* and *Rollover* of a character, the Arab oil sheikh, who was "buying up America." But it was the Hollywood image of the Arab terrorist that has been the most damaging. In the film *Black Sunday*, Arab terrorists plan to blow up a football stadium during the Super Bowl. In *True Lies* Arnold Schwarzenegger thwarts the plans of Palestinian terrorists to use nuclear weapons against the United States. Many films, for example, *Delta Force*, portrayed U.S. military forces at war with Arabs and gleefully wreaking destruction. Professor Jack Shaheen, the leading academic on anti-Arab stereotyping in film, has identified nearly a thousand Hollywood films with negative stereotypes of Arabs during the 20th century.[12]

The print and broadcast news media have tended to present Arabs almost entirely in the context of political and military conflict, and these have been almost the only images of Arabs available to the American public. Images of Arab Americans, of everyday life in the Arab world, or of Arabs as normal people have been virtually non-existent. The result has been that terrorism is often the first thought that comes to the minds of Americans when they hear a reference to Arabs, especially Palestinians, or to Muslims. These negative stereotypes have fed into the discrimination that Arab Americans face in everyday life.[13]

Hate Crimes

The 1980s saw a series of terrorist attacks and hate crimes against Arab American and Muslim communities. A building in Washington, D.C., housing several pro-Palestinian human rights organizations was firebombed. Alex Odeh, the southern California regional director of the American-Arab Anti-Discrimination Committee (ADC), was murdered when a pipe bomb was attached to the ADC office door. A police officer was injured as he attempted to defuse another bomb placed outside the ADC office in Roxbury, Massachusetts. When the United States bombed Libya and shot down Libyan aircraft in the 1980s, Arabs were beaten up in Chicago, Syracuse, and New Haven, and Arab American businesses and cars were vandalized. After an airline hijacking, bombs were thrown through the window of the Dar us-Salaam bookstore in Houston. A Jewish woman reading a book about Palestine was forced to leave an airplane. She was questioned and intimidated. There were many other incidents.[14]

Hate crimes escalated during the Gulf War. When Iraq invaded Kuwait in 1990 and when the United States began military operations against Iraq in 1991, Arab Americans were assaulted and threatened. There were arson attacks against Arab American businesses. American troops were defending Kuwait, but a Kuwaiti American pizza man was beaten. As with all forms of racism, anti-Arab bigotry was blind and violent. The ADC documented nearly 160 hate crimes during the short period of the Gulf War.[15] In 1990, prior to the invasion, there had been only four. When Timothy McVeigh bombed the federal building in Oklahoma City in 1995, "Middle Eastern–looking men" were automatically the first suspects. Supposed Middle East experts identified the bombing as clearly Middle Eastern in origin. This was widely reported in the media. In the two days before McVeigh was arrested, more than 200 hate crimes were reported to the Council on American-Islamic Relations.

Government Scrutiny and the Infringement of Civil Liberties

There were also infringements on Arab American civil liberties before the 9/11 period. On President Richard Nixon's order, the FBI began Operation Boulder following the murder by Palestinian militants of Israeli athletes at the 1972 Olympics in Munich. Numerous Arab students and Arab American activists were kept under surveillance, their phones tapped, their mail intercepted, and their speeches and writings monitored. Hundreds of people were interrogated, photographed, and fingerprinted. Some were jailed and 78 Arab nationals were deported. No terrorists were apprehended. Civil liberties lawyer Abdeen Jabara, one of the targets of the operation, filed a lawsuit that spent 10 years in litigation. Finally, the court ruled in his favor and found that the FBI had violated his constitutional rights.

In the mid-1980s, the Department of Justice (DOJ) developed a plan calling for the mass roundup of Middle East nationals in the event of a national emergency and the establishment of detention camps in Louisiana and Florida, where such individuals would be held until they were deported. In 1987, seven Palestinians and one Kenyan, who became known as the "LA-8," were arrested for their political activities. Newspaper headlines spoke of terrorism, but FBI investigations found no evidence of violent or illegal activity. All the LA-8's activities were protected by the First Amendment right to uncensored political speech and free association. For 20 years, despite repeated court rulings in favor of the defendants, the DOJ attempted to deport them. Finally in 2007, the DOJ dropped the case.

During the 1991 U.S.-Iraq war known as the Gulf War, the FBI called in numerous Arab Americans for "voluntary interviews" about what they might know about terrorist threats. The interview program identified no threats, but this was an intimidating experience for those subjected to the process and had a predictably chilling effect on the Arab American community. People thought twice before writing letters to the editor or attending demonstrations calling for negotiated rather than military solutions.

In the mid-1990s, new counterterrorism and immigration legislation created new pressures on Arab Americans, Muslims, and Arab nationals. Airline "profiling" incidents increased. Law enforcement agencies were authorized to use secret evidence in deportation proceedings. Immigrants and their lawyers were unable to mount any effective defense against unknown charges. There could be no cross examination of witnesses. After September 11, these laws became tools in the hands of federal authorities. Due process rights and procedures guaranteed by the Constitution were swept away.[16]

Arab Americans Respond

Arab Americans have long constituted a successful and vibrant community, well integrated into all aspects of American life. But until 1967, they were not politically organized. After the 1967 Arab-Israeli War, Arab American scholars and political activists formed the Association of Arab-American University Graduates (AAUG) to provide an Arab voice on Middle East issues in the United States. The AAUG was later joined by the National Association of Arab Americans (NAAA), a congressional lobbying organization; the American-Arab Anti-Discrimination Committee (ADC), a grassroots civil rights organization; the Arab American Institute (AAI), which fostered Arab American involvement in the U.S. political system; and by Muslim groups such as the Council on American-Islamic Relations (CAIR), a civil liberties organization dedicated to defending the rights of Muslims.

These organizations were called into existence by events in the Middle East. Politically active Arab Americans, especially the younger generations and more recent immigrants, strongly supported

Palestinian human rights and self-determination. They learned new political skills—organizing their communities, speaking to the media, and lobbying elected officials. Their voices became increasingly audible in public discussion and in the halls of Congress. Herblock did an editorial cartoon on lobbying that depicted the Arab tortoise outpacing the overconfident pro-Israel hare. Political advocacy on issues surrounding U.S. Middle East policy became a way for immigrants to take on the role of citizen, a means of becoming more fully American.

The conflicts in the Middle East had a personal impact on Arab Americans in a multitude of ways. For some people, scenes of violence stirred uneasy memories and awakened repressed experiences of trauma. Many were deeply concerned about the lives and safety of their relatives and friends in arenas of conflict. Arab Americans also lived with the knowledge that these conflicts could affect their physical safety, their relationships with coworkers and fellow students, their careers, their treatment in public places, and the status and regard which they could claim in their communities. The conflicts heavily influenced how their ethnicity and, in the case of Muslims, their religion was presented in films, television shows, news reports, and political speeches. It worried many that there were no positive role models for Arab American children in the American media portrayal of Arabs.

THE LONG-TERM IMPACT OF 9/11

Nine weeks after 9/11 there were fewer hate crimes and incidents of discrimination being reported, but the number of incidents remained significantly higher than before September 11.[17] The position of Arab Americans, Muslims, and South Asians in American society had been altered. Arab Americans were no longer an invisible community. The meaning of the shift was still being worked out in their own circles, in American institutions, and in public life.

Arab Americans remained on the alert. Some Arab nationals simply went back home to their own countries. Thousands more were hastily deported. Students in the Arab world sent e-mail messages to Arab American organizations, asking whether it was safe for them to come to study at American universities. Large numbers of immigrants from the Arab world decided to Americanize their names. Osama became Sam. Mohammad became Mike.

But many others reaffirmed their ethnicity or religion and became more committed to building bridges to mainstream institutions and educating other Americans about the Arab world and Islam. They were becoming at the same time more Arab and more American, creatively reshaping the nature of Arab American identity. A new energy appeared in Arab American literature and the arts.

The Bush administration declared a "War on Terror" and the public was told that future acts of terrorism were inevitable. Highly publicized code yellow and code orange announcements alerted the public to the shifting level of threat, and instructions were posted in subways and airports urging people to notify authorities if they saw any suspicious activity. Periodically, headlines proclaimed the arrest of individuals or groups identified as terrorists or potential terrorists. By 2007, there had been 510 such arrests, often accompanied by dramatic headlines, but only four people were ultimately convicted of planning attacks in the United States. Once tried in a court of law, the vast majority of cases turned out to include no link to terrorism.[18] In time, it all became almost routine, and the terrorism issue became a political tool to win votes. But an underlying sense of possible danger became permanent.

It has been widely asserted that on September 11, everything changed. Many things did change, including the American people's sense of insulation from conflicts elsewhere in the world. There was a new alarm and sense of vulnerability. There was strong public support for tracking down Osama bin Laden and Al Qaeda and for overthrowing their Taliban allies. There was also initial support for the invasion of Iraq and the overthrow of the government of Saddam Hussein, even though numerous press reports, and after the war began government reports, indicated that the official claims that Iraq had ties to Al Qaeda and possessed or was developing weapons of mass destruction were untrue.

The tragic events of 9/11, followed by the U.S.-led wars in Iraq and Afghanistan and the global War on Terror against Muslim extremists, inevitably fostered negative public attitudes toward Arab Americans, Arabs, and Muslims. Ten years after, some of that negative attitude continues to prevail.

Discrimination and Violence

A 2002 poll found that 30 percent of Arab Americans reported personal experience of discrimination. By 2007 this had risen to 42 percent. For Muslims it was 58 percent, and for Muslims between ages 18 and 29, it was an extraordinary 76 percent. Nearly 30 percent of Arab American Catholics experienced discrimination.[19] Between 2003 and 2007, the American-Arab Anti-Discrimination Committee found the level of anti-Arab incidents to be higher than before 9/11.[20] Recent immigrants from the Middle East, especially Muslims, were the most vulnerable populations. They were often marked by their accents, names, dress, mannerisms, or physical appearance.

While the rates of discrimination increased, the incidence of specific problems varied from year to year. During 2003 the Committee on American-Islamic Relations (CAIR) reported a total of 1,019 anti-Muslim incidents, finding that airline profiling declined, while hate crimes doubled over the previous year. In 2005 CAIR documented a 30 percent increase in anti-Muslim incidents over 2004, a total of 1,972 incidents, the highest number it had ever recorded. In 2007 there were 2,652 incidents. Mosques and Muslim organizations were targeted in 564 incidents, which included vandalism, rock throwing, physical assaults, death threats, and the disruption of services. There were 98 cases of violence, 3–4 percent of the total, but hate crimes overall declined, while employment discrimination and airline profiling increased substantially.[21]

Even a few years after 9/11 some Arab Americans, especially recent immigrants and young males, were continuing to avoid air travel. Many stayed close to the security of the Arab American enclaves in Dearborn, northern New Jersey, or Brooklyn. People trimmed their beards, showed the flag, and stopped speaking Arabic in public. They thought twice about whether to write a letter to the editor, attend a political demonstration, or contribute to a Muslim charity.[22]

Employment discrimination continued at a high rate. The ADC received approximately 10 reports per week between 2003 and 2007. For many people, hostile comments, slurs from coworkers, and demands of women that they remove the hijab created a hostile work environment. Some employers failed to comply with the legal requirement of providing religious accommodation for Muslim religious practices, such as opportunities for daily prayer. A Sheraton hotel employee sent death threats to her Arab American supervisor.

Simon Abi Nader was a port director in south Florida, directly involved in keeping terrorists out of the United States. He complained of a hostile work environment where discrimination, harassment, and humiliation based on national origin or race was a routine experience. "I was prohibited from leaving my office without notifying my immediate supervisor. On a daily basis, I had to inform him of every move I made and every person I contacted as the Area Port Director."[23] Nader filed a lawsuit against the Department of Homeland Security and the Department of Justice. The jury awarded him $305,000, more than had been requested. His lawyer felt that the jury was angered by the behavior of high-level agency witnesses, those responsible for the harassment, who they felt had lied under oath.[24]

Not surprisingly, Arab American young people felt higher levels of stress, fear, and anxiety. Arab American students continued to be subjected to beatings, threats, harassment, and bias. A Jordanian American girl in Phoenix was cursed and spit on by students after 9/11. Several years later, a boy rammed her head through a window. After the first incident, she told people that she was Italian or Hispanic. After the second, she organized an antidiscrimination club and started setting up cultural programs for the school. "I'm pretty hardheaded," she said.

Still, after 9/11, educators were among those most open to addressing the needs of Arab Americans and the Muslim community. Schools with large numbers of Muslim students and teachers began to include Islamic holidays on the school calendar and sought to accommodate Muslim needs in regard to diet and modest dress in physical education classes. The Council on Islamic Education reported "a very definite improvement" in the presentation of Islam in textbooks.

For Arab Americans "fear of flying" took on a new meaning— fear of searches, interrogations, and public humiliation, fear that their names would be too similar to ones on the watch lists and no-fly lists.[25] Airline and security personnel were influenced by the atmosphere of suspicion and hostility against Arabs and Muslims, even though the real threats could lie elsewhere. Richard Reid, the "shoe bomber," was English and Jamaican. Resources could be used more effectively by relying on the more specific and secret criteria that were identified by national security agencies to be statistically correlated with acts of violence against the public. The U.S. government itself brought lawsuits against airlines whose discriminatory practices were illegal. But the security net was cast very widely indeed. Television's *60 Minutes* found that the names on the watch lists of the Department of Homeland Security included "Gary Smith," "John Williams," and "Robert Johnson." A Google search for "John Williams," however, produces more than 6 million hits.

Media Stereotypes and Defamation

The mainstream media plays a huge role in shaping American perceptions of the Arab world and Arab Americans.[26] In post-9/11 films, television, and news coverage some things got better and some things got worse. Professor Jack Shaheen criticizes films like *The Kingdom* in which FBI agents track down terrorists in Saudi Arabia. The presence of a strong Arab character in the form of a capable and decent Saudi police officer did not offset the dramatically more intense images of mobs chanting "Death to America" and a storyline in which even Arab children could not be trusted. The television series *24* brought terrorist threats to America, often but not always Arab or Muslim, into the nation's living rooms on a weekly basis. The show also brought a new message: the apparently nice Arab immigrant family in your neighborhood may be plotting to unleash death and destruction. Arab Americans, previously invisible on television, now were presented as a danger. Shaheen also claims that there is a close connection between Hollywood films and U.S. policy in the Middle East. A century of negative portrayals of Arabs in film made it easier for the government to build public support for wars in Arab countries.

Shaheen has identified more than 100 films since 9/11 that portray Arabs and Muslims. The good news was that one-third of them could be considered even-handed or even be recommended to audiences. Arab Americans were portrayed as "decent folk" in some films. That was "refreshing," says Shaheen,[27] who can claim some of the credit. He was hired as a consultant on George Clooney's *Syriana*, yet another terrorism-themed film. *Syriana* was no mere action movie; it presented a morally and politically complex picture of wealthy oil interests, CIA intrigue, U.S. foreign policy, and hopelessness among the dispossessed. Writer and director Steven Gaghan (who previously had written the script for *Rules of Engagement*, which was widely criticized for promoting anti-Arab sentiments) had come to recognize what he called "an inherent bias against the Arab world."[28] He himself had been influenced by the distorted images of Arabs in films and television and so made sure that *Syriana* was a conscious improvement.[29]

Hussein Ibish, media commentator and director of the Hala Maksoud Foundation for Arab-American Leadership, believes Arab American efforts to educate and persuade filmmakers to end the stereotypes finally paid off. Terrorism was still the all-but-inevitable theme, but films like *Syriana* showed American audiences something much closer to the reality of the Arab world than did previous films. Films and television shows began to show positive Arab and Arab American characters and to address the difficult issue of balancing individual rights and national security.[30]

Ibish points to films like *Babel* in which a young Moroccan boy hunting jackals foolishly takes a potshot at a bus and wounds an American tourist. The world automatically assumes it was an act of terrorism and it becomes an international incident. The film's real theme was the collective and personal misunderstandings that plague an interconnected world. In *Traitor,* Don Cheadle played a Sudanese American Muslim who infiltrates an extremist group. *Rendition* showed an ugly aspect of the War on Terror, as an innocent Egyptian American is abducted by the CIA and shipped to an unnamed country to be interrogated and tortured. Oliver Stone's *World Trade Center* avoided any anti-Arab or anti-Muslim sentiments. *Paradise Now,* a Palestinian film with a suicide bombing plot, received an Academy Award nomination, a Golden Globe award as best foreign film, and theatrical distribution in the United States. Ridley Scott's medieval crusader epic, *Kingdom of Heaven,* portrayed Muslim leader Saladin as a man of great personal dignity who respects the Christian faith.

The new wave of films was far more sophisticated than the old cartoonish stereotypes of *True Lies.* Even terrorist characters were sometimes given nuance and depth. But none of these films was a real blockbuster, and they did not reach as broad a public as their predecessors. While there was overall improvement in even-handed portrayals of Arabs in the entertainment industry, Ibish argues that the locus of anti-Arab defamation has shifted from entertainment to anti-Arab ideologues, columnists, and commentators, and certain religious and political leaders who express their views in other mainstream media. This new wave of defamation focused less on Arab identity and more on Islam.

Islamophobia

Anti-Muslim feelings after 9/11 led to the popularization of a new concept—Islamophobia.[31] This term refers to fear, prejudice, and discrimination against all Muslims or against Islam as a religion. After 9/11, combating Islamophobia became the greatest challenge facing Arab and Muslim Americans; for this reason, their community organizations devoted their resources toward educating Americans about Islam.

Polls validate the pervasiveness of Islamophobia. By 2007, 58 percent of Americans still said that they knew "little or nothing" about Islam. From 2005 to 2007 the proportion who said that their own religion had "little or nothing in common" with Islam rose from 59 percent to 70 percent. The Pew Research Center found that 30 percent of Americans associated Islam with fanaticism, radicalism, and terrorism. Only 15 percent had positive word-associations with the religion. Some 35 percent had a negative view of Muslims.[32]

Islamophobia was further worsened by anti-Muslim political and religious ideologues and the media's use of phrases like "Islamic terrorism" that failed to distinguish traditional Islam from political extremists or terms like "Islamofascism" that stoked fears of a worldwide takeover by Islam. Sensationalized commentaries about Muslim extremists fanned public fears about Muslims in general. Some called for "a complete ban on Muslim migration to the Western world." Others publicly advocated genocide and "nuking" the Middle East. Views that had previously been marginalized were now heard in the mainstream media. Arab American leaders suspect that the goal of the idealogues has been to exclude American Muslims from public and political life and to prevent them from influencing U.S. Middle East policy.[33]

It is no longer publicly acceptable for political commentators, television personalities, religious leaders, public intellectuals, or radio talk show hosts to defame other races or religions. But in the political climate after 9/11, blatant derogatory comments about Islam or slurs about Arabs or Muslims have been tolerated in public discourse. There was no public outcry, other than from the Arab American community or Muslim American organizations, to public statements in the media referring to Arabs as "ragheads," Islam as "wicked," and Muhammad as "demon possessed," or advocating for internment of all Arab or Muslim Americans. Public personalities who made statements of this nature did so with impunity, moving along uncensored and unscathed in their careers.

The Affirmative Response

Arab Americans and Muslims definitely face challenges. The increased hate crimes, discrimination, cultural stereotyping, and public acceptance of open bigotry have been major setbacks. Yet, despite such problems, 86 percent of Arab Americans in a 2003 Detroit area study still felt "at home in America" and 94 percent felt "proud to be an American" even though they remain a community "defined as essentially foreign." Eighty-six percent felt confidence in their local police and 66 percent felt confidence in the U.S. legal system, a higher level of confidence than felt among the non-Arab Detroit population. A 2002 poll found that about 40 percent of Arab Americans were more likely than before to discuss the Middle East with friends and acquaintances.[34]

In the aftermath of 9/11, Arab American organizations, churches, mosques, student groups, educators, and individuals set out to create or strengthen bonds of solidarity with fellow Americans. They decided not to allow their ethnicity or religion to be defined either by violent extremists in the Arab and Muslim worlds or by hostile and uninformed Americans. And their outreach efforts have been well received. Invitations have poured in from schools, universities, churches, community groups, corporations, and government agencies. Some governmental agencies began their own constructive outreach to Arab Americans and Muslims.

At the national level, the civil rights divisions of federal agencies extended their outreach to the Arab American, Muslim, and South Asian communities. The Department of Justice began regular interagency meetings with representatives of "heritage communities" to discuss civil rights and civil liberties issues. The Equal Employment Opportunity Commission took a strong stand in opposing anti-Arab discrimination. After various organizations documented numerous incidents of illegal airline profiling, the Department of the Treasury instituted lawsuits against those airlines. The Department of Homeland Security appointed an Arab American leader to its advisory board and created incident management teams ready to respond in moments of crisis and promote coordination with Arab American and Muslim leaders.

Arab American organizations held cultural sensitivity workshops for thousands of police, FBI, and other law enforcement officers, training them to recognize the difference between actual threats and cultural norms associated with Arab culture and Islam. The organizations helped to organize the first FBI training camp for high school seniors at the FBI Academy. They saw the need for more Arab American and Muslim representation in law enforcement and encouraged young people to pursue law enforcement careers.

These programs helped restore trust. Important new bridges were built during a time of multiple dangers and the efforts by Arab Americans paid off. The 2007 Pew research project found that knowing a Muslim was associated with more favorable views about Muslims. Those without personal contact, who relied on the mass media for their knowledge about Islam, had more negative views.

The Arab American community remained vulnerable, but in many ways their institutions were in a position of greater strength and had greater access to policy makers than before 9/11. There were new mechanisms in place to prevent and counteract violations of civil rights. Arab Americans had won new friends, allies, and public recognition.[35]

CONCLUSION

Conflicts in the Middle East and South Asia have generated streams of immigrants to the United States. Lebanese, Palestinians, and others fled wars, civil wars, oppressive regimes, military occupations, and poverty; they sought and found political freedom and economic opportunity as new Americans. But events in their home countries—and the U.S. policies that helped shape those events— affected how Americans of Arab descent were regarded by their fellow citizens, portrayed in the media, and treated by their government. Middle East conflicts led to the increased discrimination, cultural stereotyping, and political surveillance in the 1970s, the anti-Arab terrorism of the 1980s, the first big wave of hate crimes during the Gulf War, and the anti-Muslim bias that became so vehement after 9/11.

On September 11, 2001, a few Arab Americans and Muslims were called on to be among the heroes and rescuers; others were among those who were lost. Many were the victims of hate, discrimination, and the violation of civil liberties. All of them felt the impact of those events. Their stories too should be part of the national memory of 9/11.

Since 9/11, the role of Arab Americans and Muslims in their society was altered. They were no longer invisible, although some tried to make their ethnic or religious identity less obvious. Others responded by boldly reaching out to their neighbors, community institutions, and law enforcement and government agencies. They found many new opportunities for heightened engagement in public life. While many people encountered hate and discrimination, the American commitment to the civil rights and civil liberties of all was reaffirmed.

NOTES

1. *University of Massachusetts Magazine Online* (Winter 2002). Accessed 2/5/10 at http://www.umassmag.com/winter_2002/OBITUARIES__ 1976_99_257.html.

2. "Street Renaming Honors Arab American Victim of 9/11," *Aramica,* August 5, 2005, accessed online 2/10/09 at http://74.125.93.132/ search?q=cache:-PgEKvhbeFsJ:www.indypressny.org/nycma/voices/ 128/briefs/briefs_3/+%E2%80%9CStreet+Renaming+Honors+Arab+A merican+Victim+of+9/11%E2%80%9D&cd=1&hl=en&ct=clnk&gl=us; "Our Towns: For Arab-Americans, Flag-Flying and Fear," *New York Times,* September 14, 2001, accessed online 2/11/09 at http://query.nytimes.com/ gst/fullpage.html?res=9404E0DF1E38F937A2575AC0A9679C8B63& sec=&spon=&pagewanted=all.

3. Barbara Ferguson, "US Honors Muslim Police Officials," *Arab News,* February 3, 2002, http://archive.arabnews.com/?page=4&section=0&arti cle=12531&d=3&m=2&y=2002.

4. "Chapter Reports," *ADC Times,* October–November, 2001, 27–34; "Orlando Arab Americans Donate $50,000 to Red Cross Fund, ADC Times," September 2001, 7; Michael S. Lee, *Healing a Nation: The Arab American Experience after September 11* (Washington, DC: Arab American Institute, n.d.); *Profiling and Pride: Arab American Attitudes and Behavior Since September 11* (Washington, DC: Arab American Institute Foundation, 2002), accessed online 3/9/09, at http://aai.3cdn.net/d7083bd00cf4ce3240_ wfm6ii8b7.pdf.

5. Unless otherwise indicated, the hate crime and discrimination incidents cited in this section are drawn from *Report on Hate Crimes and Discrimination against Arab Americans: The Post-September 11 Backlash,* edited by Hussein Ibish, principal researcher Ann Stewart (Washington, DC: ADC Research Institute, 2003), accessed online 2/09 at http://adc.org/ index.php?id=3302.

6. "NYPD Holds Annual Pre-Ramadan Conference," *New York Times,* September 1, 2002, accessed online 2/12/09 at http://www.nyc.gov/html/ nypd/html/pr/pr_2008_034.shtml.

7. Quoted in Aladdin Elaasar, *Silent Victims: The Plight of Arabs & Muslims in Post 9/11 America* (Bloomington, IN: privately printed, 2004), 215–216.

8. Private communication to the author at the office of the American-Arab Anti-Discrimination Committee in the days immediately after 9/11; Ibish, *Report on Hate Crimes and Discrimination,* 134.

9. Ibish, *Report on Hate Crimes and Discrimination,* 135.

10. Ibish, *Report on Hate Crimes and Discrimination,* 135.

11. Gregory Orfalea's *The Arab Americans: A History* (Northampton, MA: Olive Branch Press, 2006) provides an excellent account of the Arab American community and the challenges it faced. See also *Congressional*

Hearings on Anti-Arab Violence, Special Report, edited by Larry Ekin and Leila Gorchev (Washington, DC: ADC Research Institute, 1986); *1991 Report on Anti-Arab Hate Crimes,* Special Report (Washington, DC: ADC Research Institute, 1992); *Hate Crimes, Discrimination, and Defamation of Arab Americans* (Washington, DC: ADC Research Institute, 1995); Ghada Khouri, ed., *1996–1997 Report on Hate Crimes and Discrimination Against Arab Americans* (Washington, DC: ADC Research Institute, 1997); Hussein Ibish, ed., *1998–2000 Report on Hate Crimes and Discrimination against Arab Americans* (Washington, DC: ADC Research Institute, 2001), accessed online 2/20/09 at http://adc.org/index.php?id=3302.

12. Jack G. Shaheen, *Reel Bad Arabs: How Hollywood Vilifies a People* (Northampton, MA: Interlink Publishing Group, 2001); Jack G. Shaheen, *Arab and Muslim Stereotyping in American Popular Culture* (Washington, DC: Georgetown University Center for Muslim/Christian Understanding, 1997). The latter covers film, television, and news broadcasts.

13. Hussein Ibish, "Defamation in the Media," in Ibish, ed., *2003–2007 Report on Hate Crimes and Discrimination against Arab Americans* (Washington, DC: American-Arab Anti-Discrimination Committee Research Institute, 2008), 75–94, especially 75–76, 81–94.

14. "ADC Harassment and Violence Log" (American-Arab Anti-Discrimination Committee, no date). Covers cases in 1985 and 1986. *Congressional Hearings on Anti-Arab Violence: A Milestone for Arab-American Rights* (Washington, DC: ADC Research Institute, 1986).

15. Larry Ekin and Leila Gorchev, eds., *1991 Report on Anti-Arab Hate Crimes: Political and Hate Violence against Arab-Americans* (Washington, DC: ADC Research Institute, 1992).

16. Hussein Ibish, ed., *1998–2000 Report on Hate Crimes and Discrimination against Arab Americans* (Washington, DC: ADC Research Institute, 2001), 23–32.

17. Unless otherwise indicated, the incidents of hate crimes and discrimination in this section are drawn from Hussein Ibish, ed., *2003–2007 Report on Hate Crimes and Discrimination against Arab Americans* (Washington, DC: American-Arab Anti-Discrimination Committee Research Institute, 2008).

18. According to a study by the Center for Law and Security at New York University. "Law Center: Little Evidence of Jihadists in the U.S.," CNN.com, 10/16/07; accessed online 2/25/09 at http://www.cnn.com/2007/US/10/15/terror.study/index.html.

19. "Profiling and Pride: Arab American Attitudes and Behavior Since September 11," *Arab Americans: An Identity Survey* (Zogby International, 2007); accessed online 3/9/09 at http://www.aaiusa.org/page/-/Polls/AAIIdentity2007Final%20Report.pdf.

20. Unless otherwise cited, the cases mentioned in this section are from Hussein Ibish, ed., *2003–2007 Report on Hate Crimes and Discrimination Against Arab Americans.*

21. For information on CAIR's annual reports since 1996, see "The Status of Muslim Civil Rights in the United States: Without Fear of Discrimination," accessed online 2/26/09 at http://www.cair.com/CivilRights/CivilRightsReports.aspx.

22. Rick Hampson, "Fear 'as Bad as after 9/11,'" *USA Today,* December 20, 2006, accessed online 2/25/09 at http://www.usatoday.com/news/nation/2006-12-12-arab-americans-cover_x.htm.

23. Hussein Ibish, ed., *2003–2007 Report on Hate Crimes and Discrimination Against Arab Americans,* 34–35.

24. Ibid.

25. Andrea Elliott, "After 9/11, Arab-Americans Fear Police Acts, Study Shows," *New York Times,* June 12, 2006, accessed online 2/26/09, at http://www.nytimes.com/2006/06/12/us/12arabs.html.

26. Much of the material in this section is drawn from- "Reel Bad Arabs: How Hollywood Vilifies a People," Democracy Now radio, October 19, 2007, accessed online 2/28/09, at http://74.125.47.132/search?q=cache:Q0um0PmrSfgJ:www.democracynow.org/2007/10/19/reel_bad_arabs_how_hollywood_vilifies+%22jack+shaheen%22+%22the+kingdom%22&hl=en&ct=clnk&cd=2&gl=us.

27. Shaheen, Jack G., *Guilty: Hollywood's Verdict on Arabs after 9/11* (Northampton, MA: Interlink Publishing, 2007), xv.

28. Stephen Gaghan, advance promotional commentary for Shaheen's *Guilty.*

29. Shaheen, *Guilty,* 38–39, 169–171.

30. Huseein Ibish, ed., *2003–2007 Report on Hate Crimes and Discrimination.*

31. For a broader, global perspective on Islamophobia, see the numerous documents on the topic from the Organization for Security and Cooperation in Europe (OSCE): http://www.osce.org. For example, Imam Abduljalil Sajid of the World Congress of Faiths provides detailed analysis and documentation of the phenomenon in "Islamophobia: A New Word for an Old Fear," a paper presented at an OSCE "Conference on Anti-Semitism and on Other Forms of Intolerance," June 8 and 9, 2005. Accessed online 1/4/12 at http://www.osce.org/cio/15618.

32. "Public Expresses Mixed Views of Islam, Mormonism," Pew Forum, September 25, 2007, accessed online 2/25/09 at http://pewforum.org/surveys/religionviews07/.

33. For fuller discussion of this issue and examples of hate speech in the media, see the chapter "Defamation in the Media" in Ibish, *2003–2007 Report on Hate Crimes and Discrimination against Arab Americans,* 81–94.

34. "UM Detroit Arab American Study Portrays a Complex Population," University of Michigan News Service, July 29, 2004, accessed online at http://www.umich.edu/news/index.html?Releases/2004/Jul04/r072904 and "Profiling and Pride: Arab American Attitudes and Behavior Since Sep-

tember 11" (Washington, DC: Arab American Institute Foundation, 2002); accessed online 1/4/12 at http://www.aaiusa.org/reports/profiling-and-pride-arab-american-attitudes-and-behavior-since-september-11/.

35. For fuller detail on the work with federal agencies, see Hussein Ibish, ed., *2003–2007 Report on Hate Crimes and Discrimination against Arab Americans*, 95–97.

3

THE FAMILY

Randa A. Kayyali

At dawn on the day after September 11, 2001 (9/11), raids and interrogations by INS officers began in some Arab American homes, pulling all family members out of bed, questioning the adults about their citizenship status and acquaintances. These raids were traumatic for all, but particularly for the children. In addition, federal authorities detained 2,000 men, leaving families in a constant state of anxiety and often with financial problems. For the most part, today such raids have ceased and Arab Americans in the United States have resumed their daily lives. The events of 9/11 led to a greater visibility of Arabs in the American public sphere and media and to higher rates of discrimination and hate crimes. Arab Americans have been unevenly impacted by these incidents and have responded in a variety of ways. In terms of identity, reactions have ranged from hiding identity to highlighting their origins so as to educate others. However, the family—nuclear and extended—has remained strong. In close-knit families, discrimination against a family member can feel more personal, so after 9/11, close relatives experienced hate crimes and discriminatory treatment directly as well as indirectly.

The events of 9/11 have not altered the importance of family for Arab Americans. The intense level of contact and interactions between mothers, fathers, brothers, sisters, and cousins can be described as interconnected, or very close.[1] The hierarchal structures of Arab American families generally favor older members of the household, and the decision maker may be the father or mother, who generally carries a larger burden of child care. The rates of marriage as well as household sizes for Arab Americans exceed the national average due to larger families living together under one roof. The larger size of households generally means that siblings and cousins are in close proximity to each other. Arab American families congregate with plenty of food and fellowship at dinnertime or at holidays and on special occasions such as weddings, funerals, and births. Research has found that the events, traditions, and relationships that make Arab American family life so interconnected have not changed in frequency after 9/11.

DOCUMENTING ARAB AMERICAN FAMILY LIFE

Arab American is a broad label, used to describe immigrants from the Arabic-speaking countries of the Middle East and North Africa living in the United States. The U.S. Census Bureau defines "Arab" as a person "of Arab ancestry" who "reported being Arab, Egyptian, Iraqi, Jordanian, Lebanese, Middle Eastern, Moroccan, North African, Palestinian, Syrian and so on."[2] However, there are many who hail from the region but do not identify as Arabs. Non-Arab minorities such as Kurds, Berbers, and Chaldeans tend to continue to identify primarily with their ethnicity after migration. Minority Christian groups from the Middle East and North Africa, such as Maronites and Copts, may also not self-identify as Arab for historical and contemporary reasons. Beyond the issue of defining who is an Arab, it is hard to generalize about which family traditions are Arab because many traditions are rooted in specific, subnational locales and customs, and are affected by the family's socioeconomic realities. Arab American families reflect the diverse customs relating to food, dress, language, religious practices, and moral values in the Arab world.

This chapter is based on both nationwide statistical research and local ethnographic research in the Washington, D.C., metropolitan area. The quantitative data is from the decennial U.S. Census of 2000 and the 2005–2007 American Community Survey (ACS) that is conducted by the Census Bureau but is taken on an annual basis on a much smaller scale.[3] Census Bureau data is not a perfect reflection of the Arab American population because Arab Americans constitute less than 1 percent of the U.S. population, and statistics based on a small population percentage-wise can be skewed. For the purposes of this discussion Census Bureau information was supplemented with qualitative research: 12 in-depth focused interviews in the summer of 2009 in the District of Columbia and the neighboring suburbs of Virginia and Maryland. Metropolitan Washington, D.C., has a large, dispersed Arab American population, with a socioeconomic profile that indicates that it is, on average, a wealthy and educated group. The respondents—men and women—included Muslims and Christians, although only one wore an outward expression of her religious affiliation. While this sample group of interviewees is small, it was supplemented by ethnographic research in homes and social gatherings over an 11-year period.

THE AVERAGE ARAB AMERICAN HOUSEHOLD

Today, most Arab American families consist of married parents and children living at home. The average family and household size for Arab Americans increased between 2000 and 2007 and remained larger than the average American family and household. According to the Census Bureau, a family is "a group of two people or more (one of whom is the householder) related by birth, marriage, or adoption and residing together" and a household "consists of all the people who occupy a housing unit."[4] The Census Bureau's definition of family is based on consanguinity as well as residence and is usually interpreted to mean two or more nuclear family members who live together. According to the Census Bureau, only about two-thirds of U.S. households are defined as family units; because "households" include people who live alone or with nonrelated housemates, households are, on average, smaller than families.

As Table 3.1 shows, since 9/11 the average Arab American household and family size have grown proportionately more than the average U.S. population equivalents, indicating that Arab Americans are living with more relatives and nonrelatives. In addition to having larger families, the interconnectedness of Arab Americans encourages adult children to continue living with their families after the age of 18.

Table 3.1 Family and Household Sizes

	Census 2000		American Community Survey 2005–2007	
	Arab Americans	U.S. population	Arab Americans	U.S. population
Average household size	2.88	2.59	3.02	2.6
Average family size	3.51	3.14	3.71	3.19

Source: U.S. Census Bureau, Population Division. Census 2000 statistics from "We the People of Arab Ancestry in the United States" Report #22 by Brittingham and de la Cruz 2005, Table 2, page 19, available at http://www.census.gov/popula tion/www/cen2000/briefs/index.html#sr); and Table S0201, "Selected Population Profile in the United States," from the 2005–2007American Community Survey three-year estimates, available at http://factfinder.census.gov.

THE EXTENDED FAMILY HOUSEHOLD

In comparison to the U.S. national average, the larger family size for Arab Americans may be due not just to having more children but also to differing definitions of family households. In many Arab American families, there is an expectation that adult children will live at home until they get married, even if they are older than their late teens or early 20s. Another reason for the larger family size is that relatives often live with each other or visit, sometimes for extended periods of time. In-laws, grandparents, aunts, uncles, and cousins often live in a single household and the lines between nuclear family, family household, and extended family often blur. When asked to define their family, respondents mentioned cousins, uncles, grandparents, and great-aunts; and one respondent described a "second ring" of family that included additional paternal cousins and great-aunts as well as family friends. Another subject defined family as including "up to the progeny of my cousins." Spouses and fiancées were rarely mentioned as counting as family, perhaps implying a heavier emphasis on shared blood as a factor in definitions of family.

Children sometimes spend their childhood living with relatives who are better able to take care of their needs than are their parents. Depending on the strength of family relationships, aunts and uncles can step in to help bring up children and be there for life events such as graduations and birthdays, as a parent might. U.S.-born children and Arab American adults return to visit relatives and friends in Arab countries for weeks, or even months, in the summertime when school is out, bringing presents with them and attending family events such as weddings. After choosing to leave her nuclear family in the United States and attend the American University in Beirut, one respondent lived in the city with her grandmother, aunt, and cousins, creating what she described as "a reconstructed family" in Lebanon.

In the United States, with the exception of the year 2003, the number of individuals from Arabic-speaking countries admitted as immigrants or who became legal permanent residents has remained level post-9/11.[5] This is significant for Arab American families since family reunification is usually an important factor in the choice to migrate. In addition, young single Arabs and young families who immigrate often support family members who remain in their countries of origin, separating adult children from their parents, aunts, uncles, grandparents, nephews, and nieces. After securing U.S. citizenship or permanent resident status, family members can sponsor visas for their close kin (parents; husband/wife; children and siblings) living in the Arab world, often leading to chain migrations from their country of origin to a specific locale in the United States, such as the Detroit and New York/New Jersey metropolitan areas as well as the Orange County, California area.

FAMILIES IN ARAB AMERICAN COMMUNITIES

Many Arab Americans have tried to maintain the traditional interconnectedness of the Arab family in their lives in the United States. New immigrants tend to move to neighborhoods where they will be close to people from their family, village, or city of origin. These traditional networks may be further expanded to include Arabs who are not from their family or neighborhood so as to maintain a social life based on familiar traditions, language, and customs. Living with family members usually eases the new immigrants' transition to the United States and helps them feel more grounded by providing psychological and financial support. Many of the new immigrants, particularly those fleeing war or harsh economic conditions, arrive in the United States with little money and no job or insurance. Family members and networks can help new immigrants by loaning them money, providing lodging, or giving guidance on the procedures for renting apartments and enrolling in schools or universities. Arab American small business owners sometimes hire family members and friends, making it easier for the immigrant to find their first job in the United States, particularly if they are unskilled and have poor English-language skills.

There are only a few highly concentrated Arabic-ethnic communities or ethnic enclaves in the United States with specialty grocery stores, bakeries, restaurants, and Arabic-language bookshops and stores that cater predominantly to an Arab American clientele. The most prominent of these is Dearborn, Michigan. In 2000, the city of Dearborn had a total population of approximately 100,000, of which 30 percent were Arab American.[6] Community leaders in this suburb of Detroit established the Arab Community Center for Economic and Social Services (ACCESS) in the early 1970s and founded a Family Support Center, which provides social services and assistance to people of Arab and Chaldean origins.[7]

In contrast to the situation in Dearborn, in Chicago, particularly on the southwest side that is home to the largest concentration of Arabs in the greater Chicago area, the "ethnic safety net" deteriorated in the late 1990s. In 1997, there was greater than a 60 percent underemployment or unemployment rate in these Arab American households and a high instance of children living at or below the poverty level.[8] The surrounding neighborhood problems with crime and drugs impacted the Arab American community, particularly affecting the youth. The rise in juvenile detentions and dangers in the neighborhood heightened tensions within families, and parents felt unable to effectively discipline or monitor their children. Alcoholism, drug abuse, domestic violence, and broken families became common, interrelated problems. Sixty percent of Arab Americans in a survey taken at that time reported having ongoing domestic problems that required outside help.[9] When compared with Dearborn, the situation in Chicago in the late 1990s suggests that an ethnic-based safety net was crucial to the ability of the community to survive and repel serious problems within the family.[10]

CARING FOR ELDERLY PARENTS

One major issue for Arab American families has been how to care for aging parents and grandparents. In Arab countries, nursing homes are rare and the elderly are kept at home where they are either cared for by a family member or a hired caregiver. Although senior living facilities are common in the United States, none are designated to serve the Arab community specifically. One woman who was interviewed equated putting the elderly in retirement homes with abandoning and uprooting them; she stressed the importance of keeping the elderly living in a comfortable family setting. Another said that after much deliberation by family members, they were forced to put her paternal grandmother in a home because "people were no longer able to take care of her the way that she needed to be taken care of." The solution that they found was to transition her into a senior daycare facility that had a live-in component and gradually move her from visiting to living in the home. However, most of the families of the interviewees rotated parents and grandparents among the homes of their children, moving them every three to four months. With adult children living in many countries, these households can be spread over continents and require complex travel and visa arrangements.

Upholding the family responsibility for taking care of elderly parents can be challenging in the United States. If the elderly parents' English-language skills are poor and they have no form of private transportation, they may be unable or unwilling to leave the house without their adult children even if they wish to be independent.[11] In homes where all family members work, the daily activities for these housebound parents are watching television, cooking, and cleaning. The elderly are concerned that they are a burden and have to rely on their children and grandchildren to socialize with them and take them on outings after they return from work or school or on the weekends. As a result, many elderly immigrants feel lonely and yearn for the time when they were self-sufficient and mobile. While there is a strong sense of having a filial duty to take care of parents in the home, the onus of this duty can be substantial. Regardless, one respondent described this duty as one that she and her siblings happily take on; they were all there for their father in the hospital "100 percent." There was a definite reciprocity in how the adult children felt—their parents and grandparents had brought them up and taken care of them and now it was their turn to do the same for their elders out of respect, love, and a sense of responsibility.

MARRIAGE

Between 2000 and 2005–2007 the statistical trends related to marriage among Arab Americans were similar to those of the general

U.S. population: married-couple households decreased slightly, the number of responses from women in households that had no spouse present (female householder) rose, and the percentage of nonfamily households—meaning living in a home without relatives but with other people—also increased. Although the American Community Survey eliminated the category of male householder (no spouse), it is interesting to note that according to the 2000 Census Arab American men were more likely than the average American male to live without a spouse or family. This stands in contrast to Arab American women, who were less likely to live alone than the average American. The fact that the figures on Arab American households mirrored changes in the total U.S. population seems to indicate that 9/11 did not have an exceptional impact on Arab Americans in terms of household type and composition.

As Table 3.2 shows, both before and after 9/11, Arab Americans had a 5 percent higher incidence of married-couple households than the average American, partially as a result of the importance placed

Table 3.2 Household Type

Household type (in percentages)	Census 2000		American Community Survey 2005–2007	
	Arab Americans	Total U.S. population	Arab Americans	Total U.S. population
Married couple	58	52.5	56.4	49.8
Female householder (no spouse)	6.9	11.8	7.9	12.5
Male householder (no spouse)	5.3	4.1	n/a	n/a
Nonfamily household	29.9	31.5	30.2	33.1

Source: U.S. Census Bureau, Population Division. Census 2000 statistics from "We the People of Arab Ancestry in the United States" Report #22 by Brittingham and de la Cruz 2005, Table 2, page 19, available at http://www.census.gov/popula tion/www/cen2000/briefs/index.html#sr); and Table S0201, "Selected Population Profile in the United States," from the 2005–2007American Community Survey three-year estimates, available at http://factfinder.census.gov.

on family and marriage. When marital status is further explored, on average, Arab Americans are less likely to be separated, divorced, or widowed than Americans (see Tables 3.3 and 3.4). This statistical finding was supported in the research for this chapter; almost all of the households visited were composed of married couples of varying ages or of adult children living with their parents, who were married.

The ethnographic research component of this study makes clear that there is a less parental pressure to marry among Arab Americans in the metropolitan Washington, D.C., area due to support for their children's higher education and career ambitions. Some women as well as men in their 20s are choosing to move out of their parents' home and buy condos of their own. However, one of the interviewees—a 31-year-old woman, who is engaged—lives with her mother but will move out after the wedding. Another said that she continues to live with her fiancé despite pressure from her mother to set a wedding date. In more traditional Arabic communities, particularly in ethnic enclaves, adherence to the cultural norm of the girls living at home until marriage and marrying earlier for the purpose of starting a family is more predominant.[12]

Table 3.3 Marital Status*

	Census 2000		American Community Survey, 2005–2007	
	Arab Americans	Total U.S. population	Arab Americans	Total U.S. population
Now married	57.5	54.4	55.5	50.5
Separated, widowed, or divorced	12.5	18.5	12.6	19.1
Never married	30	27.1	31.9	30.4

*Population 15 years and older

Source: U.S. Census Bureau, Population Division. Census 2000 statistics from "We the People of Arab Ancestry in the United States" Report #22 by Brittingham and de la Cruz 2005, Table 2, page 19, available at http://www.census.gov/popula tion/www/cen2000/briefs/index.html#sr); and Table S0201, "Selected Population Profile in the United States," from the 2005–2007American Community Survey three-year estimates, available at http://factfinder.census.gov.

Table 3.4 Breakdowns of Separated, Widowed, and Divorced

American Community Survey 2005–2007	Arab Americans	Total U.S. population
Separated	3.9	6.4
Widowed	7.1	10.5
Divorced	1.6	2.2
Total % of separated, widowed, and divorced in the U.S. population	**12.6**	**19.1**

Source: U.S. Census Bureau, Population Division. Census 2000 statistics from "We the People of Arab Ancestry in the United States" Report #22 by Brittingham and de la Cruz 2005, Table 2, page 19, available at http://www.census.gov/popula tion/www/cen2000/briefs/index.html#sr); and Table S0201, "Selected Population Profile in the United States," from the 2005–2007American Community Survey three-year estimates, available at http://factfinder.census.gov.

Based on the interviews for this study, Arab American parents expect their children to get married and to have children as the ideal norm. Homosexuality is generally strongly discouraged. Adoption is also rare. An emphasis on family and marriage combined with a conservative approach to sexuality can create tension and misunderstanding between Arab American parents and their gay and lesbian children. These tensions are further magnified by the intense interconnectivity of Arab American extended families.

INTERCONNECTED FAMILIES

A study based in Lebanon found that the family was defined by a patriarchal connectivity that "operated effectively in part because both men and women were socialized to view themselves relationally" and that individuals internalized the importance of family relations as well as the accompanying gendered and aged hierarchies.[13] While the gendered hierarchies were more mixed in the United States among Lebanese Americans, status as a parent remains a vaunted position for Lebanese living in America, underlining the continuing importance of age in the hierarchical family order.

Many interviewees highlighted the fact that the extensive interconnectivity and emphasis on the importance of family for Arab

Americans was something that set them apart culturally from other Americans. One woman compared Arab Americans with the general American society, by saying, "As a family, you are more interlinked." This interlinking can result in positive, healthy relationships or it can put pressure on the individual to live with tension-filled relationships. One woman described her mother as "my closest confidante and friend" while another described her family relations as "strained and at times dutiful" and her family as "fractured." Family dynamics, as with all ethnicities, fluctuate and differ according to specific circumstances and times.

PATRIARCHY

The Arab family structure has been described by many academics, such as Hisham Sharabi, as patriarchal.[14] Patriarchy is "the privileging of males and seniors and the mobilization of kinship structures, morality, and idioms to legitimate and institutionalize gendered and age domination."[15] From the interviews done for this chapter, it seems that the patriarchal family structure has lost some of its power among Arab Americans. Although three respondents stated that their families were patriarchal, an equal number countered with a description of their family as matriarchal, an alternative structure that will be discussed in the next section.

In the self-described patriarchal families mentioned in the interviews, the father was the first and ultimate authority in terms of making decisions and the main income earner, while the mother stayed at home with the children when they were young (although she may have worked when the children were older). In a series of in-depth interviews and fieldwork with Arab Americans, as well as surveys, Jen'nan Ghazal Read found that although Arab American women have higher average educational attainment, English-language ability, and household income, they have lower employment rates than most other groups of U.S. women, regardless of their religious affiliation.[16] The factors that influence whether or not an Arab American woman works outside the home are homogamous marriages, beliefs in conservative interpretations of the Bible or Qur'an regarding gender roles, and expressions of an ideological support of patriarchal gender roles. Read found that attaining a bachelor's or master's degree does not necessarily lead to high rates of employment or a career because a woman's education is often seen as a resource that aids both the family and the community by allowing women to "marry up," be worldly, and later educate their children rather than for the purpose of pursuing their own career path.[17]

The persistence of patriarchy is more likely to occur in the United States in areas where there is a high density of Arab Americans, such as in Detroit, and thus more obligations to extended kin and community networks. For example, in low-income Lebanese and Yemeni families in Dearborn, women often do not work outside the home, despite the financial strains this places on the family.[18] In places such as the Washington, D.C., metropolitan area, with a less dense concentration of Arabs but with stronger educational backgrounds, there may be fewer family and community obligations and more opportunities to work outside the home. However, more research needs to be done on the myriad of socioeconomic factors that contribute to the choices made by Arab American women regarding employment.

MATRIARCHY

Some Arab Americans described their family structure as matriarchal, defying the stereotype of Arab patriarchy. While the mother was seen as the compliant nurturer in the patriarchal families, in self-described matriarchal families, the mother was the authority figure, and sometimes the main or equal breadwinner. In these matriarchal families, the mother made the major decisions, controlled household finances, and maintained her power by staying in close contact with her adult children. All of the respondents in the interviews reported that they spoke with their mother at least once a week, but not with their father. Often mothers continued to guide their children's decisions even as adults, despite living in a different city or on a different continent, implying a continuation of authority that dovetails with the age component of the definition of patriarchy. One interviewee said simply, "I'm a momma's boy. All Arab boys are momma's boys. That's where they [women] get their power."

In those families in which mothers have the central role in the family structure, many of the respondents considered their mothers "the glue, the cohesion" for the family and thus central to its interlinking. Even if the mothers worked outside the home and were part of a working partnership with their husbands, they seemed to prioritize their obligations to the family and dominate the household. The interviews also revealed that the more traditional stay-at-home mothering role often itself underscored women's authority in the family and household during their children's childhood. However, dominance in the household or over family matters does not necessarily mean equality between men and women.

CHILDREN

Census statistics show that overall Arab Americans are a young population. The median age of Arab Americans was five years younger than the national median age, remaining at 30.8 years in both 2000 and 2005–2007. According to the American Community Survey data in Table 3.5, 31 percent of Arab Americans are under 18—substantially more than the national average of 25 percent. The high proportion of under-18-year-olds was present before 9/11 and continues to be an important demographic factor for Arab Americans.

The high rate of under-18-year-olds and the relatively youthful age of the Arab American population means that Arab American families tend to have a larger number of children. Depending on the specific circumstances and family location, socializing within the extended family can be so extensive that cousins can be as close as siblings, growing up together from childhood and into adulthood.

Table 3.5 Age Distribution

	Census 2000		American Community Survey, 2005–2007	
	Arab Americans	Total U.S. population	Arab Americans	Total U.S. population
Under 18	29.9	25.6	31	24.7
18 to 64	62.9	61.9	61.6	63
65 and older	7.2	12.4	7.5	12.5
Median age (years)	30.8	35.4	30.8	36.4

Source: U.S. Census Bureau, Population Division. Census 2000 statistics from "We the People of Arab Ancestry in the United States" Report #22 by Brittingham and de la Cruz 2005, Table 2, page 19, available at http://www.census.gov/popula tion/www/cen2000/briefs/index.html#sr); and Table S0201, "Selected Population Profile in the United States," from the 2005–2007American Community Survey three-year estimates, available at http://factfinder.census.gov.

SIBLING RELATIONSHIPS

The tension between interconnectedness and power dynamics is reproduced in family relationships among peers within the family group, such as when brothers and sisters concurrently fight and are close. Sibling and cousins are often very important relationships for Arab Americans: brothers, sisters, and cousins can be an individual's closest confidantes from youth until old age. As siblings age, they usually continue to be involved in each other's lives and decisions, even after getting married and having their own children. However, not all siblings and cousins get along. There are often rifts within the nuclear and extended family, based on personality and family politics. These conflicts and their associated alliances may shift or continue throughout life, but the importance of the interconnectivity of family is often passed down from generation to generation.

Age and gender hierarchies exist within many Arab American families. People with three or more siblings reported that age hierarchies between siblings formed because parents gave more authority to the elder sibling, who in turn bossed around or bullied younger brothers and sisters. Many studies on the Arab American families conclude that boys are given more latitude and playtime, while girls are more closely monitored and required to help out with daily household chores, thus reproducing traditional gender roles and dynamics in which boys have more freedom and girls are kept closer to the home and within the family. Research on the Shi'a community in Dearborn concluded that the disparate gender-specific treatment of children caused boys to "take on more of the social characteristics of the dominant American society, whereas anti-assimilationist pressure is exerted on the girls through careful monitoring of social activities."[19] This implies that the girls were protected within the family and community of Dearborn while the boys dodged the traditional, authoritative role assigned for men and instead took on more of the social characteristics of the dominant U.S. society. This study on Shi'a in Dearborn stands in contrast to the ethnographic fieldwork in Washington, D.C., undertaken for this essay. I found that both adult men and women were active in the public sphere, working and socializing with non-Arab Americans, regardless of gender.

FRIENDSHIPS ACROSS ETHNIC LINES

Of course, Arab Americans have friendships and relationships that exist across many racial and ethnic lines. In the interviews, all reported having daily interactions with non-Arab colleagues at work or school, regardless of their religious affiliation. One respondent explained that he had two pools of friends: one, mostly Arabs, was the source of his close, deep friendships, while another bigger and less intimate pool of friends were Asian, African American, Italian American, 'white', and Indian American. One post-9/11 study on American Muslims found that young people have felt socially excluded in high schools and limited their friends to fellow South Asian Muslims, finding that a "shared religious identity as Muslim has increasingly come to underpin friendships."[20] For some Arab Americans religion does indeed play a role in choosing friendships, but for others shared ethnicity plays a more important role so Arab American Muslims and Christians share social circles. For still others, race, ethnicity, and religion play no role in the choice of friendships.

FAMILY HONOR

Honor plays a central role in regulating life in the Arab world. A person's honor is shown through his or her behavior and is considered an extension of the family's honor. As with other immigrant communities, there is often a rift between immigrant parents and U.S.-born children that reflects generational divides in assessments of norms and acceptable behavior. Parents sometimes insist on certain types of dress or behavior because of a desire to maintain the good reputation of the family. If the Arab American family is part of a larger circle of family or friends from the Arab world (which was not always the case), there is a certain amount of pressure placed on children and youth to behave in specific, culturally appropriate ways. The interconnectedness of the community in high-density Arab American locales means that there are gossip grapevines that serve to inform the family of misbehavior. These gossip grapevines can even reach family residing overseas. All of the interview respondents who grew up in the United States said that their parents were more worried about what other Arabs in the community thought than they were concerned about "regular Americans." This is partially because news can reach family members and friends quickly and so impact family honor, as interpreted in that setting. However, there is no single Arab moral framework—norms and rules differ from family to family and community to community. For example, while some observant Muslim families discourage their adult children from socializing at any party or gathering where alcohol may be served, for other Arab American families—Christians and more moderate Muslims—alcohol is less of an issue, increasing the number of acceptable venues for socializing outside of the family setting.

CHILDREN AND DISCIPLINE

As is the case with all families, Arab American parents have to discipline their children at times. Many of the interviewees reported that in their childhood, their fathers and mothers sometimes hit them as a disciplinary measure. One woman reflected on episodes from her childhood when her mother "would give us *the* look and if *the* look didn't work then [she laughed loudly] she would pinch us" on the arm. Although this woman did not resent being pinched as a child, she would like to think that she would never hit her own son because, she reasoned, "I don't think it was really effective." An expectant father, however, anticipated that he would spank his child if the child misbehaved, even though the current debates in the United States about the legitimacy of spanking as a form of discipline are certainly impacting the choices made by Arab American parents.

Socializing with peers can be a source of contention between teens and their parents, particularly for girls. Most of the female and some of the male interviewees said that their "extremely protective" parents in some way restricted their interaction with peers. The strictness of parents varied dramatically. Some parents allowed sleepovers and gave their children "lots of leeway" in terms of making their own decisions about socializing. Other parents did not allow their children to see movies at the theater after 7:00 P.M. or spend the night at a friend's house, and insisted on chaperoning them when out with friends at night. In one case parents refused their child's request to go to the prom but relented at the last minute. For other parents the freedom and latitude given to their children depended on the family knowing and trusting their children and their children's friends. Of course, this latter option is more possible when there is a sense of community between sets of Arab American parents and their teenage children.

DATING

In areas with high concentrations of Arab Americans, parents tend to worry about what people will say and how teen behavior will reflect on the family's reputation, particularly if their daughters are rumored to be having premarital sex. Although some Arab American girls are sexually active, even dating is usually considered taboo, particularly for girls in conservative families.[21] Boys are less likely than girls to be punished or admonished for dating, but if a girl thinks that the dating issue is negotiable, or that the relationship is leading to marriage, she might introduce the boy to her parents and may then be allowed to see him with their blessing. Many of the respondents said that dating was actually a nonissue in their teen years because they were not interested in dating in high school—not really out of deference to their parents but more in response to the lack of attractive mates in school.

The cultural taboo on dating in conservative Muslim and Christian families means marriage could happen at a young age, but the increasing desire among Arab American women for higher education and a career have pushed back the age of marriage somewhat. Although generally supportive of their children's desire to attend college, many Arab American parents prefer to send their children to nearby universities so that they can live at home or visit on the weekends. The cost of tuition and housing can be major factors in this choice, but parents also often want their children to continue living in the same household as a protective measure. Affluent and liberal Arab American parents are more likely to allow their children to go away for college and live in college dorms.

At schools and universities, Arab Americans have set up and joined clubs tagged by ethnicity or religion, such as an Arab students club or the Muslim Students Association—a national organization with chapters at universities and colleges across the United States. In the post-9/11 atmosphere of negative perceptions, fear, and intimidation, some Arab American students have chosen to speak out on political issues, particularly the struggles in Palestine and Iraq, while others concentrate on social activities—hosting *haflas* (parties), inviting non-Arab members of the college community and serving Arabic food, bringing in live Arabic music or a disc jockey. Through these clubs, Arab American youth establish friendships and relationships that may lead to engagements and marriage.

WEDDINGS

In addition to the university clubs mentioned above, there are many semi-supervised events that parents may feel are appropriate places for their children to meet a potential spouse, such as weddings and weekend conferences held by national associations. At the local and regional levels, church events and civic associations often organize *haflas* as a place for their members to find partners. Parental permission and approval is sought before marriage, and without it the bride or groom may be ostracized from the family. Under Islamic law and traditions, it is not permissible for a Muslim woman to marry a non-Muslim man, which has led to the conversion of some fiancés to Islam before the wedding in order to secure the approval of the parents and the sheikh from the mosque who marries the couple.

The traditional wedding consists of two parts: the actual marriage ceremony and the *hafla* that follows it. The choice of ceremony varies from a small recitation of vows presided over by a minister, priest, or *imam* to a traditional church wedding. For Muslims, a *sheikh* or *imam* performs the marriage, usually in the privacy of a home with a small group of family members as witnesses. This is called *kitab al-kittaab*—literally meaning "the writing of the book"— in which the couple reads the first verse of the Qur'an with the imam and signs the marriage contract. In the United States an Islamic marriage contract is usually a one-page document that includes the signatures of the couple, the imam, and two witnesses, plus a statement that says that the marriage is governed by Islamic law. It includes the amount of the *mahr*, or dowry, which can be a monetary or a nonmonetary gift given by the groom to the bride at the time of the marriage, and the amount of the *muta'akhir*.[22] The *muta'akhir* is in effect a prenuptial agreement between the couple in case they get divorced and covers financial arrangements to be made if one spouse dies. In addition, a marriage contract can also stipulate that the woman has the right to obtain a divorce. Although signing the *kitab al-kittaab* means that the couple is married according to Islam, this ceremony can take place a year or more before the wedding *haflas*, which marks the social recognition of the marriage. The size of the *haflas*, or reception that celebrates the marriage, varies. Large wedding parties of 500 guests or more are usually community events, with an extended list of invitees, and do not require a formal RSVP.

Although most Arab American weddings and receptions happen in the United States, some couples may choose to get married in their hometowns and hold receptions in the big hotels of Cairo, Beirut, or Amman. As part of the celebration, there are sometimes stage performances, as well as musical bands and/or DJs to play Arabic music, while people talk, sing, or dance late into the night.

An Arab American *hafla,* or wedding reception. For the most part, Arabs have adopted the European tradition of white wedding dresses for women and tuxedos for men. Although it is not common, here, the bride, Ramiah Ali Qasem, and her groom, Raoof Qasem, are accompanied by brides-maids Reema, Manzila, and Dhafer's wife; and groomsmen Dhafer, Amar, and Ali Baleed Almaklani. (Courtesy Arab American National Museum)

Food and desserts are plentiful but alcohol may or may not be served, depending on the beliefs of the bride and groom's families. Also, more conservative Muslims may not approve of singing and dancing at weddings and so might leave halfway through the party. There is an increasing trend towards smaller *haflas* of less than a hundred guests in a home or smaller reception hall, usually with some dancing and music. Although some Islamic centers in the United States have a space to hold a reception or party, wedding ceremonies and processions are generally held at halls or hotels rather than in mosques. A honeymoon trip generally follows the wedding.

BIRTHS, DEATH, AND FUNERALS

Births are celebrated with rituals, gifts, and special foods. Before the baby is born, family, friends, and coworkers hold a baby shower to give gifts such as clothes, toys, and baby gear to the mother, as is common in the United States.

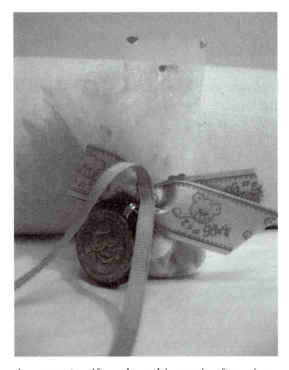

A memento gift such as this one is often given to guests who either attend a baby shower prior to a birth or visit the home of the parents after the birth of a baby. This favor consists of Jordan almonds (sugared almonds) wrapped in tulle and secured with a ribbon that says, "It's a Boy!" or "It's a Girl!" Attached to the ribbon is a flat blue glass bead that is associated with the warding off of the evil eye, and an inscription of the baby's name in Arabic. This gift was given to guests at the 2001 baby shower for Amal Sabag and her son, Zain, of Ann Arbor, Michigan. (Courtesy Arab American National Museum)

Once the baby is born, Muslims usually make it a point to first of all whisper the call of prayer in the baby's ear so that the first thing she or he hears is the "words of God." Babies are sometimes also given pendants with the evil eye (usually a blue glass bead with a white circle) to ward off jealousy and evil spirits. For Muslims the evil eye may be embellished with phrases and verses from the

Qur'an. Before the mother and baby leave the hospital, the pediatric surgeon circumcises both Muslim and Christian boys. Once home, it is traditional to hold a two-day open house in which visitors can congratulate the parents. The new parents serve their guests finger foods and *karawya aka moughli*—a pudding made of crushed rice or cornstarch, sugar, cinnamon, and crushed caraway seeds topped with raw peeled nuts, such as almonds, walnuts, or pistachios, served either hot or cold in small dessert bowls or glasses. Children are often named after dear family members, and traditionally, the first son is named after the father or grandfather (on the father's side) and all the children take the father's first name as their middle name. Christian babies may have a "churching" shortly after their birth, where they are carried into the church with their family at the beginning of the Mass or service. Babies are baptized according the family church's specific traditions, usually within the first few months.

At the other end of life, the traditional Arab funeral includes a religious service in a mosque or church, a burial in a cemetery, and a mourning period. In a church, the service includes an open casket and eulogies for the deceased, as well as readings from the Bible, presided over by a priest or minister. In the mosque, the service is a special group prayer called *salaat al-janazah* that may be attended by men and women, although women pray in a section at the back or to the side of the men. The body of the deceased may or may not have an open casket and is placed in front of the imam.

After the service, the deceased is buried in a cemetery of their denomination. In accord with the guidelines laid down in the Qur'an, Muslims avoid embalming and strive not to unduly disturb the body of the deceased. This has meant that while Christian burials may be delayed for a few days to gather family and friends from afar, Muslim funerals happen shortly after death. Autopsies are discouraged but may be performed, if necessary, with the utmost respect for the dead. Some families choose to send the bodies of the deceased overseas for interment, usually in family cemeteries in their place of origin. Because of the similarity of their liturgical practices and ecclesiastical affiliations, some Melkites, Maronites, and Chaldeans have been buried in Roman Catholic cemeteries in the United States. As the Arab immigrants of the 1960s and 1970s pass away, there has been a growing demand for Muslim burial grounds. Traditionally, a Muslim corpse is washed and wrapped in a white cloth (except in Indonesia), placed directly in the ground and laid on its right side, facing Mecca. American Muslims have had to adapt to U.S. laws that require a simple casket, but they strive to follow the other Islamic guidelines for burials. Mosque committees focused on this issue have bought land for Muslim cemeteries; they have also endorsed the interment of bodies in Jewish and multidenominational cemeteries according to Islamic laws.

After the service and burial, the closest family members to the deceased open their house for three days, hosting family and visitors who come to express their condolences in an *'azza*, or mourning reception. Depending on the local customs in the Arab country of origin, female family members may sit apart from the men and wail to show their emotions, adorned with no jewelry and wearing black clothing to repel death and symbolize their sadness over the loss of a loved one. The mourning period lasts for 40 days, during which the widow and close female relatives of the deceased are expected to wear black. In the United States, women may show less emotion, as marked by wailing, and wear black for less than the traditional 40-day period. For both Christians and Muslims the *'azza* is becoming less formal, and according to one respondent, at an *'azza* he attended, visitors were not divided by gender but by age, with the younger generation sitting outside of the formal guest-receiving area.

KITCHEN CULTURE

Arabs' renowned hospitality has been brought to the United States by Arab Americans. Like a few other communities in the United States —Italian Americans, for example—food is a major cultural expression among Arab Americans: recipes are passed down from generation to generation, refrigerators are usually full of homemade dishes, and dinner is the locus for daily family gatherings. Food plays a chief role in all Muslim and Christian celebrations including Ramadan *iftars, Eid al-adha, Eid al-fitr,* Christmas, and Easter, as well as Thanksgiving. Egyptian Americans also hold a celebration at the beginning of spring called *Sham el-Nassim,* in which the family congregates and eats special foods such as *faseekh* (salted fish), onions, lettuce, and boiled eggs. Usually more food is served than can possibly be eaten—the quantity and variety of dishes prepared and served is understood to signify generosity, respect, and love for those sharing in the meal. Although in traditional homes it is the women who generally cook, among the younger and second generations, men are cooking more.

Families often gather to share food on American holidays as well as religious feast days. Here, the Fakhouri family enjoys *mansaf*, a festive dish of Bedouin origin made from flatbread, lamb, and roasted almonds and/or pine nuts, topped with a yogurt sauce. It is traditionally eaten with the right hand, molded into a ball in the hand, and then fed to others around the tray of food as a sign of affection and love. (Courtesy Arab American National Museum)

Some second- and third-generation Arab Americans describe their Arabic-language skills as "kitchen Arabic," meaning that they know only the common colloquial language they picked up in the kitchen and home, rather than through formal language training. Arabic dishes and the terms used to describe them vary from country to country, and even within a country, but in American popular culture there has been a standardization of what is commonly known as Arabic food. The rise in the popularity of ethnic food and the establishment of Lebanese restaurants has led to the presence of hummus, grape leaves, and tabbouli in American grocery stores. Ethnic Arab restaurants, usually labeled Lebanese or Mediterranean, are generally owned and managed by recently immigrated Arab American families who come from a variety of Arab countries and serve popular dishes, including falafel, kebob, and *shwarma* that have grown popular in American culture.

The increase in demand for Arabic prepared products has been simultaneously fueled by the growth of specialty food production plants and grocery stores. Arabic specialty grocery stores carry sweets such as baklava, olive oil from Lebanon and Palestine, orange and green lentils, canned and dried hummus and fava beans, spices including sumac, cumin, and *za'atar*, and freshly baked pita bread, among other items. Specialty stores that cater to Muslims specifically may carry only religiously permissible, or halal, food. Shellfish, alcohol, and meat not slaughtered in the way prescribed by the Qur'an are not considered halal. Halal butchers have increased in number in the last few years and are mostly located in areas with concentrated Muslim populations. The demand for halal food by Muslim Americans not living in such areas has also grown and food production companies that offer frozen halal meat products have flourished in the United States and Canada. Muslim dietary restrictions can limit the ability of practicing Muslims to eat in restaurants or in the homes of non-Muslims, so some American Muslims have adapted by bringing a dish cooked with halal meat with them to potluck gatherings. However, Muslims have also adapted their dietary restrictions by carefully choosing vegetarian and kosher items in restaurants. (Both kosher and halal meats are butchered in a similar fashion.) Some Muslims do not follow the halal food guidelines very strictly or do so only during Ramadan and on feast days. The growth of Arabic-identified restaurants and halal specialty stores as well as items in large chain stores indicates an increased mainstreaming of Arabic culture within American culture.

SPEAKING ARABIC

The continuous inflow of new immigrants to the United States from the Arab world ensures that there are native speakers who speak Arabic in the home, with friends, and on the phone. There is a certain sense of intimacy and exclusivity in speaking with family in a language other than English that can be comforting and a way of bonding. Family terms of endearment are used such as *mama* (mother), *baba* (father), *sitti* or *sito* (grandmother), and *jedo* (grandfather) in the Lebanese, Syrian, and Palestinian dialects. Arab immigrants, like most other immigrant groups, quickly lose their mother tongue, switching to English after one to two generations. However, as Table 3.6 shows, approximately 55 percent of Arab Americans speak more than English at home, in marked contrast to the total U.S. population. This means that Arabic (or another language) is mostly spoken in Arab American households and in 18 percent of households there is no English spoken.

Table 3.6 Language Spoken in the Home

	Census 2000		American Community Survey, 2005–2007	
	Arab Americans	Total U.S. population	Arab Americans	Total U.S. population
Only English at home	45.4	82.1	45	80.5
Non-English at home/ English spoken "very well"*	35.8	9.8	55	19.5
No English at home/ English spoken less than "very well"*	18.8	8.1	18.9	8.6

*There is a problem with comparing these figures because the 2000 Census focused on languages spoken in the home but ACS survey changed the wording and categorizations to ask about the respondent's level of English-language comprehension.

Source: U.S. Census Bureau, Population Division. Census 2000 statistics from "We the People of Arab Ancestry in the United States" Report #22 by Brittingham and de la Cruz 2005, Table 2, page 19, available at http://www.census.gov/population/www/cen2000/briefs/index.html#sr); and Table S0201, "Selected Population Profile in the United States," from the 2005–2007American Community Survey three-year estimates, available at http://factfinder.census.gov.

The type of Arabic spoken in homes reflects the divides and complexities of the Arabic language in general. While the written form of Arabic is more standardized, there are many colloquial dialects and even other primary languages spoken in the Middle East and North African region. Arab Americans who speak Arabic use colloquial dialects that are broadly classified as part of the Arabic language. These colloquial dialects reflect the family's particular national and subnational origins in the Arab world. To prevent the linguistic loss of formal, written Arabic, immigrant parents may either bring in a tutor to the home or send their children to learn written Arabic at community language schools, which are held at Arabic churches and especially at the local mosque or Islamic center due to the importance of learning Arabic to recite the Qur'an.

In the years directly following 9/11, many Arab Americans reported that they were self-conscious about speaking Arabic outside the home, but are more comfortable with it today. However, among interviewees there was not a simple public/private dichotomy as to where one felt comfortable speaking Arabic. One respondent said that she felt that "people looked at us" in New York City when she spoke Arabic with her sister on the street. Many also reported that they felt that their phones were tapped and felt that speaking Arabic was viewed negatively in the United States. Still, some respondents resort to Arabic as a secret language, incomprehensible to others, and useful to communicate about the price of things in a store, private matters, or people in the neighborhood. Many Arab Americans in D.C. report that they now feel comfortable speaking Arabic in public.

CLOTHING

Clothing and jewelry worn in public are identity markers that can reflect racial or ethnic origins. Arab American parents can have a range of reactions about their children's clothing, often linking their pleas for compliance with their wishes to the idea of maintaining the family's reputation and honor. How parents define revealing clothing or insist on their daughters' wearing the hijab depends on the family. However, it should be noted that many young women chose to wear the hijab on their accord. As is the case in all families, children's defiance of their parent's wishes may cause fights and misunderstandings between the generations. While the hijab or other types of veiling are Muslim rather than distinctly Arab, they are one way in which Arab American Muslims have been able to show their religious affiliation in public. Many of the younger generation of women are donning the hijab over the objections of their more secular parents. Christians, who do not veil, may wear a cross around their neck or hang rosaries on their rearview mirror as a religious rather than an ethnic symbol. Kaffiyehs (white and black or red checkered scarves) have traditionally been a pro-Palestinian political statement in the United States but are now a fashion accessory worn by celebrities such as Rachel Ray or Paris Hilton. Thus the kaffiyeh lost its political significance for one of the interviewees, and she stopped wearing it. One soccer fan wore the jerseys of the French national soccer team player Zinedine Zidane, who is originally from Algeria, as a public display of his Arab ethnicity. A woman whose family is originally from Ramallah, in the

West Bank, wore pro-Palestinian T-shirts and Bedouin jewelry. A Palestinian man wore political T-shirts and put a Palestinian flag on his car's rearview mirror. However, most people do not show their ethnicity in overt ways. The respondents said that they were quick to explain their Arab or national origins, if asked. However, perhaps by not wearing clothing that identifies them as Arab with regularity, they are choosing when and to whom to show their ethnicity.

CONCLUSION

Family remains central to Arab American lives, regardless of the events of 9/11. The description by Arab Americans of their close-knit family ties indicates that family relationships are important for the individual and the strong familial interconnectedness can bring together siblings, parents, children, elderly parents, and grand-parents, cousins, aunts, and uncles in uneven but complex ways. Siblings can remain close into adulthood when parental authority continues to prevail. Individual families also have hierarchies that generally respect age, but gender dynamics are more complicated. Indeed, the family structure for Arab Americans is mixed between patriarchal and matriarchal forms that indicate who is the head of the household and main decision maker. However, women tend to carry the heavier burden in the realms of child care and domestic chores.

Arab Americans have a higher marriage rate in comparison to the average national rates. While many mothers and women do work outside the home, under certain circumstances—homogamy, belief in conservative interpretations of gender roles in the Bible or Qur'an, and the ideological support of patriarchy—they are less likely to do so. However, Arab Americans on average have larger household and family sizes than the average American, and quali-tative research indicates that this difference is attributable to larger families, children staying in the home longer, and extended family both visiting and living in the family household.

Colloquial Arabic dialects are used extensively in the home in the form of "kitchen Arabic" and food is a central motif in Arab American family life. While special food is prepared for holidays, families also bond over dinner on a daily basis. As with all fami-lies, events such as weddings, births, and funerals have particular importance. In some families, weddings have become smaller while in others they are large community-wide celebrations. While 9/11 has had some social and psychological impact on Arab Americans, the interconnectedness of families continues and remains strong in the United States today.

NOTES

1. The term *interconnected* is borrowed from Suad Joseph's concept of interconnectivity in *Intimate Selving.*

2. Angela Brittingham and G. Patricia de la Cruz, *The Arab Population: 2000* (Washington, DC: U.S. Census Bureau, 2003), 1.

3. All statistics for the Census 2000 are from Angela Brittingham and G. Patricia de la Cruz, *We the People of Arab Ancestry in the United States: Census 2000 Special Reports* (Washington, DC: U.S. Census Bureau, 2005), Table 2, page 19: www.census.gov/prod/2005pubs/censr-21.pdf. American Community Survey data is from a table generated from American Community Survey section on the Census Bureau's website, www.census. gov.

4. U.S. Census Bureau, *Current Population Survey (CPS)—Definitions and Explanations,* http://www.census.gov/population/www/cps/cps def.html.

5. Randa Kayyali, "The People Perceived as a Threat to Security: Arab Americans Since September 11," *Migration Information Source* (July 2006), http://www.migrationinformation.org/Feature/display.cfm?ID=409.

6. Angela Brittingham and G. Patricia de la Cruz, *The Arab Population: 2000* (Washington, DC.: U.S. Census Bureau, 2003), www.census.gov/prod/2003pubs/c2kbr-23.pdf.

7. Barbara C. Aswad, "Challenges to the Arab-American Family and ACCESS," in *Family and Gender Among American Muslims: Issues Facing Middle Eastern Immigrants and Their Descendants,* ed. Barbara Bilge and Barbara C. Aswad (Philadelphia: Temple University Press, 1996).

8. Louise Cainkar, "The Deteriorating Ethnic Safety Net among Arab Immigrants in Chicago," in *Arabs in America: Building a New Future,* ed. Michael W. Suleiman (Philadelphia: Temple University Press, 1999), 192–206. Cainkar defines ethnic safety net as "cohesion, safety, security and prosperity of Arab families through interaction, assistance and intervention" (193).

9. Cainkar, "Deteriorating Ethnic Safety Net," 198.

10. Randa A. Kayyali, *The Arab Americans* (Westport, CT: Greenwood Press, 2006), 67.

11. Kristine Ajrouch, "Arab-American Immigrant Elders' Views about Social Support," *Aging and Society* 25, no. 5 (2005): 655–73.

12. Loukia Sarroub, *All American Yemeni Girls* (Philadelphia: University of Pennsylvania Press, 2005), 29, and 140n3.

13. Suad Joseph, *Intimate Selving in Arab Families: Gender, Self, and Identity in Arab Families* (Syracuse, NY: Syracuse University Press, 1999), 13.

14. Hisham Sharabi, *Neopatriarchy: A Theory of Distorted Change in Arab Society* (New York: Oxford University Press, 1988).

15. Joseph, *Intimate Selving*, 12.

16. Jen'nan Ghazal Read, *Culture, Class, and Work among Arab-American Women* (New York: LFB Scholarly Publishing, 2004).

17. Jen'nan Ghazal Read and Sharon Oselin, "Gender and the Education-Employment Paradox in Ethnic and Religious Contexts: The Case of Arab Americans," *American Sociological Review* 73, no. 2 (2008): 296–313.

18. Barbara C. Aswad, "Attitudes of Arab Immigrants toward Welfare," in *Arabs in America: Building a New Future*, ed. Michael W. Suleiman (Philadelphia: Temple University Press, 1999), 177–91.

19. Kristine Ajrouch, "Family and Ethnic Identity in an Arab-American Community," in Suleiman, *Arabs in America*, 138.

20. Katherine Pratt Ewing, *Being and Belonging: Muslims in the United States since 9/11* (New York: Russell Sage Foundation, 2008), 96.

21. Evelyn Shakir, *Bint Arab: Arab and Arab American Women in the United States* (Westport, CT: Praeger, 1997), 186.

22. Azizah Y. al-Hibri, "Muslim Marriage Contract in American Courts," paper read at the Minaret of Freedom Banquet, May 20, 2000, T.C. Williams School of Law, University of Richmond, http://www.mina ret.org/azizah.htm.

4

RELIGIOUS LIFE

Anan Ameri

In the United States there are an estimated 4.2 million Arab Americans, who primarily practice two religions: Islam and Christianity. In the United States, the majority of Arab Americans are Christians. According to a 2002 Zogby International survey, 63 percent of Arab Americans are Christians, 24 percent are Muslim, with the remaining 13 percent belonging to other religions or not practicing any faith. In some states or cities, such as Dearborn, Michigan, or Brooklyn, New York, the percentage of Arab American Muslims may be higher than 24 percent. The same might apply to some recent Arab immigrants who have come from war-devastated regions such as Palestine, Lebanon, or Iraq.

Arab American Christians and Muslims share many beliefs and values with other Americans. Although the United States is often perceived as a Judeo-Christian nation, in fact, Islam and Muslim Americans have been part of this country since its inception. Furthermore, Islam is one of the world's three Abrahamic religions, also referred to as the monotheistic religions, which include Christianity and Judaism in addition to Islam. These three religions have much more in common than is often understood.

Islam is believed to be the second-largest religion in the United States, although estimates from various sources had varied significantly from 2.4 million to 6 million adherents.[1] American Muslims comprise many different national and ethnic backgrounds, including African American, Arab American, Asian and Southeast Asian American, as well as European American. Arab Americans have established their own religious institutions, including charities, churches, and mosques, as well as schools and youth clubs. These institutions provide their constituencies with a place to worship, learn about their religion, socialize, and meet people who share their values.

"We are a nation of Christians and Muslims, Jews and Hindus, and nonbelievers. We are shaped by every language and culture, drawn from every end of this Earth."

Excerpt from 2009 Presidential Inaugural Address by President Barack Obama

---

ARABS, ARAB AMERICANS, AND ISLAM

The word *Islam* is a derivative of the Arabic word *Salam,* which means peace; it can also refer to a Muslim's submission to the will of God. Islam refers to the religion itself, like the terms Christianity and Judaism, while the word Muslim refers to the followers of the Islamic faith. Islam is the fastest-growing religion both in the United States and in the world. The total number of Muslims worldwide is estimated at 1.2–1.5 billion. As the second largest religion after Christianity, Muslims comprise about 20–22 percent of the world's population.

It is important to distinguish Arabs from Muslims. One common misconception is that all Muslims are Arabs, and all Arabs are Muslims. While the Arabic language is the mother tongue of Islam, Arabs are actually a minority among Muslims, not exceeding 20 percent of the world's Muslim population. The largest Muslim country is Indonesia. Other Southeast Asian countries with large Muslim populations include India, Pakistan, and Bangladesh. The majority of the population of the African countries of Nigeria, Senegal, and Mali are Muslims, and a sizable percentage of the people of Ghana, Uganda, Kenya, and Tanzania are also Muslim. Muslims are also found in many European countries. The majority of the population in Turkey, Bosnia, and Albania are Muslims, and certain regions in Russia have majority Muslim populations. Like Christians, Muslims are found in almost every nation around the globe.

SEPTEMBER 11 AND ARAB AMERICANS

Before September 11, the 4.2 million Arab Americans were, to most Americans, invisible. Like the rest of us, Arab Americans woke up on that morning to face a new day. They got their kids out of bed and got them ready to go to school, young adults went to their colleges and universities, and men and women went to work. For some, work was at the World Trade Center or at a police or a fire station in New York City. Consequently, Arab Americans were among the direct victims of the 9/11 attacks or they died or got injured as they were part of the rescue efforts that day. Like all Americans, Arab Americans mourned the tragedy of that sad day. However, within a few hours, and regardless of their faith or how long they or their ancestors lived in the United States, Arab Americans found themselves treated or perceived as non-Americans, as outsiders, or even as the enemy. They were viewed by many of their fellow Americans as if they were responsible for what happened on 9/11.

MUSLIM ORGANIZATIONS
RESPOND TO SEPTEMBER 11

As soon as September 11 happened, many Muslim Americans issued statements condemning these attacks and hoped that the U.S. government would to do whatever it took to pursue the perpetrators.[2] Muslim American organizations issued statements on that day urging their followers to extend all possible help to the victims of the attack. Arab Americans were as horrified and angered as other Americans by these events, but they were also horrified because these crimes, committed by Muslims, violate the very basic tenets of their faith that prohibit the killing of civilians. One verse of the Qur'an, the holy book for Muslims, states, "That who takes an innocent life, as if he has killed the whole humanity, and that who saves an innocent life as if he has saved the whole humanity" (chapter 5, verse 32).

Because most Americans knew very little about Arab and Muslim Americans, it was easy to target anger toward them and to treat them with suspicion. Many Muslim and Arab American organizations felt the need to issue condemnation statements immediately after the tragic events of September 11. Fear of attacks by angry individuals prompted these organizations to also call upon on Federal Bureau of Investigation (FBI) and other U.S. government agencies for added security to protect their communities. An example of such a statement, issued by the American Muslim Council, reads,

[We] call upon the members of the Muslim community to come together at this tragic time where so many of our fellow Americans have been killed and injured. The American tragedy affects all of us and we should do whatever we can to help save lives of the injured victims. AMC urges Islamic Centers to start blood drive campaigns and to encourage everyone to visit hospitals and medical centers in the capitol and New York City to donate much needed blood to those who are required to receive immediate medical assistance.[3]

The following are excerpts from the Council on American Islamic Relations (CAIR) statement issued on September 11:

- Called on Muslims nationwide to offer assistance to the victims of the terrorist attacks in New York and Washington, D.C. Muslim medical professionals were encouraged to go to the scenes of the attacks to offer aid and comfort to the victims.
- Muslim relief agencies were urged to contact their counterparts to offer support in the recovery efforts.
- Individual Muslims were asked to donate blood or funds to the local office of the Red Cross.

Additionally, CAIR's statement also asked community members to report incidents of anti-Muslim harassment or attacks. It also suggested steps to increase security around mosques and Islamic centers. Security precautions suggested by CAIR's alert advised American Muslims to consider staying out of public areas for the immediate future, if they were wearing traditional Islamic attire.

- Request additional police patrols in the vicinity of mosques.
- Post mosque members at entrances and parking areas during prayer times.
- Report suspicious packages to police.
- Document descriptions of suspicious people or vehicles.[4]

THE U.S. GOVERNMENT AND MUSLIM AMERICAN CHARITIES

The fear within the Arab and Muslim communities was often reinforced by government actions, particularly the closure of many Muslim American charities. The USA PATRIOT Act passed by the Congress on April 18, 2002, made it easy for government agencies to target and disable Muslim organizations and individuals based primarily on suspicion and with little evidence. A few months after the 9/11 attacks, a number of American Muslim charities' offices were invaded by the FBI and other law enforcement agencies, their assets were frozen, their staff was arrested and investigated, and their operations were disrupted or stopped. These actions violated the rights of Americans Muslims to create their own organizations and to engage in the charitable giving that is mandated by their religion. They also violated the legal due process granted to all American citizens.

Charity (*zakat*) is one of the Five Pillars of Islam. It is mandatory for all Muslims who are able to do so to give annually of their income and/or wealth to charity. Although Muslims can give *zakat* at any time, most people give at the end of the month of Ramadan. Some give to poor family members, neighbors, or friends; others give to the charitable organizations found in almost every country that has a Muslim population. Like Americans of other faiths, Muslim Americans have built and supported charitable institutions. Many give their annual *zakat* to these institutions, rather than to particular individuals. Others, especially recent immigrants who came from poor or war-torn countries, send money to charitable organizations in their country of origin or send it directly to poor family members, friends, and neighbors who remain there.

Six Muslim charitable organizations were closed by the U.S. government, including the Holy Land Foundation based in Dallas, Texas, which was the largest Muslim American humanitarian organization, as well as the Global Relief Foundation, based in Chicago, the second largest. In 2002, the U.S. government announced that they had placed an additional five Muslim charities under investigation. These actions not only damaged the reputation of Muslim charities but also reinforced the public suspicion of Arab and Muslim Americans.

Even though most Muslim Americans were convinced that Muslim charitable organizations had been unfairly targeted by the U.S. government, they became reluctant to donate to them out of fear of being targeted or subjected to investigation themselves. As early as November 2002, members of Arab and Muslim American organizations expressed concern to the U.S. Department of Treasury about the drastic decline in charitable giving by members of their communities.[5] In June 2009, the American Civil Liberties Union (ACLU) issued a lengthy report titled *Blocking Faith, Freezing Charity*,[6] concerning discrimination by the U.S. government toward Muslim charitable giving. The report was based on interviews with more than 120 Muslim community leaders, as well as experts on antiterrorism laws and regulations. According to the ACLU report, the U.S. government had damaged the reputation of most Muslim charities without affording these organizations or individuals a day in court or any other opportunity to clear their name. The report clearly reveals how discrimination and a lack of due process starved Islamic charities of money and impeded Muslims' ability to fulfill *zakat*. The report also notes that independent bodies like the 9/11 Commission found that evidence used to seize assets was often kept secret, making it impossible to challenge, and has in some cases included hearsay or been based on news reports. In his June 6, 2009, speech at Cairo University in Egypt, President Barack Obama made reference to this situation: "In the United States, rules on charitable giving have made it harder for Muslims to fulfill their religious obligation. That is why I am committed to working with American Muslims to ensure that they can fulfill *zakat*."[7]

ARAB AMERICANS ARE DIVERSE

In the Arab world, the majority of the people are Muslims. However, there are sizable Christian communities in many Arab countries. While most people in the United States think of Christianity as a Western religion, in fact, Christianity started in the Arab world. Arab Christians are descended from the world's earliest Christians, and the churches in some Arab countries are the world's oldest.

Arab Muslim and Christian Americans are as diverse as America itself. They come from various national backgrounds, including all of the 22 Arab countries. They live in every state of our nation, including small towns and large cities, as well as suburbs. Some have been in the United States for many generations, others are more recent immigrants. Some Arab Americans are upper- and middle-class, while others are struggling to make a living. They can be found in every profession; some are factory workers or migrant farmers in the valleys of California, while others are doctors, engineers, scientists, and educators. Some own their own businesses or work in family businesses such as hotels, restaurants, or grocery stores. The same educational and professional diversity can be found among Muslim and Christian Arab American women. While some are working women, others stay home and care for their families.

Regardless of their religious affiliations, Arab Americans, and those who look like them, were subject to harassment and discrimination after the tragic events of 9/11.

"Arabs, Chaldeans and others of Middle Eastern descent have been singled out for public scrutiny and government surveillance," said University of Michigan sociologist and business professor Wayne Baker, who led the research team[8] for a 2004 study by the University of Michigan on the Arab and Chaldean communities in the Detroit area. The study found that 15 percent of Arabs and Chaldeans had encountered some hostile experience after 9/11, including verbal insults, workplace discrimination, targeting by law enforcement or airport security, vandalism, and, in rare cases, physical assault. This number was probably much higher in other states because in the Detroit area where there are large Arab and Chaldean American communities, many non-Arabs are much more familiar with the culture and probably have a friend, a classmate, or a colleague who is an Arab or Chaldean American. In fact, the study also showed that 33 percent of those interviewed said that they have received expressions of support from non-Arabs.[9]

The University of Michigan study also found that Muslims in particular worry about their future in the United States.[10] "Forty-two percent of Muslim Arabs feel that their religion is not respected by mainstream society, compared to just 11 percent of Christian Arabs and Chaldeans," said Princeton University political scientist Amaney Jamal, a member of the study team.[11] The study also found that 58 percent of Arab American Muslims and 31 percent of Arab American Christians worry about the future of their families in the United States.[12]

Arab American Christians

Christian Arabs were among the earliest Arabs to come to the United States, some arriving as early as the 1850s. Although a small number came from Palestine, most of these immigrants were from Syria and Lebanon, which at the time was part of the region known as Greater Syria. Later, Arab Christian immigrants came to the United States from other countries such as Jordan, Iraq, and Egypt. The Christian Arabs who came from Iraq are known as Chaldeans. They are an ethnic minority in Iraq who trace their origins to the ancient inhabitants of Mesopotamia. Although they speak Aramaic, a majority of Chaldeans speak Arabic as well. Chaldean Americans share basic cultural characteristics with Arab Americans, but many do not identify as Arabs.

Antonius Bishallany was among the very early Arabs from Lebanon to come to the United States. His arrival was facilitated by U.S. Protestant missionaries in Lebanon. Bishallany arrived in 1854 to study, with the intention of going back to his home country as a Protestant missionary. Upon his arrival he received a scholarship to study at the Armenian Seminary in upstate New York where, in return, he would give Arabic lessons to missionaries preparing to go to the Arab world. Before he could finish his studies, he became ill and died from tuberculosis. Bishallany is buried with a Bible at Greenwood Cemetery in New York City.

Adele L. Younis, *The Coming of the Arab-Speaking People to the United States* (Centre for Migration Studies, 1995), 96–106.

Arab American Churches

Christian Arab immigrants who came to the United States have been members of a variety of denominations. Initially, because many of them were peddlers, they either worshiped at home or attended whatever church was in their neighborhood, regardless of the domination. Once their numbers increased, they started to build churches of their own. The first Arab American churches were established along the East Coast because that is where many of the early immigrants settled. Between 1880 and 1895, three Arab American churches were built in New York: one Maronite, one Melkite, and one Eastern Orthodox (Antiochan). A Maronite church was built in Boston in 1890 and another one in Detroit in 1898. The establishment of three Maronite churches in this period reflects the large size and relative prosperity of the Arab Christian community who belonged to the Maronite church. Today, there are thousands of Arab churches located in every city and major town in the United States. Arab American churches can be divided into two main groups, Eastern Rite Catholic and Eastern Orthodox.

The Eastern Rite Catholic Churches include the following:

- **Maronite:** Most of the followers are of Lebanese origin, having descended from some of the earliest Arabs to immigrate to the United States. The first church was founded in Boston, Massachusetts. Today Maronite churches can be found in every major U.S. city.
- **Melkite:** Church members also trace their origins to the early immigrants who came mostly from Syria, Lebanon, and Palestine, with fewer numbers from Jordan and Egypt. The first Melkite church was founded in the early 1900s, in Lawrence, Massachusetts. In the early 1900s, Melkite churches were founded in Los Angeles, Detroit, and Boston. Today, churches are found in many other U.S. cities. The Melkite patriarch resides in Damascus, Syria.
- **Syrian Catholic:** Most of the followers are from Syria, Lebanon, and Iraq, and the first church was built Jacksonville, Florida, in the 1950s. Today, Syrian Catholic churches can be found in Detroit, Los Angeles, and New York.
- **Chaldean Catholic:** Almost all of the followers came from three small villages in northern Iraq, but a few came from Syria. The first Chaldean congregation was founded in Michigan in 1947. Today, the Chaldean Diocese of the Catholic Church has parishes in Michigan, California, Illinois, and Arizona, with their patriarch in Baghdad, Iraq.

The Eastern Orthodox Churches include the following:

- **Coptic Orthodox:** Most followers are Egyptian. The first Coptic church was built in the 1960s in California and New Jersey. Today, Coptic churches are found in Detroit, Los Angeles, New Jersey, and New York. The Coptic patriarch is in Alexandria, Egypt.
- **Antiochan Orthodox:** Most of the followers are originally from Syria, Lebanon, and Palestine. Their first church was established in the 1890s in New York City. Large communities are found in Detroit, New York, Boston, and Los Angeles. The patriarch lives in Damascus, Syria.
- **Syrian Orthodox:** Followers are Syrian, Lebanese, and Iraqi. The first church was established in New Jersey in 1927. The patriarch is located in New Jersey. Today, a number of Syrian Orthodox churches are found in all major U.S. cities.

Christian Holidays

Like the rest of American Christians, Arab American Christians celebrate the major Christian holidays, including Christmas and Easter; they also observe other holidays such as the Feast of Saint Barbara, celebrated in the fall, and the Rogation on Nineveh, observed mostly by Chaldean Americans.

Christmas and Easter are mostly celebrated by Arab Americans in the same way as the rest of American Christians. As Arab Americans adjusted to life in America, they began to celebrate Christmas in the same fashion as other American Christians, although a few, especially members of the Coptic Church, continue to celebrate Christmas on January 7, and gift giving is usually limited to children. In the Arab world, however, Easter is considered more important than Christmas.

For many Arab Christian families, the Easter season is a special time of year, and for my family, this is exactly the case. In our home, not unlike those for Christmas, preparations for the Easter season last for weeks, and there is much anticipation leading up to that special Sunday. The reward of the Easter season is not just the religious celebration of Christ's resurrection—which is celebrated with services rich in meaning and symbolism, including Palm Sunday and Holy Saturday—it is the special foods, clothes, and other cultural traditions that make the holiday so special for my family.

Food. The word stands on its own, really, because so many of my family's celebrations center around the preparation and, of course, the eating of certain foods. For the 40 days before Palm Sunday and the Holy Week leading up to Easter, we observe the Lenten season, which means we abstain from certain foods, including meat and dairy. Since the fast is a challenge for many, breaking the fast is an important and tasty part of the celebration. One food that my mother labors over is the traditional sweet known as *ca'ak be ajweh,* a date-filled cookie made with semolina flour and lots of butter. The time-consuming process involves the whole family, as each cookie must be individually formed and decorated, and dozens of cookies are made. But the end results, including the amazing smells that waft through the house, are well worth the time and energy.

In addition to cooking and eating, shopping for a new Easter outfit is a regular part of the season. As little girls, my three sisters and I would wear the obligatory flowered dresses, adorned with lace and fluff, and often accessorized by a hat, gloves, and white shoes, which to me signified the beginning of spring and the celebration of Palm Sunday. My two brothers usually got new suits. To commemorate the arrival of Christ into Jerusalem we always go to church in these fabulous new outfits, carrying candles that are just as festive as the dresses.

Palm Sunday begins Holy Week, the last week leading up to Easter. The main service happens the Saturday night before Easter. The service, which usually starts around 10:00 P.M., is beautiful, but long. There is a moment when the service turns from somber to celebratory, and the clergy and parish break out into a song that starts "Christ is risen from the dead" and is sung in English, Arabic, and Greek. When the service is over, our church serves a traditional Arabic breakfast to break the fast. It doesn't matter that it's nearly 1:00 A.M. by this point; Arab mealtimes do not have a deadline.

Finally, on Easter morning, we wake up to do, what else, eat. This time though, we eat all the things we haven't eaten for the last month and a half, which when we were younger, included candy from Easter baskets that my mother always made, along with hiding the candy in plastic colored eggs throughout the house. These egg hunts were the highlight of Easter when I was little. While today we no longer hide plastic eggs or decorate elaborate baskets, we still eat the candy, and once again through food, the tradition carries on.

Sonya Kassis, interview by author, Arab American National Museum, Dearborn, Michigan, September 4, 2009.

Arab American Christian holidays are occasions for family members to get together and celebrate. Traditional Arabic food is cooked for these occasions which usually include lamb, ham, and rice cooked with nuts, stuffed grape leaves, *kibbeh,* and tabbouli salad. Also, special cookies stuffed with dates or nuts are made for special occasions. Another traditional dessert served is baklava, layers of filled thin dough stuffed with nuts.

As far as the observation of Lent, some Arab Americans continue to observe Lent in the traditional way observed in their country of origin, by fasting for 40 consecutive days before Easter. This includes abstaining from all animal products, including meat, milk, butter, and eggs, except for eating fish on Fridays. Others may fast for periods during the 40 days before Easter. Many of the younger generations observe Lent by giving up one item of their favorite food.

The Rogation on Nineveh is celebrated by Chaldean Americans three weeks before Lent. This holiday commemorates the time that God sent a warning to the people of Nineveh through the prophet Jonas that in order to avoid the destruction of their city they should repent of their sins. People fast for three days from midnight to midday and follow the same restrictions on animal products as for Lent.

ARAB AMERICAN MUSLIMS

The first significant number of Muslim Arabs came to the United States during the Great Migration of 1880–1924. Their number has been estimated at just 5–10 percent of all Arab immigrants. Like their Arab Christian contemporaries, these Muslim immigrants came mostly from rural areas in Syria, Lebanon, and Palestine, and had limited formal education. They were members of all the major sects of Islam: Sunni, Shiite, and Druze. They worked in a variety of trades—as peddlers and assembly line workers, in the lumber, mining, and shipping industries, and in transportation, building both roads and railroads. Some even homesteaded in South Dakota. The largest Muslim Arab community in the early 1900s was found in Chicago.

Because of their small number and scattered locations around the country, it was very difficult for Muslim Arab immigrants to establish their own places of worship. They often practiced their religion at home or at the home of an elder who led the Friday and holiday prayers. Early Arab Muslim immigrants had a much harder time practicing their religion than Arab Christians. Not only did they not have a place to worship, they were a very small minority in a country with a majority Christian population. The first mosque built by Arab Americans, most of whom were Lebanese, was constructed in 1923[13] in Highland Park, Michigan. It survived for only four years until the community moved to Dearborn, Michigan, for well-paying jobs at Ford Motor Company's new Rouge Plant. In 1925, an Arab mosque was built in Michigan City, Indiana, which is still in use today. Another Arab mosque and community center was established in Cedar Rapids, Iowa, in 1934 and rebuilt in 1971. In 1952, the Federation of Islamic Associations in America was founded; its membership included 25 mosques, a majority of which were Arab American. Unlike mosques in the Arab world, which serve primarily for religious practice, mosques in the United States soon acquired social and cultural functions as Muslim Arab Americans struggled to maintain their Arab and Muslim identities and culture. Today, there are hundreds of Arab mosques in the United States, with at least one in almost every major city.

Between World War I (1914–1918) and World War II (1939–1945), restrictive immigration laws allowed few Arab immigrants, Muslim or Christian, into the United States. After World War II, however, the United States encouraged highly educated people such as

The Founding Women's Club of the American Bekaa Moslem Society in 1938. At the time, Muslims were a minority among Arab Americans. Many Muslims settled in the Detroit enclave of Highland Park, Michigan, and took jobs with Ford Motor Company in Highland Park and later, at the automaker's massive Rouge Complex in Dearborn. (Courtesy Arab American National Museum)

physicians, engineers, and scientists to come to the United States, regardless of their religion or national background. As a result, many Muslim Arab professionals from various Arab countries came to the United States. Because of their higher level of education and income compared to earlier Muslim Arab immigrants, they were able to assimilate quickly and settle in suburban America, rather than in Arab American neighborhoods.

The most recent Arab immigrants, who began arriving here in the early 1970s, included a larger number of Muslims coming mostly from war-devastated nations like Palestine, Lebanon, and Iraq. This wave of immigrants also included small numbers of Muslim immigrants from the African Arab countries of Morocco, Tunisia, Algeria, Sudan, and Somalia. Today, the largest Muslim Arab communities are found in major metropolitan areas including Detroit, New York City, Washington, D.C., Los Angeles, Chicago, and Houston.

ISLAM: RELIGION, POLITICS, AND THE CLASH OF CIVILIZATIONS

For more than a century, Arabs and Muslims have been widely misrepresented and misunderstood within the United States. The mainstream media depicts the violence of minority extremists as an inherent characteristic of Islam. Hollywood films often portray Arabs and Muslims as a terrorist threat to our national security. Scholars that are widely read, such as Samuel Huntington and Bernard Lewis, claim that the culture and values of Arabs and Muslims are incompatible with those of the West, leading to a "Clash of Civilizations." As a result, Islam is not seen in relation to the other monotheistic faiths of Christianity and Judaism, but rather as an opposing force and at the root of world conflict. Advocates of these views ignore the fact that in the last century, and for long before that, most world conflicts, with their accompanying death and destruction, were not the result of clashes between Muslim countries and the West, but rather between Western nations, where the majority of the population is Christian. Additionally, despite the diverse experiences and realities of the estimated 1.2–1.5 billion Muslims worldwide, the same few stories that highlight violence, oppression of women, irrationality, and incompatible differences are circulated over and over again.

This distorted view of Arabs and Muslims has been exacerbated by the terrorist attacks of 9/11 and the War on Terror. The continued depiction of Arabs and Muslims as fundamentally different from "us" and as "the enemy" reinforces the conviction that war and confrontation with Muslims and Arabs are inevitable. Broad and inaccurate generalizations further legitimize the opinion that Muslim societies are inherently undemocratic, and therefore undeserving of human rights, recognition, or understanding.

Islam and Violence

An objective examination of Islam and Muslim nations strongly suggests that Islam is neither more nor less violent, or more political, than any other religion. As with most religions, some Muslims use their religion to justify their political or social convictions or to justify the violence, racism, and oppression of others. It is true that in the last few decades, especially since the 1970s, political Islam had emerged as a force in the Muslim world. However, it is important to differentiate between Muslim political parties and organizations that seek political power through democratic elections, as is the case with the ruling party in Turkey, and other Muslim political parties that rule by force or use their own interpretation of Islam to justify their violence and repression. Secular Muslims have more often been the target of these fringe groups, and the overwhelming majority of Muslims around the world condemns their actions and resents the fact that violence has been committed in the name of their religion. Between 2001 and 2007, the U.S.-based Gallup organization conducted the largest and most comprehensive study of contemporary Muslims ever done. It ran surveys in 35 predominantly Muslim nations. The research was published in a book entitled, *Who Speaks for Islam? What a Billion Muslims Really Think*, which identified the following interesting similarities between Muslims and Americans

- Radical Rejection: Muslims and Americans are equally likely to reject attacks on civilians as morally unjustified.
- Admiration of the West: Muslims around the world say what they most admire about the West is its technology and its democracy—the same two top responses given by Americans when asked the same question.
- Critique of the West: Muslims around the world say what they least admire about the West is its perceived moral decay and breakdown of traditional values—the same responses given by Americans when posed the same question.[14]

THE RELIGION OF ISLAM

Islam is the youngest of the three monotheistic religions. Muslims believe that their religion is an extension of the Abrahamic tradition that includes Judaism and Christianity. Muslims believe that there is only one God; they also believe in angels, books of revelation, individual responsibility, the Day of Judgment, and an afterlife.

Islam recognizes all the biblical prophets found in the Hebrew scriptures but believes that the prophet Muhammad, born in 570 CE in Mecca, in present-day Saudi Arabia, is the last of these prophets. Muslims believe that at age of 40, Muhammad began receiving revelations from God. These revelations, or the words of God, which were revealed to Muhammad over the next 23 years, comprise the Muslim holy book, the Qur'an (also spelled Koran.). Qur'an, which means recitation, was originally revealed to Muhammad in his mother tongue, Arabic. Muslims around the world, regardless of their nationality or native language, recite parts of the Qur'an in Arabic during their prayers.

Muslim Sects

Islam has two main branches or sects: Sunni and Shi'a (pronounced SHE-ah). Roughly 85 percent of the world's Muslims are Sunni and 15 percent are Shi'a. A relative comparison is the two main branches of Christianity: Catholic and Protestant. Today the majority of Shi'a reside mainly in Iran, Iraq, and Lebanon.

This division between Muslims happened in the late seventh century shortly after the death of Muhammad. The Muslim community was relatively small at the time and had a disagreement about who should lead Muslims after Muhammad's death. The followers who came to be known as the Shi'a believed that the Prophet had appointed his nephew and son in-law, Ali Bin Abi Taleb, to be the religious and political leader of the Muslim community. The followers who became known as Sunni disagreed and selected Abu Bakr Al-Sideek, a friend and confidant of the Prophet, who was also the first person to believe in Muhammad and his new religion, Islam. Although each group has its own mosques and ceremonial traditions, both Sunni and Shi'a adhere to the Five Pillars of Islam and have more in common than they do differences.

In addition to these two major divisions, there are many smaller Muslim sects, whose differences from the two main branches of Islam are often based on various interpretation of the Qur'an or the way the religion should be practiced. One large sect among Arab American Muslims is the Druze, who trace their origins to Egypt. The Druze sect started as a reform movement in the 11th century. In addition to the Qur'an, the Druze have a collection of about 30 other manuscripts that guide them through their daily life. Today there are more than a million members of the Druze community; the majority of them reside in Lebanon, Syria, and Israel. There is also a sizable Druze American community, with their own associations and clubs.

Another important sect in Islam is Sufism, a mystical movement. Followers of Sufism aspire to have a direct relationship with God by focusing on the spiritual aspects of the faith.

The Five Pillars of Islam

All Muslims must fulfill five religious requirements; these comprise the foundation of Islam and are known as the Five Pillars of Islam:

1. Declaration of Faith (*Shahada*): This is the belief in one God and in Muhammad as God's last messenger. If a person wants to become a Muslim, he or she has only to believe in and recite the *Shahada:* "There is no God but God, and Muhammad is his messenger."

2. Prayer (*Salat*): Observant Muslims pray five times a day: at dawn, noon, mid-afternoon, sunset, and nightfall. Before praying, Muslims perform the ritual of personal cleansing called *wudu*. Prayers usually take a few minutes and can be performed at home, at work, or at school. On Friday, the Muslim holy day, people go to the mosque for noon prayer.

3. Fasting (*Soum*): During the month of Ramadan, Muslim adults are expected to fast by abstaining from eating and drinking between sunrise and sunset. Exceptions are made for pregnant or nursing women, the sick, the elderly, children, and travelers. Through fasting, Muslims come to understand and empathize with people who are less fortunate, while also experiencing self-restraint. The ritual of breaking the fast is usually shared with members of the extended family, as well as neighbors and friends.

4. Charity (*Zakat*): Capable Muslims are required to give annually to those who are less fortunate or to charitable organizations. Traditionally, people give their *zakat* during the month of Ramadan. Some Muslim scholars specify that the amount to be given should be 2.5 percent of an individual's wealth, while other interpretations say to give 2.5 percent of one's income.

5. Pilgrimage (Hajj): Muslims who are physically and financially capable are required to perform the hajj once in their lifetime. This annual ritual takes place in Mecca during the last month of the Islamic (lunar) calendar. An estimated three million pilgrims arrive in Mecca each year. During the hajj, all pilgrims wear simple white garments that are intended to erase distinctions of wealth and create a feeling of equality in front of God. Muslims believe that the Ka'ba, a black stone structure in Mecca, is the first house of worship built by Adam, and later rebuilt by Abraham and his son Ishmael.

Dietary Restrictions

Most world religions have some kind of dietary restrictions; Islam prohibits its followers from the consumption of alcohol, pork, blood, and any animal that has been found dead. In addition, animals must be slaughtered in a quick merciful way (halal) for

Man praying at Medina, Saudi Arabia. Medina and nearby Mecca are the two holiest cities in Islam and the focus of activities surrounding the hajj, the pilgrimage all observant Muslims, including Muslim Arab Americans, must make once in their lifetimes. (S.M. Amin/Saudi Aramco World/ SAWDIA)

meat; the procedures used are similar to those used for Jewish kosher meat.

Practicing Religion

As is the case with the followers of all other religions, some Muslims are more devout than others and strictly follow the Five Pillars of Islam, while others might practice only one or two components of the faith, such as fasting during Ramadan or praying occasionally. Some might celebrate the holidays but forego other practices. For some, Islam is more of a cultural identity. There are many Muslims who are secular or nonbelievers who might limit their religious participation to celebrating the holidays. As in all religions, this diversity in practice can be found within each community, among the members of extended families, or even within a single household. It is not unusual to find a husband who fasts during Ramadan while his wife does not, or to find two sisters, only one of whom wears the modest style of Islamic dress and the head covering called the hijab.

Muslim Holidays

Throughout the year, Muslims around the world celebrate a number of religious holidays. One of the most important is *Eid al-Fitr* (Breaking the Fast), which comes immediately after the fasting month of Ramadan. It is a three-day holiday, also called *Eid al Sageer,* or the small holiday. The second major Muslim holiday is *Eid al-Adha* (the Holiday of Sacrifice,) which marks the end of the hajj. This four-day holiday is also called or *Eid al Kebber,* or the big holiday. *Eid al-Adha* commemorates the Prophet Abraham's willingness to sacrifice his son Ishmael, because God willed it.

These two holidays are as important to Muslims as Christmas and Easter are to Christians. Both are celebrated similarly, although the particulars of how Muslims around the world celebrate may vary according to culture and tradition. Most celebrations include family visits, communal activities, and gift-giving, especially for children. On the first day of *Eid al-Fitr* and *Eid al-Adha,* many practicing Muslims start their holiday by attending the *Eid* prayer at a mosque. Visiting the elderly and the sick on the first day of the *Eid* is also common practice and some go to the cemetery to visit the graves of their loved ones. The usual Arabic greeting for both holidays is *Eid Mubarak* (Blessed Holiday) or *Kul sana wa inta salem* (May you be safe this year and every year).

The *Eids* are also an occasion for family members and friends to come together around a meal. As with Arab American Christian holidays, traditional Arabic food is usually served, although Islam prohibits Muslims from eating pork or drinking alcohol, and meat dishes served need to be *halal*. Other Muslim holidays include the lunar New Year, the birthday of the prophet Muhammad, and the 27th day of Ramadan, when Muslims believe that the Prophet ascended to heaven.

Ramadan

While the month of Ramadan is not considered a holiday, it does have a festive feel as family members and friends come together to break the fast and visit the elderly and the sick. Ramadan is also a time when rules are bent a little for children, as they are allowed to stay up longer at night to socialize with visitors. The latter part of Ramadan is particularly joyful because it is the time when people start to get ready for the *Eid*. Preparation includes buying gifts and new clothes as well as cooking and baking in preparation for the large number of visitors expected to come by.

Commemorating Ashura

The Arabic word *Ashura* is derived from *ashra*, which means 10 because there are 10 days of mourning that take place on the first 10 days of the Islamic lunar month of *Muharram*. This is a sad occasion that commemorates the death of Hussein, the grandson of the prophet Muhammad. This period of mourning is observed mostly by Shi'a Muslims. During these days, many Muslim Shi'a go to the mosque to recount and remember the tragic loss of Hussein, who was killed in the battlefield.

The Lunar Calendar

All Muslim holidays including Ramadan and the hajj occur according to the lunar calendar in which a year has only 354 days, 11 days fewer than the Gregorian calendar used in most of the world. The lunar calendar is also used in other cultures and religions; both Jewish and Chinese holidays follow the lunar calendar. While the 12 months of the Gregorian calendar are based on the

365-day rotation of the earth around the sun, the lunar calendar months start with each new moon and run 29 or 30 days. Muslim holidays always fall on the same date on the lunar calendar, but fall 11 days earlier than the previous year on the Gregorian calendar. For example, if Ramadan began on August 15 in 2009, it will begin on August 4 in 2010. This means that Ramadan "migrates" through the seasons, rather than being always celebrated at the same time of year. For this reason, daytime fasting lasts less time when Ramadan falls during winter, and many more hours if it occurs during the summer.

Celebrating Muslim Holidays in the United States

Until the last few years, Muslim holidays were rarely mentioned by the media or noticed by the general public in the United States. Also, most Muslims have to work and go to school during their holidays. In some cities, where there is a large concentration of Muslim students, as for example in Dearborn, Michigan, schools do close on the main two Muslim holidays *Eid al-Fitr* and *Eid al-Adha*. Also many working Muslims take a day or two off, usually as personal or vacation days, to celebrate their holidays with their families.

After a diligent campaign by Muslim Americans, in 2007 the U.S. Post Office issued a stamp that had *Eid Mubarak* in Arabic and "Eid Greetings" written in English. Also, under the Bush administration, the White House began to hold a special *iftar*, "breaking the fast," dinner and invited members of various Muslim communities to attend. These efforts have raised awareness among the general public about Arab and Muslim Americans.

Muslim Holy Sites

There are three important religious sites for Muslims, all of which are located in the Arab world where Islam originated: Mecca, Medina, and Jerusalem. Many Muslims make it a point to travel to all of these locations because of their historical and religious significance.

- *Mecca* is in present-day Saudi Arabia. It is considered a holy site because it is the birthplace of the prophet Muhammad and the place where he first received revelations from God. Muslims around the world face Mecca when they pray.
- *Medina* is also in present-day Saudi Arabia and is the city where the Prophet took refuge along with his followers to escape persecution

by the powerful elite of the Mecca, who felt threatened by the emergence of Islam. Medina is also where Muhammad died.

- *Jerusalem* is home to the Al-Aqsa Mosque and the Dome of the Rock, built in the seventh century, from which Muslims believe that the Prophet ascended to heaven. Before Muslims began praying in the direction of Mecca, they prayed facing Jerusalem.

- *Karbala,* a city in Iraq, is home to the shrine of the Prophet's grandson Hussein and is considered a sacred site by Shi'a Muslims.

ISLAM: CULTURE AND CIVILIZATION

Motivated by the new faith of Islam, Arabs established a political empire that flourished between the 8th and 17th centuries. This new empire extended from southern Europe and North Africa to central Asia. Islam was the official religion of the empire, and Arabic was its official language, as well as the language of commerce and science. People who lived in this empire were Arab, Spanish, Persian, Pakistani, Turkish, and Indian; and they practiced many religions: they were Muslims, Christian, Jews, and Hindus. The cultural and religious heritage of these communities was an important element in this new Arab-Islamic world.

Scholars who lived in the Arab-Islamic Empire contributed enormously to the world's civilization. They preserved the ancient knowledge of the previous civilizations of Greece, Rome, Persia, and India by translating important works, in a variety of fields, into Arabic. Additionally, scholars of the Arab-Islamic Empire made significant discoveries in the fields of medicine, science, mathematics, astronomy, and architecture. Much of this knowledge was later shared with Europe through Latin translations. One of the most celebrated legacies of the Arab-Islamic period took place at the time when Arab Muslims ruled southern Spain, known as Al-Andalus, or Andalusia. To this day, life under Arab Muslim rule of Al-Andalus is considered one of the world's best examples of how people from various faiths and cultures can coexist and flourish.

ISLAMIC ARTS

In many respects, Islam is not only a religion but also a culture. Today, many museums throughout the world hold vast collections of Islamic art. These artifacts, which sometimes include large rooms with decorated walls and center fountains, reflect the richness of Islamic art and architecture. Other items in these museums include calligraphy, jewelry, weavings, mosaic, glass, and pottery. These collections reflect the deep diversity in Islamic culture and the complexity of its artistic style. Islamic art does not necessarily refer to art based on religion, but rather based on the culture. Islamic art also refers to Islamic architecture, considered one of the most beautiful styles in history. Among the most famous Islamic monuments are the Dome of the Rock Mosque in Jerusalem, which dates from the 7th century; the Alhambra Palace in Cordoba, Spain, from the 14th century; and the Taj Mahal in Agra, India, built in the 17th century. It is important to note that Islam discourages the paintings or sculptures of people, especially prophets and leaders, in order to discourage the worship or idealization of human beings, since only God can be worshiped. Because of this restriction, other forms of Islamic art flourished, such as calligraphy, geometric designs, and tile painting.

THE THREE MONOTHEISTIC RELIGIONS

Judaism, Christianity, and Islam, the three major monotheistic religions, all originated in what is known today as the Arab world. Monotheism literally means "the belief in only one God." The central values of family, charity, and respect for others are shared by these three religions. Throughout history, these religions have spread from their birthplace, crossing the boundaries of race and ethnicity, and now have followers in nearly every country in the world.

Although the focus is often on the differences between them, there are many commonalties that exist between Judaism, Christianity, and Islam:

- All have roots in what is known today as the Arab world.
- All are monotheistic religions holding the belief that there is only one God.
- All are Abrahamic religions, recognizing the prophet Abraham as the founder of monotheism.
- All recognize a holy book considered to be the word of God. For Jews it is the Torah, for Christians, the Bible, and for Muslims, the Qur'an.
- All have a creation story in which God created the universe out of nothing.
- All believe that God sent prophets to spread his word.
- All consider Jerusalem to be a holy city. For Jews, it is home to the Wailing Wall, the holiest site in Judaism, and the Temple Mount,

the site of the first and second temple in ancient times. For Christians, the city contains the Church of the Holy Sepulcher, believed to be the site where Jesus was entombed after his crucifixion. For Muslims, Jerusalem is home to the Dome of the Rock, where the prophet Muhammad ascended to heaven, and the Al-Aqsa Mosque, the third holiest site in Islam.

- All believe that individuals will be held accountable for their actions.
- All believe in charity, with the requirement of giving to those in need.
- All have different branches, sects, and schools.

RELIGION AND IDENTITY

Particularly since 9/11, the popular conception generated by the media, and some politicians, as well as by religious extremists, is that the Muslim religion is the single source of identity for a large number of people from various cultural, ethnic, and national backgrounds. But in fact, the personal identity of all individuals, including those referred to as "Muslim," is rather complex and multifaceted. For most people, their religious faith is just one element or dimension among the many that define them, including their gender, socioeconomic status, political affiliation, profession, and place of residence. For that reason some Muslims may not identify themselves as Muslims, in spite of the fact that they belong to the Muslim faith. This is not because they want to deny the fact that they are Muslims, or because they want to distance themselves from Islam, but because other components of their identity are more important to them. For example, an Arab American Muslim may have much more in common with an Arab American Christian than he or she might have with a Muslim from Bosnia or Somalia; or a Muslim female doctor who lives in a Los Angeles suburb may share more in terms of personal identity with her Christian or Jewish medical colleagues who live and work in the same neighborhood, than with her Muslim cousins living in rural America.

Also, a person's culture embodies a much more complex set of norms and traditions, which includes religion, family, and community relationships, food, dress, work ethic, dance, music, and more. For that reason, it is important to remember that American Muslims, like all members of American society, are complex people whose religious affiliation may or may not define who they are.

CONCLUSION

Among the more than 300 million people living in the United States today, an estimated 4.2 million are of Arab descent. Arab Americans have been present in the United States since its inception. Although the majority of people in the Arab World are Muslim, the majority of Arab Americans are Christian. Arab immigrants, both Christian and Muslim, started to come to the United States in significant numbers during the Great Migration of (1880–1924). At that time, Muslims comprised only 5–10 percent of Arab immigrants. Because Christianity originated in the Arab World, Arab Christian immigrants brought with them their own denominations, including the Roman Catholic and Eastern Rite churches. Between 1880 and 1895, three Arab American churches were built along America's East Coast—one Maronite, one Melkite, and one Eastern Orthodox. The first purpose-built Arab American mosque was erected in Highland Park, Michigan, in 1923; in 1925, another mosque was built in Michigan City, Indiana. Today there are hundreds of Arab American churches and mosques in almost every major U.S. city.

Regardless of religious affiliation or how long their families have been in the United States, the lives of Arab Americans—and those Americans whose appearance might be stereotypically classified as Arab—were forever changed by the horrific events of September 11, 2001. Many perceived the public and the government had assigned them the blame, as if Arab Americans were somehow responsible for what happened on that tragic day. Many Arab American mosques and Islamic schools were vandalized and threatened, and the U.S. offices of most Muslim charities were closed by government agencies. These actions took place despite the absence of any evidence proving these charities or their donors were involved in any illegal activity. The Muslim charities that have remained open continue to suffer from decreased funding because their donors fear potential persecution by the U.S. government.

What made such actions possible is the lack of public knowledge about Arab Americans and the prevailing stereotypes about the Arab world, Arab Americans, and Islam. Very few Americans realize that Islam has been part of the fabric of American society for centuries, and that today, Islam is the second-largest religion in the United States, with an estimated following of six to seven million adherents. While many Americans believe "Arab" and "Muslim" are interchangeable terms, the majority of the world's Muslim population is not ethnically Arab. The same applies to the majority of Muslim Americans, whose origins may reach back to Africa, Southeast Asia, the Arab World, and even Europe. In fact, the first mosque in America, established in 1915, was formed by European Americans from Albania.

Although many Americans believe Islam is a radically different religion from Judaism and Christianity, these three monotheistic faiths actually have a great deal in common. They all originated in what is known today as the Arab world. They all believe in a single deity and his messengers, and all embrace Abraham as God's prophet. The core values of family, charity, and respect for others are shared by these three religions. The three religions also have a holy book, a communal place to worship, some form of fasting and important holidays. Throughout history, these religions have radiated from their birthplace, crossing boundaries of race and ethnicity, with followers in nearly every country in the world.

NOTES

1. Pew Forum on Religion and Public Life, http//pewforum.org/surveys/muslim-america.

2. Statement from Council on American Islamic Relations (CAIR) on the Tragedy of September 11; press release from CAIR on September 11; Statement from Islamic Society of North America (ISNA) on September 11, Cair.com, http://www.cair.com/AmericanMuslims/AntiTerrorism/ISNAJoinsAMPCCinCondemningTerroristAttacks.aspx.

3. "Muslim Americans Condemn Attack," IslamiCity.com, December 9, 2001, http://www.islamicity.com/articles/articles.asp?ref=am0109-335.

4. Ibid.

5. "Response to Inquiries from Arab American and American Muslim Communities for Guidance on Charitable Best Practices," The Office of Public Affairs, November 7, 2002, PO-3607, www.treas.gov/press/releases/docc.pdf.

6. "Blocking Faith, Freezing Charity: Chilling Muslim Charitable Giving in the 'War on Terrorism Financing,'" American Civil Liberties Union, June 2009, http://www.aclu.org/human-rights/report-blocking-faith-freezing-charity

7. http://www.whitehouse.gov/blog/NewBeginning/.

8. U-M Detroit Arab American Study (pdf), Report Summary of the Arab American Study, July 29, 2004, 1, http://www.ns.umich.edu/index.html?Releases/2004/Jul04/r072904.

9. Ibid.

10. Ibid., 2

11. Ibid.

12. Ibid.

13. Interestingly enough, the first mosque in America was built by Albanian Muslims in Maine in 1915; Polish-speaking Tatars built a mosque in Brooklyn in 1926. Neither of these populations is Arab.

14. John Esposito and Dalia Mogahed, *Who Speaks for Islam? And What a Billion Muslims Really Think* (Gallup Press, 2008), xii.

5

ARAB AMERICANS AND THE AMERICAN EDUCATIONAL SYSTEM

Janice J. Terry

Arab culture places a great deal of emphasis on education. Two aspects of education are important in understanding the daily life of Arab Americans. First, Arab Americans have disproportionately high levels of education, compared to the national average, which helps them assimilate as immigrants and achieve economic success. Secondly, education has been an area where Arab Americans have both encountered and fought prejudice. Facing discrimination in American society, Arab American organizations, institutions, scholars, and educators have used the intellectual sphere as a platform to foster understanding of the Arab world, Islam, and Arab American life. Although raising awareness and fighting discrimination have been important to Arab Americans for many years, this has become particularly important since the September 11, 2001, terrorist attacks, when Arab Americans faced a backlash from the general American public. Furthermore, 9/11 brought about a heightened interest in the Arab world and increased the U.S. government's need for regional experts. The response to these dynamics at the primary and secondary levels, as well as at institutions of higher learning, has impacted the educational life of Arab Americans.

EDUCATIONAL LEVELS AMONG
ARAB AMERICANS

According to the 2000 U.S. Census some 85 percent of Arab Americans have a high school degree and 4 out of 10 have a bachelor of arts or higher degree, compared to 24 percent of the general U.S. population. Seventeen percent of Arab Americans have a postgraduate degree compared to 9 percent of Americans. Among Arab American students, 13 percent are in preschool, 58 percent in elementary or high schools, 22 percent in college and 7 percent in graduate studies.[1] Among American Muslims, of whom only a minority are Arab Americans, a 2001 poll conducted by Zogby International found that 58 percent had graduated from college and 24 percent had some college courses.[2] In comparison, Pew Research Center polls found that only 25 percent of the general public in the United States had graduated from college and 24 percent had some college education.[3] Statistics from the Prejudice Institute, a nonprofit organization dealing with minorities, issued similar

Graduation ceremony at Fordson High School in Dearborn, Michigan, 1988. When the school, a local landmark, opened in 1928, its students were primarily of Italian and Greek origin; in recent decades, the student body has become more than 90 percent Arab American. (Millard Berry/Courtesy Arab American National Museum)

statistics regarding the educational levels of Arab Americans on its website, indicating that 36 percent of Arab Americans have earned a bachelor's degree or more and 15 percent have earned a graduate degree[4] Although both Arab Americans and Muslim Americans clearly have a higher than average level of education, professionally only 6 percent of American Muslims are involved in education or in the field of teaching.[5] With regard to involvement in K–12 education and support for local schools, evidence indicates that Arab Americans have almost the same relatively low involvement in PTA activities as the general public with 14 percent of the Detroit Arab Americans polled being active in PTA as compared to 18 percent of the general population.[6]

REFLECTIONS ON THE ROLE OF EDUCATION IN MY LIFE

I grew up hearing the expression "education first." As a third-generation Arab American Muslim woman, my parents saw my education as more than a rite of passage, a degree, or a formality; it was essential to cultivating my identity. It was understood that an education would create access and opportunity. As the eldest and only girl, with three younger brothers, I was a role model for them. Going to college was never an option; it was an expectation. There was never less emphasis on the completion of my education than on that of my brothers; in fact, there was more, because I am a woman and therefore, part of a more vulnerable demographic that is still plagued by the glass ceiling.

I am the product of a Muslim grade school, a Montessori middle school, a Catholic all girls' high school, two public universities, a private Mennonite university, and countless Arabic tutors. Having been exposed to an array of academic experiences, I quickly realized that an education was more than what one found in the classroom alone; education came through life experiences and opportunities as well. Having the support and encouragement of my parents to study abroad and move out of state for my graduate studies was essential to my development. I have also been fortunate to live in a household where the advancement of oneself is defined not

---

(Continued)

only by academic achievement but also through extracurricular activities and unique life experiences.

Our parents gave each of us unspoken permission to find ourselves. Because I was not athletic like my brothers, I found my niche in the arts. As a family we could be found on the sidelines of a soccer or basketball field, or at the boards of a hockey game, supporting my brothers. My family could also be found sitting in the audience of a play or musical that I was not even starring in, as I was often working behind the curtain, as a member of stage crew.

Beyond my degrees, activities, and experiences, my most prized education has come from my home. Some young people can't wait for the chance to break free of their families to move out and seek autonomy, but I had no need to find myself when I finally landed in a big city; I was able to be my best self there. Granted, we are all constantly growing and changing, but my core values are something I learned in my home. Compassion for others and honoring one's dignity is something that I learned from my mother. From my father, I learned to not be naïve but to still dream and that generosity and a sense of justice are not just beliefs; they have to be actively lived out. What it means to be a woman, a member of a family, a member of a community, and an American Arab Muslim is not something that can be taught in a classroom alone. In combination, the many aspects of my educational life have provided me with the ability to create meaning around these roles. My worldview is constantly growing, because I was taught that it should never be stagnant and as I have new experiences, my education continues.

Nadia Bazzy, interview by author, Arab American National Museum, Dearborn, Michigan, December 15, 2009.

IMPACT OF 9/11

Arab Americans, especially the youth, have faced a wide array of new challenges in schools and universities since 9/11. Arab Americans have had a long struggle against the negative stereotypes and ethnic racism that are deeply engrained in American culture. However, threats of physical violence, harassment, bullying, and racial slurs against Arab American students increased in the weeks following the September 11 attacks.[7] The subsequent War on Terror, the Iraq War, and the unresolved Arab-Israeli conflict contributed to the increase of negative attitudes, even at the highest levels of academic life. Many Arab Americans have had to bear the brunt of the hostile feelings that the political tensions in the Middle East have engendered. Islamophobia, or fear of Islam as a religion and Muslims as believers, has also become a serious problem in the United States.

In a 2003 Pew Research Center survey, 44 percent of American respondents believed Islam encouraged violence; this demonstrated a notable increase from the 25 percent recorded in the 2002 poll.[8] The Council on American-Islamic Relations (CAIR) poll in 2004 found that more than 25 percent of those polled had negative attitudes toward Muslims.[9] Further, Pew Research indicated that 25 to 30 percent of Americans polled had unfavorable views of Muslims as compared to 10 to 18 percent with negative attitudes toward Protestants or Catholics.[10] Interestingly, an even greater percent—over half—of the respondents held negative views of atheists.[11] A substantial percentage, between 25 to 46 percent, believed Islam was more likely to encourage violence than other religions.[12] Since many Americans equate being Muslim with being Arab, these negative attitudes clearly have implications for Arab Americans. A 2006 *USA Today*/Gallup poll indicated that 39 percent of Americans were prejudiced against Arabs. A frighteningly similar percent believed that all Muslims, even U.S. citizens, should carry special IDs.[13] These trends have had a long-term impact as indicated by a 2009 *Washington Post*-ABC News poll showing that 3 in 10 (29 percent) believed Islam advocated violence against non-Muslims; however, on the positive side 58 percent thought it was a peaceful religion.[14]

Stereotypes and Discrimination in K–12 Education

Instances of discrimination were documented in school systems across the country following the September 11 attacks.[15] There were numerous reports in K–12 school systems of Arab American children being bullied or harassed. Girls wearing the hijab were often singled out for unfair treatment. Although harassment, bullying, and racial taunting were the most common problems, occasionally the attacks escalated into actual physical violence. Some Arab American students also retaliated with physical attacks. Arab

American students reported feeling higher levels of stress in the immediate aftermath of the September 11 attacks. These stresses are well described in *How Does It Feel to Be a Problem? Being Young and Arab in America* by Moustafa Bayoumi. In this moving book, Bayoumi tells the life stories of several young Arab Americans living in Brooklyn. The narrative captures how these young people navigate the complexities of overlapping identities (American, Arab, Muslim, male and female) as well as how they cope with the public taunts or hostility that were prevalent in the aftermath of the September 11 attacks. The book received the 2009 Arab American National Museum Book Award for the best adult nonfiction work by an Arab American author or about Arab Americans.

The Civil Rights Division of the U.S. Department of Education has investigated schools where there have been allegations of discrimination. Under the Bush administration, Secretary of Education Rod Paige sent a letter to school districts across the country after the September 11 attacks to encourage them to take action to prevent anti-Arab actions or attacks on Muslims.[16]

Countering Negative Stereotypes

Countering negative perceptions at the earliest stages of education is important to fight stereotypes. But some efforts to change curriculums that would include objective materials on Islam and Arabs as well as the Arab-Israeli conflict have met with opposition by organized political and religious groups and sometimes by parents. Although the number of complaints has been relatively small, such pressure has often prevented open debate on key issues in the classroom. Teachers in general have reported that maintaining objectivity and civility in discussions of controversial issues regarding the Arab and Muslim worlds has been extremely difficult. However, in spite of complaints by parents or political and religious groups, most school systems and many teachers have made proactive attempts to include objective material on Islam and Arab history and culture in the curriculums. Organizations such as ACCESS (Arab Community Center for Economic and Social Services) have developed curriculum supplements and programs on Arabs and Arab culture for use in elementary schools. ACCESS was established in 1972, in Dearborn, Michigan, in response to the increased number of immigrants who were arriving in the area at the time. While the main mission of ACCESS is to help new immigrants adjust to life in America, the organization recognized that its work would be much more effective if the American public could have a better understanding of the Arab world and Arab American history and culture. As early as 1987, ACCESS started to provide educational workshops and materials, including curriculum supplements, to elementary and secondary schools and to college students and educators. As the demand for these services continued to grow, ACCESS established the first and only Arab American National Museum in Dearborn. The museum's mission is to document, preserve, and educate the public on Arab American history, culture, and contributions. Today, more than 60,000 people visit the museum annually.

Another organization dedicated to educational outreach is AWAIR (Arab World and Islamic Resources), founded by Audrey Shabbas in 1990 and based in New Mexico. The educational resources available from AWAIR are used around the country, and the organization operates an online resource center as well as offering one- and two-day staff development programs on Islam and the Arab world. These workshops have provided useful teaching tools and curriculum for teachers nationwide. For more information you can go to http://www.awaironline.org/aboutus.htm.[17] School systems have also established multicultural programs to educate students about a wide range of peoples and cultures including Arabs and Islam.

Tension and Controversy on College Campuses

The effects of 9/11 on Arab American students and intellectuals, as well as programs that educate about the Middle East and the Arab world, have been profound. The post-9/11 period was simultaneous with a breakdown in peace initiatives between Israel and the Palestinians and the start of the U.S.-led Iraq War in 2003, causing increased tension between special-interest groups on U.S. college campuses. Programming around issues important to Arab Americans at the university level faced new challenges. Harassment of students attending forums on the Middle East with speakers who were critical of U.S. policies or of Israel was commonplace. Scholars and experts who presented the Arab point of view, or who were even sympathetic to that view, were similarly attacked. Although some universities stood up to outside pressures, others withdrew invitations to so-called controversial speakers.[18] The so-called Islamo-Fascism Awareness Week that took place on several American college campuses in 2007 and 2008 is an example of blatantly anti-Arab and anti-Muslim programs that used the educational setting as a platform to promote fear and bigotry.

Arab American intellectuals have made major contributions across many fields in American scholarship. But the fear brought about by 9/11 led to organized attacks and increased scrutiny of the work of many Arab American professors, usually centered on their treatment of the contentious Arab-Israeli conflict. Interest groups established websites and watch groups to monitor classes, professors, and programs dealing with the Middle East, and lists were issued naming professors, both Arab and non-Arab, who were accused of presenting materials or views that questioned or opposed Israeli policies. A number of professors were accused of bias in their classrooms or of intimidating students who did not adhere to their political beliefs, sometimes leading to university investigations that deemed the charges baseless. Since 2001, there has been heightened interference by interest groups in academic appointments and tenure decisions at American universities through exerting pressure and influence on university administrators and donors. In hiring and tenure decisions, both Arab and non-Arab professors have been targeted with increased attention to the candidate's position on Middle East issues.[19]

Academic freedom and the ability openly to debate political issues that include an Arab perspective were challenged on multiple fronts during this period. It is impossible to ascertain to what extent these campaigns affected the willingness of professors, especially untenured ones, to engage in discussion of controversial issues as they pertain to the Arab world, Arab Americans, and Muslims. However, these campaigns have undoubtedly had a chilling effect on the freedom of speech and have certainly increased the stress felt by Arab American and Muslim students and professors.

Academic freedom was further threatened in 2003, when a congressional bill was proposed that targeted area studies programs at the university level that receive government Title VI funding. The bill would have subjected academic programming and curricula to oversight by a government-appointed advisory board. Although the bill easily passed through the House of Representatives, scholars and others lobbied against it on the grounds that had the potential to censor or limit freedom of speech and scholarly research on key issues involving the Middle East, Arabs, and Islam. Owing in part to grassroots opposition from Arab Americans and others, the bill died in the Senate. Opposition to this bill was also organized by the Middle East Studies Association (MESA), a nonpolitical academic association dedicated to promoting excellence in scholarship to foster understanding of the Middle East and its peoples. In recent years, MESA has continued to organize its membership around the defense of academic freedom, not only in the United States but also in Arab states and other Middle Eastern nations.

Effect on Foreign Students

Following 9/11, increased security regulations also made it much more difficult for foreign students, especially Arabs and those from predominantly Muslim countries, to study in the United States. In the years immediately following the September 11 attacks, the number of foreign students in U.S. universities dropped markedly. By 2006 the number of foreign students began to rebound and owing to a concerted effort by the Saudi government there was a significant increase of students from Saudi Arabia.[20] The number of students from North Africa also increased by 4 percent in 2007–2008.[21] Foreign students help to provide diversity and a means for American youth to learn more about Arabs and Muslims. Since the overwhelming majority of international students were either privately financed by their families or their governments, they also yielded economic benefits to U.S. universities, colleges, and local communities, especially since they pay high "out of state" tuition.[22]

PROGRAMS ON ARABS AND ARAB AMERICANS IN HIGHER EDUCATION

The events of 9/11 brought to light Americans' serious lack of knowledge about the Arab world, and yet, education is a crucial means of fighting misperceptions, disseminating knowledge, and raising awareness. Polls have consistently indicated that American youth of both genders and all ethnic backgrounds were more open to diversity and much less likely to hold stereotypic views and hostile attitudes toward Arabs and Muslims. Pew Center Research polls also found that college-educated young Americans were more likely to have positive views of Muslims than those without university educations.[23] These findings reinforced the general belief among scholars in the field that knowledge about the Arab world and Islam, as well as firsthand contact with Arabs and /or Muslims, is the best means of fighting racism and discrimination.

The lack of expertise in the Arabic language and Arab history or culture among job applicants poses a major problem for the U.S. Department of State and other government agencies and for businesses with contracts in the Arab world. The lack of input by experts on the region with Arabic-language skills has had a negative impact on the formation and implementation of U.S. policies and actions throughout the Arab world. After September 11, there were only a handful of qualified experts fluent in Arabic in either the State Department or the Pentagon. Figures in *The Digest of Education Statistics* indicated that only 26 PhD degrees in Arabic were awarded by U.S. universities in the 1970s, as compared to more than 1,800 in French.[24] During the same timeframe, only 10 PhD degrees were awarded in Islamic studies and 102 in Middle Eastern studies (an area that includes Iran, Israel, Turkey, and Afghanistan).[25] In 2006 the Bush administration attempted to redress this problem by announcing a National Security Language initiative to encourage increasing numbers of American students to learn Arabic and several other "critical need" languages such as Russian, Chinese, Farsi, and Hindi.[26]

After 9/11, the sharp increase in the need for regional experts and Arabic language speakers to work in the government and the military highlighted the vital role played by the Middle East Centers found at many American universities. Because many graduates from these area studies programs go on to serve in the public sphere, Middle East Centers can be funded through government Title VI funding. Typically these centers have an array of national and international scholars who teach in a number of disciplines as well as graduate students who serve in a number of professions, but often in academia or public service.

ARAB AMERICAN INTELLECTUALS

The late Edward Said (d. 2003) was for many years the preeminent Arab American scholar. In his groundbreaking books *Orientalism* (1978) and *Culture and Imperialism* (1993), Professor Said explored the themes of culture, imperialism, and racism, laying the foundation for a new generation of scholarship regarding Western attitudes and the Arab world. In *Orientalism,* Said challenged the narrow ethnocentric depiction of the Arab world found in much of Western literature, art, media, and scholarship. He offered a nuanced critique of the Orientalist approach to the Arab world from the 18th through the 20th centuries. In his prolific scholarly publications and in his political life, Said advocated for the "decolonizing" of Western depictions of Arabs; he argued that "the goal of Orientalizing the Orient again and again is to be avoided. . . . Without 'the Orient' there would be scholars, critics, intellectuals, human beings, for whom racial, ethnic, and national distinctions were less important than the common enterprise of promoting human community."[27] Said was also well known for his passionate support of the Palestinian cause, as well as for his defense of civil liberties for oppressed peoples around the globe. After his death, some old political antagonists attempted without great success to tarnish his intellectual contributions. However, Said's scholarly analyses continue to resonate in academic fields to the present day.

Since Said's death, Rashid Khalidi, Joseph Massad, and other Arab American academics have continued his work in deconstructing Western stereotypes and approaches to the Arab world, as well as presenting more objective analyses of Arab history, politics, and society. Rashid Khalidi holds the Edward Said Chair in Modern Arab Studies at Columbia University in New York City. Before moving to Columbia, Khalidi taught at the University of Chicago. He has published a number of scholarly studies focusing on Palestinian history and U.S. foreign policy in the Middle East. His publications include *Palestinian Identity: Constructions of Modern National Consciousness* (New York: Columbia University Press, 1997) and *Resurrecting Empire: Western Footprints and America's Perilous Path in the Middle East* (Boston: Beacon Press, 2005). His most recent book, *Sowing Crisis: The Cold War and American Dominance in the Middle East* (Boston: Beacon Press, 2009) traces U.S. involvement in the Middle East from World War II to the end of the Cold War within the context of the rivalry between the two superpowers of the era, the United States and the Soviet Union. Khalidi is a frequent commentator on U.S. involvement in the Middle East and ongoing crises in the region in the *Nation* and the *New York Times* as well as on National Public Radio broadcasts.

Joseph Massad is associate professor of Modern Arab politics and intellectual history at Columbia University. His work deals primarily with Palestinian, Jordanian, and Israeli nationalism. His publications include *Colonial Effects: The Making of*

(*Continued*)

National Identity in Jordan (New York: Columbia University Press, 2001) and *The Persistence of the Palestinian Question: Essays on Zionism and the Palestinians* (New York: Routledge, 2006). In *Desiring Arabs* (Chicago: University of Chicago Press, 2007), Massad builds on the work of his mentor, Edward Said, to provide a sophisticated, interdisciplinary theoretic discussion of the sexual representation and creation of Arab sexual identity by earlier generations of Western scholars. Like Khalidi, Massad frequently speaks about current events in the Middle East and about the Palestinian cause at public forums and debates.

Other Arab American scholars have reinforced Said's arguments while making original contributions of their own. These included Ibrahim Abu Lughod, Hisham Sharabi, Michael Suleiman, Naseer Aruri, Samih Farsoun, and Elaine Hagopian among others. These Arab American scholars also mentored a new generation of Arab American academics, including Ghada Talhami, Jamal Nassar, and William Haddad.

In his groundbreaking work, *Reel Bad Arabs,* Jack G. Shaheen documented the pervasive negative stereotyping of Arabs in Hollywood films. His subsequent work has extended and updated this line of inquiry. Based on his personal experiences as an Arab American and his scholarship in cutting-edge literary theory, Steven Salaita's *Anti-Arab Racism in the USA* offered a provocative and thought-provoking analysis of the deeply embedded racism among Americans against people of color, including toward Arabs. In *Race and Arab Americans before and after 9/11,* edited by Amaney Jamal and Nadine Naber, a number of scholars offer provocative discourses on the issues of "blackness," "whiteness," and "otherization," as they pertain to and affect Arab Americans.

With the proliferation of scholarly publications and conferences, an entire new field surrounding the study of Arab Americans as a distinct group within the larger American mosaic has been created. Alixa Naff and Michael W. Suleiman were pioneers in the creation of the new field of Arab American studies from the 1960s to the present day. They helped to pave the way for other Arab American scholars who specialize in Arab American studies; these include Barbara Aswad, Nabeel and Sameer Abraham, May Seikaly, Suad

Joseph, and others. Their work has enlarged and expanded the field. Over the past 20 years, young Arab American scholars, including but not limited to Nadine Naber, Gregory Orfalea, and Evelyn Sultany, have authored studies about Arab American immigration to the United States, Arab American culture, daily life, and gender issues. More recently Arab American scholars Lisa Majaj, Rosina Hassoun, Steven Salaita, Randa Kayyali, and others have dealt with issues as diverse as gender, health, aging, and racism. The expansion in this field demonstrates the recognition of the unique Arab American experience in the American mosaic.

ARAB AMERICAN ACADEMIC ORGANIZATIONS

Arab Americans in the field of education have founded a number of organizations to network and promote understanding of issues that are important to them. Following the disastrous defeats by the Arab states in the 1967 Arab-Israeli war, a number of Arab American scholars organized to educate Americans about the Arab world and the Palestinian cause. Established in 1967, the Association of Arab-American University Graduates (AAUG) was for many years the foremost Arab American organization dedicated to publishing and distributing scholarly information on the Arab world and Arab Americans.[28] From the late 1960s through the 1980s, the AAUG published a massive number of books, information papers, and newsletters. The AAUG also held an annual national conference, where renowned Arab and Arab American scholars and writers, as well as leading politicians and public figures, were featured. These conferences provided a venue for Arab American academics and others to present their latest research and to debate crucial issues facing Arab Americans, American foreign policy in the Middle East, and developments in the Arab world. For the last decade or more, the AAUG has been largely moribund, but a handful of AAUG members have continued to support and publish the organization's flagship journal, the *Arab Studies Quarterly (ASQ)*. The *ASQ* is a quarterly scholarly publication that issues peer-reviewed essays by scholars, including a number by young Arab American academics, and is the largest circulating journal in English devoted to the Arab world. After the 9/11 attacks, *ASQ* published special issues on terrorism, global relations, human rights in the Arab world, and other articles of topical interest, including critiques of the United Nations' 2002 *Arab Human Development Report.*

The Middle East Studies Association (MESA), the largest U.S. organization of academics involved with Middle East studies, also regularly includes panels or discussions about and by Arab Americans at its annual conference and in its academic publications. Annually MESA holds a well-attended conference; it also publishes its own journal, drawing upon the best scholarship in Arab and Arab American studies in America.

ARAB AMERICAN STUDENT ORGANIZATIONS

On university campuses Arab students have long been active in a wide variety of Arab organizations. In the 1960s and 1970s, the Organization of Arab Students (OAS) was particularly active on U.S. campuses. The OAS adopted a strong pan-Arab stance and generally adopted programs in keeping with the policies of Egypt under Gamal Abdul Nasser. During the same time frame, the General Union of Palestine Students (GUPS) was established in Cairo in 1959 and had chapters on a number of U.S. campuses. Although it was composed primarily of Palestinian students, some other Arab American students joined GUPS. From the 1980s forward, some Arab American Muslim students also joined a variety of Muslim student organizations that are well represented on campuses across the country.

However, these organizations tended to focus on specific political or religious issues within the Arab world, not specifically on issues pertaining to Arab American students. Established in 1996, the Union of Arab Student Associations (UASA) specifically provides a venue for young Arab Americans to network and exchange. With chapters in more than 40 universities, it holds an annual national conference featuring well-known keynote speakers as well as panels and opportunities for its members to meet with government officials and to develop strategies for activist programs. Its sister organization, the Network of Arab-American Professionals (NAAP), established in 2001, supports the programs of UASA. Also, NAAP hosts cultural events; its members are available for outreach programs to educate Americans about Arab Americans and Arab culture. On some campuses, such as that of Brown University, Arab American and Arab students have merged to form one umbrella organization. But on most campuses, multiple Arab, Muslim, or Arab American student organizations continue as separate entities, although they may sometimes cooperate or sponsor joint programs and events. Tufts University, the Universities of Michigan, Texas, and New York, George Mason University, and a number of other universities have Arab student associations. There are also a number of Egyptian student organizations across the country. Harvard and the Massachusetts Institute of Technology also have Arab alumni associations.

Like all student organizations, Arab American student groups face the ongoing problem of maintaining continuity of leadership and programming. As students graduate and enter the professional world, they almost inevitably drop their affiliations with university groups. The next group of students must step in to fill the void and to continue the programming and outreach of the various Arab American or Arab student organizations.

ARAB AMERICAN ORGANIZATIONS' OUTREACH PROGRAMS

For decades the Arab Community Center for Economic and Social Services (ACCESS) in Dearborn has sponsored outreach programs on Arab Americans and the Arab world for teachers, law enforcement personnel, and community leaders in Michigan. In 2005 ACCESS established the Arab American National Museum. The museum's Education Outreach programs serve thousands of people annually in Michigan and in other states through exhibits, educational and cultural events, as well as publications that focus on Arab American history, culture, and contributions. Other Arab American organizations have held similar programs from California to Chicago. Arab American and Muslim groups on university campuses have also regularly organized programs to counter stereotypes and bigotry and to educate their classmates about themselves and the Arab world. Arab and Muslim Americans are also regularly included as participants in many multicultural programs and events across the country.

Arab Americans and Muslims have been proactive in speaking out against anti-Arab and Islamic events or campaigns on college campuses. In 2007, the American Arab Anti-Discrimination Committee (ADC) contacted all the universities named as hosts for Islamo-Fascism Awareness Week to warn of the potentially racist nature of the program. The ADC National Executive Director, Kareem Shora, noted concerns over the "racist, bigoted, Islamophobic, and anti-Semitic speakers . . . [who] promote hatred and spread misinformation and lies."[29] Students on some campuses sponsored counter programs to feature more balanced presentations about

Schoolchildren take a docent-guided tour of the Arab American National Museum, the only such institution among the 17,500 museums in the United States. Education is at the heart of the museum, where more than half of the 50,000 annual visitors are students of all ages and their instructors. (Courtesy Arab American National Museum)

the Arab and Muslim world. Many Arab American events also highlighted both sides of the conflict between the Israelis and Palestinians.

Since 2005, the Middle East Teacher Resource Project (METRP), sponsored by the American Friends Service Committee, has provided information from a wide variety of sources to K–12 educators; the Arab American National Museum has sponsored similar programs. These programs typically include Arab food and music, an excellent means to make the Arab world more accessible to teachers and students. These events also include lectures by scholars on culture, history, Islam, and current events in the Arab world. Teachers who attend these programs typically receive packets of information that include readings from published sources, bibliographies of books for further reading, and videos on Arab Americans and the Arab world.

The Arab-American Historical Foundation (AAHF) was established in Los Angeles by Joseph Haiek in 1978. The AAHF is an organization dedicated to research and to preserving and disseminating information about Arab American history. In 2008, it sponsored a national conference that included top scholars in the field. Presentations included research findings on family histories, culture, and the political engagement of Arab Americans. In 2008, the state of New Jersey created an Arab American Commission with 25 members to coordinate events and assist in the dissemination of materials to schools as a means of educating teachers and students about the rich history and culture of Arab Americans and the Arab world. When signing the executive order to create this commission, New Jersey Governor Jon S. Corzine stressed that the commission was "an important step in recognizing the economic, social, and cultural contributions of Arab-Americans and . . . will provide opportunities to education the general public and our students about these contributions."[30]

In the 1980s, a small group of Arab American women also challenged the more traditional discussions regarding feminism and women of color at the annual National Women's Studies Association (NWSA). Arab American women have since become an integral part of feminist discourse in the United States. In *Bint Arab: Arab and Arab American Women in the United States*, Evelyn Shakir traced the personal stories of a number of Arab women in the United States from the late 19th century through the 20th century. A growing number of research materials and scholarly publications on Arab American women are now more regularly included in women's studies programs. In 2009, Michael W. Suleiman, Distinguished Professor of Political Science at Kansas State University, organized a highly successful national conference on Arab American women. More than two dozen academics, many of whom were Arab Americans, gave scholarly presentations on history, society, politics, and religion at the well-attended event. Selected papers from these presentations will be published in a book.

EDUCATIONAL OUTREACH BY AMERICAN UNIVERSITIES

The growing interest in Arab Americans is reflected in the establishment of a number of new programs about Arab Americans in universities. The study of Arab Americans as a defined ethnic group has become part of the much older and sometimes well-funded programs on other immigrant and ethnic groups. In 2007, the Asian and Asian American Studies (AAAS) organization reached out to Arab Americans by sponsoring a plenary session on Arab American

identity at its annual conference. This was an opening to an ongoing debate over the question of whether Arab Americans were also
part of the larger Asian construct. Academic organizations and researchers are currently exploring the issues of race and Arab Americans and how the two may or may not interrelate within the United
States.

Established in 2000, the Center for Arab-American Studies
(CAAS) at the University of Michigan–Dearborn offers a full range
of academic courses. This center also hosts film festivals, occasional
exhibits, and conferences such as the 2006 International Conference
on Mapping Arab Diasporas.[31] The University of Minnesota's Immigration History Research Center (IHRC) has established an endow-
ment for the preservation and promotion of Arab American history.
To further this mission, the center offers the annual Francis Maria
Graduate Fellowship in Arab American Studies, with the goal of
"stimulating and nurturing new research talent."[32] Arab American
experiences and history are now frequently included in courses on
ethnic studies and the immigrant experience. In 2004, Tufts University sponsored a highly successful conference, Arab American
Writing Post-9/11.

CONCLUSION

The value of education is deeply rooted in Arab culture; Arab
American families place great emphasis on their children's educations. As a result, Arab Americans have higher than average levels
of education. However, and in spite of their high level of education,
Arab American continue to face discrimination and hostility in
schools as well as at the work place. Discrimination and stereotyping of Arab and Muslim Americans escalated after the tragic events
of September 11. Those most frequently victimized have been school
and university students, who continue to face a wide range of hostile activities including bullying, violence, and racial slurs. At the
same time, efforts have increasingly been made by student organizations and educational institutions to provide programming,
materials, and curriculum about the Arab world, Arab Americans,
and Islam. Also at the university levels many courses about the Arab
world, Arab Americans, and Islam have been introduced.

After September 11, university campuses, especially Centers for
Middle East Studies, as well as professors who expressed views
that were critical of Israel or the United States' Middle East policies, were scrutinized or attacked. This created an intimidating

atmosphere and threatened censorship in educational institutions, which are supposed to provide a safe space for people to develop their critical thinking and explore various points of views. Arab American scholars and intellectuals like Edward Said, Rashid Khalidi, and Jack Shaheen have addressed the issue of stereotyping of Arabs, Arab Americans, and Islam, which existed before 9/11 and has dominated American popular culture for decades.

Arab American organizations also play an important role in providing workshops, seminars, and educational materials that can help the public better understand the Arab world, Arab Americans, and Islam. Since September 11, these organizations, including community-based, civil rights, and student organizations, increased their efforts and have reached out to a large number of students, educators, law enforcement, and government officials. Arab Americans are now a recognized part of the mosaic that constitutes American history and culture, and this is increasingly recognized in programs on all educational levels and in scholarly publications. These positive developments will make important contributions toward the further integration and understanding of Arab American young people in future years.

NOTES

1. Angela Brittingham and G. Patricia de la Cruz, *We the People of Arab Ancestry in the United States: Census 2000 Special Report* (U.S. Census Bureau, March 2005), www.census.gov/prod/2005pubs/censr-21.pdf; see also Michael W. Suleiman, "A History of Arab American Political Participation" in *American Arabs and Political Participation,* ed. Philippa Strum (Washington, DC: Woodrow Wilson International Center for Scholars, 2006), 5.

2. Zahid H. Bukhari, "Demography, Identity, Space: Defining American Muslims," in *Muslims in the United States: Identity, Influences, Innovation,* ed. Philippa Strum and Danielle Tarantolo (Washington, DC: Woodrow Wilson International Center for Scholars, 2003), 12.

3. Bukhari, "Demography, Identity, Space," 12.

4. "Fact Sheet 5: Arab Americans," The Prejudice Institute, http://www.prejudiceinstitute.org/Factsheets5-ArabAmericans.html.

5. Ibid.

6. Ronald R. Stockton, "Arab-American Political Participation: Findings from the Detroit Arab American Study," in Strum, *American Arabs and Political Participation,* 57.

7. Hussein Ibish, ed., *2003–2007 Report on Hate Crimes and Discrimination against Arab Americans* (Washington, DC: American-Arab Anti-Discrimination Committee Research Institute/ADC-RI, 2008), 2 and 10.

8. Scott Keeter and Andrew Kohut, "American Public Opinion about Muslims in the U.S. and Abroad," in Strum and Tarantolo, *Muslims in the United States*, 55.

9. "Poll: 1-in-4 Americans Holds Anti-Muslim Views," CAIR Poll, October 4, 2004, www.cair-net.orgdownloads/poliresults.ppt. Accessed October 5, 2004.

10. Keeter and Kohut, "American Public Opinion about Muslims in the U.S. and Abroad," 53.

11. Keeter and Kohut, "American Public Opinion about Muslims in the U.S. and Abroad," 52.

12. Keeter and Kohut, "American Public Opinion about Muslims in the U.S. and Abroad," 55.

13. "USA's Muslims under a Cloud," *USA Today*, August 10, 2006; see also Paul Findley, "Inglorious Steps on the Path to Victory," *Washington Report on Middle East Affairs* (January/February 2009).

14. "ADC LEOP Continues to Lead Fight against Ignorance and Intolerance," ADC Press Release, www.adc.org, April 8, 2009. Accessed April 9, 2009.

15. "ADC LEOP Continues to Lead Fight," 47–74.

16. Marvin Wingfield, "Arab Americans: Into Multicultural Mainstream," *Equity and Excellence in Education* 39 (2006): 259.

17. http://www.awaironline.org/workshop.htm.

18. *2003–2007 Report on Hate Crimes and Discrimination Against Arab Americans* (Washington, DC: American-Arab Anti-Discrimination Committee Research Institute/ADC-RI, 2008), 63–74; "Academic Freedom and Columbia University" http://www.academicfreedomcolumbia.org; Victoria Fontan, "McCarthyism and Middle Eastern Studies: A Frenchwoman's Disillusioning Journey from Iraq to an Upstate N.Y. Campus," *CounterPunch* 16, no. 6 (March 16–31, 2009).

19. Daniel Pipes, "Redeeming the Wayward University," *New York Sun*, November 28, 2006, http://www.danielpipes.org/4167/redeeming-the-wayward-university; "Islamo-Fascism Week Backfires," *The Washington Report on Middle East Affairs*, December 2007, p. 82; Joan W. Scott, "Middle East Studies Under Siege," *The Link* 39, no. 1 (January–March 2006).

20. Patricia Chow and Rachel Marcus, "International Students in the United States: Open Doors Survey," *International Higher Education* 55 (Spring 2009): 13, http://www.bc.edu/bc_org/avp/soe/cihe/newsletter/Number55/Number55.htm, accessed July 3, 2009.

21. Chow and Marcus, "International Students in the United States," 13. See also John Owens, "Foreign Students Facing post-9/11 Rules," *Chicago Tribune*, October 6, 2002, http://www.opendoors.iienetwork.org/?p=29534, accessed July 3, 2009.

22. Mary Beth Marklein, "Report: USA Sees First Increase in Foreign Students since 9/11," *USA Today*, November 12, 2007, http://www.usatoday.com/news/education/2007-11-11-study-abroad_N.htm, accessed

July 3, 2009. The Institute of International Education (IIE) estimated that international students and their families spent $14.5 billion on the U.S. economy in 2006–2007 alone.

23. Keeter and Kohut, "American Public Opinion about Muslims in the U.S. and Abroad," 66–71.

24. *The Digest of Education Statistics, 1985–86* (Washington, DC, 1986); U.S. Department of Education, Office of Post-Secondary Education, *Enhancing Foreign Policy Language Proficiency in the United States: Preliminary Results of the National Security Language Initiative* (Washington, DC, 2008), 1.

25. *Digest of Education Statistics, 1985–86*

26. *Digest of Education Statistics, 1985–86*

27. Edward W. Said, *Orientalism* (New York: Pantheon Books, 1978), 328.

28. Janice J. Terry and Elaine C. Hagopian, eds., a special double issue titled "The AAUG Experience: Achievements and Lessons Learned," *Arab Studies Quarterly* 29, nos. 3 and 4 (Summer and Fall 2007).

29. "ADC Leads Effort Against Hate Campaigns on Campuses," ADC Press Release, October 19, 2007, www.adc.org.

30. Michael M. Shapiro, "Governor Creates New Jersey Arab-American Heritage Commission," November 17, 2009, http://www.thealternative press.com/article.asp?news=318. Accessed November 17, 2009.

31. "Mapping Arab Diasporas," University of Michigan Dearborn, Arab American Studies, http://www.casl.umd.umich.edu/346201/.

32. "The Arab American Studies Fund," Immigration Research Center, University of Minnesota, http://www.ihrc.umn.edu/support/arab.php.

6

PROFESSIONAL LIFE

Kathleen Marker

One reason Arab immigrants began coming to the United States in the late 1800s and continued to immigrate is for economic advancement. Work and educational opportunities have attracted Arab immigrants throughout the years and motivated them to uproot their lives and often leave friends, family, neighborhoods, and their familiar culture behind. Some immigrants moved with the promise of being able to work in the businesses of family or friends who had immigrated before them and shared their success stories. Others heard about job opportunities in corporations, agriculture, industry, or educational programs that would allow them to work in business, accounting, engineering, education, medicine, or law.

Less research has been done on the occupations and employment of Arab Americans than on other areas of Arab American life. The majority of research has been done on small groups in specific parts of the country and is not always representative of Arab Americans in other regions of the United States. Additionally, there is a shortage of large survey data on Arab Americans. While the government does conduct a survey of minority- and women-owned businesses, only blacks, Hispanics, Asians, and Native Americans are included. Furthermore, the 2000 U.S. Census does not have a category for respondents to identify their ethnicity as Arab or Arab American.

The data for this chapter relies on the limited studies that have been conducted on Arab American employment as well as the 2000 U.S. Census. Findings from interviews conducted with 100 Arab Americans who own a diverse range of businesses throughout Metropolitan Detroit, Michigan, are also used to enhance the data.[1] It is useful to study the lives of Arab Americans in Detroit because the area has one of the largest and densest populations of Arab Americans outside of the Arab world.

What is clear, however, is that Arab immigrants have often quickly found employment in American factories, businesses, and corporations. Arab Americans have excelled in their education and tend to earn good wages. Both business acumen and education are held in high regard within Arab culture. The employment and educational opportunities pursued by Arab Americans not only provide a means to make a living but also exposure to American culture, traditions, and norms. Employment also allows people to develop lasting relationships with coworkers and join workers' organizations.

Following 9/11, Arab Americans have faced new challenges. Many experienced increased ridiculous discrimination at the workplace in the backlash. Yet, as 9/11 increased the profile of Arab Americans, they seized the opportunity to reach out to fellow citizens to teach them about Arab heritage, cultures, languages, religions, and values. This recent development in the Arab American work experience is only part of a rich history of Arab American peddlers, factory workers, business people, and other professions contributing to the American workforce and economy.

EARLY ARAB IMMIGRANT EMPLOYMENT

When the first Arab immigrants arrived in America in the late 1800s, they faced the daunting task of finding employment in a country and culture they knew little about. Many spoke little English, making the process of finding a job even more challenging. Early Arab immigrants were mostly single men who migrated with the intention of earning and saving enough money to bring their families to the United States or return to their country of origin with substantial savings. The first Arab immigrants were mostly Christians from the Mount Lebanon region in the Ottoman province of Syria. Throughout the 20th century, the religious and national diversity of Arab Americans expanded to include Muslims and people from Yemen, Iraq, Jordan, Palestine, and other Arab countries.

Peddling

Despite the challenges of finding jobs in a new country, many Arab immigrants quickly found work as peddlers, selling wares throughout the United States.[2] Following their arrival at Ellis Island in New York, Boston, or other ports of entry, Arab immigrants dispersed throughout the country, moving to areas as varied as Ohio, Montana, Florida, and California. Peddling required Arab immigrants to travel to farms and small towns to sell a variety of goods such as clothing and household items to consumers who would otherwise have to travel great distances in order to find stores that sold similar goods. Constantly traveling from place to place while carrying their wares prevented many early Arab immigrants from settling down in one area for a very long time and from establishing families and homes. However, as peddlers became more successful, they often established homes and businesses. Some successful peddlers built outposts along peddlers' routes and earned their livings supplying, housing, and feeding other peddlers. A peddler could stay at an Arab-owned boarding house along the trade route and enjoy traditional Arab cooking, while speaking Arabic with other peddlers, activities that were often impossible to do while peddling in areas without significant Arab American populations. These early Arab immigrants excelled in their jobs. By 1910, they reported earnings close to three times that of the average American.[3]

Agricultural Work

The Homestead Act of 1862 was enacted to facilitate the expansion of the western United States. According to the act, potential homesteaders did not have to pay anything for their land; instead, "In exchange for a 160-acre land deed, the U.S. government required a five-year residency and cultivation of a large part of the land."[4] This encouraged immigrants, former slaves, and poor people to obtain farmland. The Homestead Act also provided subsidies for those who wanted to buy farmland, increasing land ownership opportunities for the economically disadvantaged. Moreover, in order to take advantage of the benefits of the Homestead Act one did not need to be a citizen of the United States; one only needed to live on and cultivate the land. Homesteaders produced a variety of crops for personal consumption and sale.

The majority of Arab Americans who partook in homesteading moved to North Dakota during the early wave of Arab immigration in the late 1800s. Most of these Arab immigrants came from modern-day Syria and Lebanon. Early Arab immigrant homesteaders established churches and mosques and other cultural centers. However, for many Arab immigrants homesteading was not always a welcome occupation. North Dakota's severe winters were very different from the mild temperatures and green landscapes of Syria and Lebanon, and new farmers also faced the isolation of living without a neighbor around for miles. Some lands offered through the Homesteading Act spanned up to 640 acres, making the loneliness even greater. Nevertheless, many Arab immigrant homesteaders established themselves in North Dakota and hundreds of descendants of these early pioneers continue to live there.[5]

Even if they were not homesteaders, some Arab immigrants found work in agriculture. Some of these immigrants had experience working on farms in the Middle East, but many did not. In order to work in agricultural jobs, soon after arriving in the United States, a number of Arab immigrants moved to California's San Joaquin Valley to take advantage of the economic opportunities of farm work. Later generations often remained in California and opened businesses or began professional careers.[6] However, a few Arab Americans, especially Yemenis, continue to work in California's agricultural sector, many as migrant workers.

Industrial Work

Another employment option for early Arab immigrants was to work in America's growing industrial centers. As the industrial core of America grew in the late 1800s and early 1900s, so did employment opportunities in factories. Like other immigrants, Arab immigrants typically traveled directly from Ellis Island to large industrial towns such as Detroit, Pittsburgh, Boston, or Chicago to seek work in automobile, steel, food, and clothing production factories. These jobs required few skills and little knowledge of the English language. At the same time, factory positions provided fairly high wages and consistent work, which made industrial jobs ideal for many immigrants. In 1914, Henry Ford began paying laborers at Ford Motor Company in Michigan five dollars per eight-hour workday. This

Mohammad Abdalla (left), who immigrated to the United States from Yemen as a teen, works the fields with another Yemeni in 2002. Abdalla arrived in America with just $7 and the address of a Yemeni coffee shop. There he found other Yemenis who helped him establish his new life, which grew to include a Mexican American wife and two children who are college graduates. (Donation of Mohammad and Erma Abdalla/Courtesy Arab American National Museum)

unusually high wage for manual work enabled employees to adequately support their families and encouraged many immigrants to seek out jobs at Ford and, later, at other automobile factories. Word of these high-paying and abundant factory jobs spread quickly. Even after only a few days in the United States, many Arabs were able to find employment and relocate to industrial towns.

On the downside, factory work was often physically dangerous and exposed workers to numerous long-term health risks. In the late 1800s and early 1900s, there were few safety standards for industrial facilities. The machinery and chemicals found in many factories often made for unsafe working conditions, and if a worker

Saleem (*fourth from left*), with other industrial workers, at one of his first jobs. Saleem immigrated from Jordan in 1950 and attended the University of California, Berkeley. (Courtesy Arab American National Museum)

was injured on the job, he or she was unlikely to receive proper medical care or compensation from the factory owner. These conditions and the monotony of factory work encouraged many Arab immigrants to seek out other jobs. Some Arab Americans worked in factories upon arrival in order to save up enough money to open businesses that would allow them more autonomy and more control over their working conditions and profits. Others saved money and provided their children with a better education so they would have career options other than factory work.

WORK AND THE ETHNIC ENCLAVES

Arab immigrants often moved to areas where they had family or friends, or where they knew others from their hometowns and villages had settled. This chain migration allowed many immigrants in the United States to continue their relationships with family and neighbors from their hometowns and villages. Often, this type of clustering created an ethnic neighborhood referred to as an ethnic enclave. Several of these Arab American neighborhoods were in the industrial areas such as Detroit, Boston, and New York, where many newly arrived immigrants found factory jobs. Moving to where one had connections often eased the financial and social impact of migration and helped immigrants navigate through a new country, culture, and language. Family and friends could often help new immigrants find employment in the factory where they worked or at a business they owned.[7]

Many successful peddlers relocated to Arab American neighborhoods and either brought their families from their country of origin or married another immigrant and established new families. After spending years traveling across the country with limited interaction with other Arabs, peddlers and other Arab Americans found ethnic enclaves to be ideal for raising children with Arab values and an understanding of Arab culture. Immigrants were attracted to areas where other Arabs lived not only because they could receive support in adjusting to the United States but also because it was easier to maintain their culture and traditions. Communities with large Arab American populations gave rise to Arab American organizations, churches, and mosques, as well as stores and restaurants that sold ethnically specific products and traditional foods. Living in an Arab American ethnic enclave also enabled many Arab immigrants and their children to maintain their ability to speak Arabic. Residents in ethnic enclaves are able to use their native language in daily interactions at restaurants, stores, and health clinics. Ethnic enclaves typically also include weekend language and cultural schools to ensure that the children and grandchildren of immigrants learn to speak, read, and write in the native tongue of their relatives. With residential clustering, many entrepreneurs saw a market for businesses that serviced the co-ethnic population and developed ethnic economies.

ENTREPRENEURSHIP AND BUSINESS OWNERSHIP

Arab Americans are highly entrepreneurial.[8] In fact, they are one of the most successful entrepreneurial groups in the United States. Some people have argued that this is because Arabs were used to working in sales and traveling to other parts of the world, such as Australia, Europe, and West Africa. A more likely explanation is that the value of self-employment is passed on from generation to generation. Self-employment provides the same type of autonomy as peddling, but allows for a more settled life than earlier peddlers had experienced. A third explanation for these high rates of self-employment is based on the importance of family unity in the Arab culture. Many families open and run businesses together, which provides employment to family members, eases the challenges of business ownership, and allows for success. Business ownership helps many to adjust to life in America, as new immigrants are able to quickly obtain employment with family or friends, while developing business, language, and professional skills. Furthermore, scholars argue that these high rates of family-owned businesses, and the economic opportunities and self-employment they provide new immigrants, have allowed Arab Americans to quickly adjust to American culture and lifestyles.[9]

The Daily Life of the Arab American Worker: Naser

Naser is an eye doctor who migrated to the United States from Palestine as a young child in the early 1960s. Naser went to college and medical school in the United States. After graduation, he started working as an ophthalmologist, specializing in surgical procedures that improve people's vision. After gaining surgical experience working for others, he decided it was time to open his own clinic. Naser claims that his friends from medical school thought he was going into business for himself too soon, but he explained that because his dad, uncles, and brother all had businesses, he saw it as a natural step. He feels he was able to start his medical business earlier than his medical school classmates because he had gained the necessary business knowledge working in his father's store after school and on weekends when he was growing up. In order to open his own practice, Naser used his savings from working for several years and obtained a loan from his father.

Naser reports that the majority of his patients and staff are non-Arabs. However, he does have several Arab American patients with whom he often communicates in Arabic. Expanding on his advanced surgical knowledge and use of cutting-edge technologies, Naser has been able to open several clinics in the United States and one in the United Arab Emirates. Now, he spends most of his time traveling between the two clinics. Naser says it was a challenge to open a clinic overseas. He was the sole financer and received little support from the government. Because he splits his time between the two locations, he has had to hire and train more staff than would otherwise be necessary. Fortunately, the services he offers in his clinic in the UAE have attracted patients from around the Arab world. Naser is pleased that through his expertise and hard work he has been able to improve people's vision both inside and outside of the United States.[10]

Arab American Business Owners Today

Arab Americans own a diverse range of businesses from small hair salons, restaurants, grocery stores, travel agencies, and auto repair shops to large national law firms and international medical centers. Small business ownership has proven to be very successful for Arab Americans because with a substantial time investment and the support of family, many small business owners can reap hefty profits. For example, if an Arab American couple opens a small restaurant, they often invest long hours working, and their children also frequently help out in running the restaurant and greeting customers. Hiring employees outside of the family network can be costly because the business owner has to pay for advertising the job, training employees, and monitoring the productivity of strangers, in addition to the higher wages and benefits required for nonfamily members. The significant time investment many Arab American families put into businesses allows for higher profits but can come at the cost of leisure and quality family time. However, after years of sacrifice, many business owners are able to invest in other businesses ventures, grow their businesses, or hire nonfamily members as employees.

From these investments in small businesses, many Arab Americans have used the profits to establish larger corporations that involve more risk but are potentially more profitable. Others have grown a small business, such as a small real estate or engineering firm, into a corporation with several branches across the state, the country, and the world. Using connections in their country of origin and knowledge of the business practices, language, and culture of the Arab world, some Arab Americans have developed branches of their companies in Arab countries or invested in corporations overseas. Many Arab Americans still involve family in helping run these large corporations. Furthermore, growing up working for a parents' business provided many children with essential work experience, business knowledge, and savings that enabled them to immediately open large and successful firms.

Arab Americans Doing Business in the Arab World

Many Arab Americans who own successful businesses like to diversify their businesses by opening branches of their companies or investing in other businesses in Arab countries. Some entrepreneurs have been able to establish businesses in their country of origin or another Arab country. The oil-rich Persian Gulf region and,

Mona Mulhair is surrounded by goods from her store, which features imported Egyptian handicrafts, at an event sponsored by the Arab American Chamber of Commerce. Mulhair has operated several retail outlets in Los Gatos, California, featuring unique items from her Egyptian homeland. (Donation of Mona Mulhair/Courtesy Arab American National Museum)

**FAMOUS ARAB AMERICAN ENTREPRENEURS
AND EXECUTIVES**

Steven Jobs, Founder and CEO of Apple

John Mack, CEO and Chairman of the Board for Morgan Stanley

George Maloof Jr., Real estate investor and owner of the Palms Casino Resort and the Sacramento Kings

Ned Mansour, Former President of Mattel, Inc.

Jacques Nasser, Former President and CEO of Ford Motor Company and current CEO of the mining company BHP Billiton

Paul Orfalea, Founder of Kinko's

---

in particular, the United Arab Emirates (UAE) have attracted U.S. entrepreneurs and business investors. Many entrepreneurs have developed a successful product or service in the United States and the essential business knowledge and capital that allows them to start transnational businesses in Arab countries. International business owners are often forced to split their time between managing their businesses and training employees overseas and in the United States. While rewarding, this can require extensive traveling that makes business ownership difficult and taxing on both business owners and their families. Alternatively, some entrepreneurs rely on family members to run and manage a business they have established overseas. This shared business relationship can allow for economic advancement for both parties, but can cause disagreements on how a business should be run and how profits should be spent.

Other business owners report their desire to open a new business in their country of origin, such as Lebanon, Yemen, or Iraq, or in the Gulf States. This is of particular interest to younger business owners. In contrast, older business owners often report wanting to focus on the business operations in the United States without having to deal with the extra stress that comes with expanding a business. However, the majority of entrepreneurs who would like to own a business in their country of origin or another Arab country report that they are unlikely to do so because of the political instability in many Arab countries. In recent years, Lebanon has been damaged by conflict with Israel. Similarly, while some Iraqis report that their country has become safer than it was in the early years of the Iraq War, entrepreneurs are not yet comfortable enough to invest in business opportunities in the country. Additionally, while the UAE has had a quickly expanding economy and remained peaceful, several business owners cite political unrest in the surrounding areas as a deterrent to investment. Business owners worry that it would be too hard and financially taxing to rebuild a business operation if it were destroyed by conflict. Other entrepreneurs who have developed business plans for overseas investments report having a hard time convincing other potential investors of the safety of business investments.

Additionally, the U.S. government's increased monitoring and scrutiny of Arab Americans following 9/11 has altered overseas investments and business dealings. Taken together, the monitoring of investments and personal travel and other scrutiny has deterred some business owners from making overseas investments. There have also been reports of the U.S. government confiscating the goods of owners of international import and export companies.[11] However, the development of international businesses in the Arab World could provide job opportunities and generate wealth, which may in turn improve Middle Eastern economies, infrastructures, educational systems, and social conditions.

PROFESSIONAL OCCUPATIONS

Aside from both small and large business ventures, Arab Americans can also be found working in every profession. They tend to be more educated and are more likely to have professional and managerial jobs than the average American. Arab Americans work as politicians, doctors, lawyers, engineers, scientists, writers, and teachers. According to the 2000 U.S. Census, 42 percent of Arab Americans are employed in professional and managerial positions. In comparison, only 34 percent of all Americans are employed in such positions. Similarly, 31 percent of Arab Americans work in sales, office, and administrative support positions versus 15 percent of all Americans.[12]

OCCUPATIONAL DISTRIBUTION OF ARAB AMERICANS AND U.S. POPULATION

Yet, it is important to remember that not all Arab Americans have equal access to educational opportunities that allow for professional occupations. Many Arab immigrants, even those who received advanced educations in their country of origin, frequently have difficulties finding employment and high-paying jobs after arriving in the United States. These immigrants may suffer from discrimination incurred by their accents or physical features. Many older Arab immigrants who worked in the legal, medical, or educational fields have had to learn English, take local exams, and obtain licenses to be able to practice similar occupations as those they held in their country of origin. Meeting these requirements can be quite challenging and many older Arab immigrants end up doing work unrelated to their professions. Other Arab immigrants, who have lived through war, economic hardship, and other stressful events, may have little education, few job skills, and limited occupational opportunities. In addition, emotional stress brought about by living in unstable conditions and immigration can hinder adjustment to American society and the job market. These immigrants often seek assistance from social organizations or family and friends in order to adjust to the American economic system and navigate the job market.

WORKERS' ASSOCIATIONS

Many Arab American workers have joined or helped organize workers' associations. These associations help their members de-

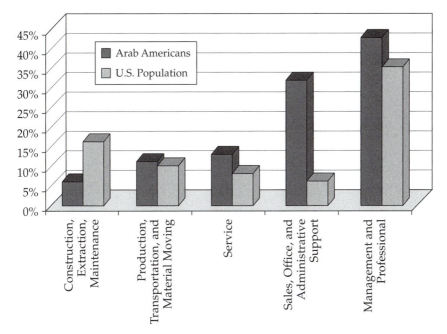

Arab Americans work in a wide range of occupations. Data indicates that they tend to be more educated and are more likely to have professional and managerial jobs than the average American. (Statistics are drawn from the 2000 U.S. Census as analyzed in Ivan Light and Steven Gold, *Ethnic Economies*)

velop relationships and further work skills and assist them in standing up for their rights in the workplace. Some of these organizations and their role in the work lives of Arab Americans are presented below.

- *United Auto Workers Union (UAW)*—After the UAW was founded in 1935, early Arab immigrants employed in the auto industry often joined. These Arab Americans fought along with other workers for safer working conditions, fair pay, better benefits, and the right to protest. Arab Americans went on to serve as officers and leaders of the UAW union. For example, George Addes was an Arab American who helped organize and grow the UAW during the early 1930s. He was born in Wisconsin to Lebanese parents and worked as a wet-sander. He became involved with the founding of the UAW in an effort to obtain better wages and working conditions for all employees. After the formation of the UAW in 1935, Addes was elected the first secretary-treasurer of the UAW and was elected for 10 more one-year terms.[13] Under his leadership, the UAW grew from 30,000 to more than 50,000 members.

- *National Farm Workers Association (NFWA)*—Under the leadership of Cesar Chavez and others, the NFWA was formed in 1962. The NFWA is well known for organizing farm workers and leading strikes and long marches against grape and lettuce growers. In the 1960s, NFWA workers protested for better pay and work conditions. Many Arab immigrants in California's Central Valley joined and even helped organize the NFWA. In 1973, Naji Daifullah, a Yemeni immigrant, was killed by police during a NFWA protest.

- *Arab American Union Members Council (AAUMC)*—The formation of the AAUMC was inspired by Naji Daifullah and other Arab American immigrants who fought for workers' rights. The organization was formed to protect the rights of Arab, Muslim, and South Asian workers. Following 9/11, the AAUMC teamed up with other labor unions and community organizations to serve as a source of support for workers who faced discrimination and inequality in the workplace.

George Addes celebrates with other industrial workers. (Donation of George Addes/Courtesy Arab American National Museum)

- *Arab American Lawyer and Bar Associations*—There are several local organizations for Arab American lawyers throughout the United States. These professional organizations allow Arab American attorneys, law students, and other legal professionals to come together for networking events to share ideas and further their professional knowledge and skills.

- *National Arab American Medical Association (NAAMA)*—The NAAMA was formed in 1975 and has chapters throughout the United States. The organization sponsors conferences and conventions for medical professionals as well as educational and charitable events.

- *Network of Arab American Professionals (NAAP)*—Formed in 2001, the NAAP holds national and local networking and educational events. The organization is also concerned with empowering the Arab American community.

- *Arab American Chamber of Commerce (AACC)*—The AACC serves the population of large Arab American business owners and entrepreneurs in the Detroit, Michigan, area. The chamber brings business owners together for networking events and even sponsors community activities. Other areas throughout the United States with significant populations of Arab Americans have established similar organizations to promote business networking.

Lama Fakih, a lawyer at New York University's Center for Human Rights and Global Justice, is seen working at her desk in 2009. (Paul Washburn)

EDUCATION

It is often easier for the children of immigrants to obtain educations and advanced degrees because they have more advantages than their immigrant parents. Immigrants often lack the financial means, language skills, and knowledge of the American educational system that is necessary to seek out educational advancement. Furthermore, some Arab immigrants who have earned advanced degrees in the Arab world have frequently been unable to apply these degrees and receive certification to work in the same professions they had before migrating. Many doctors, lawyers, teachers, and engineers have had to go back to school to meet U.S. requirements or are forced to find employment in occupations unaffiliated with their advanced educational training. Like other immigrant groups, Arab immigrants work hard at whatever jobs they can to provide for their families so that their children will have more opportunities. Education is extremely important in Arab American culture. Not only do parents stress the importance of education, but many families also provide both financial and emotional support for their children to continue in higher education.

The sacrifice of many parents and the value of education can be seen in the high rates of Arab American's educational attainment. Both Arab American men and women reach higher levels of education than the average American. According to the 2000 U.S. Census, more than 85 percent of Arab Americans complete high school with more than 40 percent going on to earn bachelor's degrees. Seventeen percent of Arab Americans pursue postgraduate degrees. In comparison, only 24 percent of the entire American population has earned a bachelor's degree and only 9 percent have gone on to earn advanced postgraduate degrees.[14] These achievements make it easier for Arab Americans to navigate the job market and find employment opportunities and financial success.

EDUCATION OF ARAB AMERICANS AND THE U.S. POPULATION ON THE JOB TRAINING

At the same time, Arab Americans are also highly entrepreneurial. While formal education is very valuable in Arab American culture, so are entrepreneurial activities and self-employment. Many Arab American children grow up assisting in a parent's business and are surrounded by extended family members and friends who work in the business. This familiarity provides Arab Americans with solid experience in business management. Some Arab American students report frustration with college business and management courses.[15] They find that working for a family business has provided them with more real-world knowledge and business experience than their instructors have. This frustration has sometimes led students to forgo school in order to establish their own businesses.

INCOME AND CLASS

According to the 2000 Census, the median income for Arab American households was $47,000, while the average household income in America was $42,000. Furthermore, 30 percent of Arab American families earn more than $75,000 a year, compared to 22 percent of U.S. families who earn more than $75,000 a year.

However, not all Arab Americans have equal access to advanced degrees, earn high wages, or enjoy the economic advantages of the middle and upper classes. In particular, recent immigrants and lower-income families often face more challenges when entering the workforce or attempting to partake in educational opportunities that will allow them to obtain high-paying jobs.

ECONOMIC IMPACT OF ARAB AMERICANS ON THE LOCAL ECONOMY

The Center for Urban Studies at Wayne State University in Detroit conducted one of the most thorough analyses of the impact of Arab Americans on a local economy for the League for Economic Empowerment.[16] The League for Economic Empowerment is an organization of Arab American professionals who are interested in promoting the economic interests of Arab Americans. According to this research, Arab Americans have significantly impacted the local economy in Southeast Michigan. Using data from the U.S. Census and a survey that was conducted for the study, the researchers estimate that of the 68,515 Arab Americans working in the state in 2005, nearly 27 percent worked in retail trade (18,636). The next most common occupations are in manufacturing and hotel accommodation and food services. The research team concluded that in Southeast Michigan, Arab American economic activity supports between 99,494 and 141,541 jobs. Furthermore, jobs either held by or created by Arab Americans are responsible for between $5.4 and $7.7 billion in wages and salaries. This money in turn generates additional employment, supports tax initiatives, and leads to additional economic growth, which also allows others to start businesses.

FAMILY AND WORK

Arab American businesses are often said to be so successful because of the strong family ties and the importance of group well-being that characterizes Arab culture. Families often work long hours together in a business in order to get ahead. The opportunity to hire family ensures that more trustworthy, dependable, and hardworking people are involved in a business operation. Staffing a business with family members cuts costs and also decreases overhead. Many family businesses are able to grow and prosper through the help, advice, and hard work of family members. When talking about why their businesses are so successful, many Arab American business owners explain that their families were always there to provide advice and support in times of need. Families offer advice on how to best start a business and Arab Americans frequently obtain loans from family, rather than from banks, which charge high interest rates and prefer not to loan to small and potentially risky business ventures. For many children who sacrificed to help their parents with their businesses, this financial support and business advice is well-deserved.[17]

The Daily Life of the Arab American Worker: Dalal

Dalal owns a real estate agency that she runs with her mother and sister. Dalal and her sister were born in the United States, but her mother emigrated from Lebanon in the early 1950s and received most of her education in the United States. In fact, once her own children were old enough to be in school, Dalal's mother returned to college and completed her college degree. In the early 1980s, she opened the real estate company. Originally, the real estate agency was run out of the family home, but as the business grew, Dalal, her sister, and her mother opened an office. In order to purchase the office space, the women tried to obtain a bank loan but had a hard time getting a business loan. They had to secure the funding for the business from family members.

Dalal says most of her clients come to their agency based on word-of-mouth recommendations from previous clients. The women rarely advertise their business. The majority of clients are Arab Americans who live in the area and Dalal claims that her family's Arab heritage helps in attracting business. According to Dalal, the community is very tightly knit and many customers feel comfortable, almost like family. When the agency needs to hire additional help they often depend on their loyal customers to recommend potential employees. Sometimes they also post advertisements about job openings in the local newspaper and Arab American newspaper. Dalal, her sister, and her mother are all bilingual, and they often speak both English and Arabic in the workplace.

On Fridays, Dalal often closes the agency for a few hours to attend Friday prayer services at the mosque. After the service the family reopens the business for the day. Dalal feels that her gender and religious faith have never cost her any customers. In fact, she feels that her customers actually like coming to the agency because it is run by women and combats typical stereotypes of Arab and Muslim women.

GENDER AND WORK

As in traditional American culture, in Arab culture, women are often considered responsible for the children and household, while men are encouraged to work as the family breadwinner. Many Arab American women work at home raising children and maintaining family life, while their partners provide the necessary financial support. Women who are stay-at-home mothers and wives may also put in hours with a family business or work a part-time job. Other Arab American women work full-time jobs outside the home while simultaneously balancing family duties. Arab American women work in a plethora of jobs. They can be viewed daily on television working as reporters, entertainers, and politicians. Their clothing designs are seen traveling down fashion runways. We read the words of Arab American women in novels and newspapers. Arab American women teach in schools and universities and care for people in hospitals. They run corporations and international charities.

Some Arab and Muslim stereotypes present Arab American women as restricted to gender roles that would prevent their education and employment. But the data do not seem to support this contention. Many Arab American women obtain high levels of education, which can provide numerous occupational opportunities and significant incomes. According to 2000 Census data, 37 percent of Arab American working-age women have earned a bachelor's degree or higher compared to 29 percent of working-age white women. Furthermore, according to Jen'nan Read, of the Arab American women who are employed "over two-thirds

---

FAMOUS ARAB AMERICAN WOMEN AT WORK

Entrepreneurs

Zainab Salbi, Activist and entrepreneur, founder of Women for Women International

Reem Acra, Fashion designer known for her bridal gowns

Writers

Helen Thomas, White House correspondent for many new organizations with a career spanning decades

Lorraine Ali, Reporter and editor for publications such as *Newsweek* and *Rolling Stone*

Naomi Shihab Nye, Poet and novelist

Actresses and Television Personalities

Selma Hayek, Actress, producer, director

Hoda Kotb, Cohost on the *Today Show* and *Dateline NBC* correspondent

Shannon Elizabeth, Actress in *American Pie, Scary Movie,* and contestant on television's *Dancing with the Stars*

Kathy Najimy, Actress in *Sister Act,* and television's *King of the Hill* and *Veronica's Closet*

(67.2 percent) occupy managerial and professional positions, a much higher proportion than for any other group of U.S. women."[18] The general trend for women who obtain an education is that they are more likely to work outside the home. Furthermore, the more education women earn, the more likely they are to work in high-paying professional positions. However, data suggest that while Arab American women often obtain advanced degrees, which are considered an important asset, many choose to stay home taking care of their children and households. Read notes that while 73.2 percent of white women, 73.1 percent of black women, 70.2 percent of Asian women, and 65.8 percent of Hispanic women work outside the home, that is the case for only 59.9 percent of Arab American women. Thus, while Arab American women are more educated than the average American woman, they are less likely than the average American woman to work outside the home. Furthermore, it seems clear that practicing Islam does not significantly influence Arab American women's rates of employment.[19]

Gender frequently influences workplace experiences. Women tend to earn less than men who hold the same position, and they are less likely to occupy the highest positions in a corporation despite having the qualifications. Women who attempt to advance in corporations often face a glass ceiling and are prevented from advancement due to bias. Race and ethnicity add to the effects of gender bias and sexism in the workplace. Arab American women who work outside the home are likely to experience workplace discrimination because they are both women and minorities.

For example, Arab American Muslim women who wear the head covering known as a hijab have reported experiencing discrimination from other employees in the workplace.[20] Coworkers may feel uncomfortable working with women who they see as different and supervisors may be afraid that religion and ethnicity will scare away customers. Some women who experience workplace discrimination report trying to downplay their religion, while others find it important to teach coworkers about their culture and religion. Arab American women who do not wear the hijab or who are Christian have also experienced discrimination based on their ethnicity and perceived cultural and political differences.

Yet, many Arab American women do not experience workplace discrimination. For example, the owner of a travel agency, whose mother worked for him and wore her hijab, explained that family and friends approached him after 9/11 with concern that his mother's presence could spark hate crimes and negatively impact business.[21] The travel agency owner reported the exact opposite. Without his mom, business was not as strong. His mother was gregarious and had developed personal relationships with customers that attracted business to the firm. This finding suggests that positive personal interaction can sometimes overshadow and combat negative stereotypes.

Arab American women are not alone in their experiences of discrimination in the workplace. Following 9/11, thousands of Arab American men and women throughout the United States were questioned by the U.S. government.[22] Some Arab Americans were even detained without cause only to later be released without any charges or explanations for their detentions. Others were deported for expired visas and minor immigration violations.

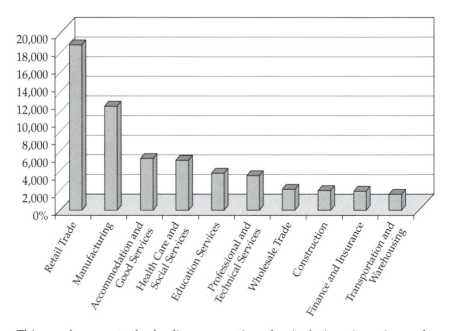

This graph presents the leading occupations for Arab Americans in south-eastern Michigan. (Data from the 2010 U.S. Census and the Arab American Institute.)

There were several cases of mistaken identity when fellow Americans, angered by the terrorist attacks and their perceptions of Arab Americans as dangerous, reacted by attacking Arab Americans and others who looked Arab. People attacked those who had darker skin, or wore a beard and a turban. Many Sikhs, who are Indian or Pakistani, experienced violent acts during this time, as a case of mistaken identity and misplaced anger.

The wars in Afghanistan and Iraq and the wiretapping, questioning, and detention of Arab Americans after 9/11 influenced the work environment of Arab Americans. Arab Americans experienced difficulties finding jobs and more discrimination in the hiring process. Some claimed to have changed their names on job applications from Muhammad or Osama to Mo or Sam, out of fear of possible discrimination. Coworkers and bosses increasingly perceived their Arab American colleagues as dangerous, backward, and different. Following 9/11, there are reports of customers asking business owners about their religious or ethnic identities and making an effort to frequent non-Arab-owned businesses or those owned by people who shared their religion.

Others felt that religion or ethnic heritage has had little impact on their businesses. Some Arab American workers experienced no discrimination in the workplace. Focusing on the increased attention and publicity, some found that people actually had an easier time pronouncing their Arab names and treated them better, although they admit this could possibly have been out of fear of lawsuits. According to interviews conducted for the Detroit Arab American Study, 33 percent of Arab Americans in Metropolitan Detroit reported receiving support from non-Arabs following the events of 9/11.[23]

CONCLUSION

Arab Americans are found in every occupation and they tend to place a high value on both education and entrepreneurship. Arab American women and men are better educated than the average American, which often results in professional and high-paying jobs. Arab Americans value the autonomy and economic opportunities that can come with entrepreneurship. As a result, Arab Americans are one of the most highly entrepreneurial ethnic groups in the United States. Their entrepreneurial activities range from small convenience stores, jewelry shops, and video production companies, to large national grocery store chains and international construction companies. These business owners significantly contribute to the American economy. They are responsible for job creation and providing employment and training to others. Additionally, Arab American entrepreneurs have developed innovative products and procedures that have changed and advanced American society.

The majority of early Arab American immigrants worked as peddlers or industrial laborers, while today's Arab Americans work in a wide range of occupations across the United States. Some continue to work as manual laborers or farm workers; some are political leaders, prominent social activists, and award-winning journalists, scientists, accountants, engineers, and teachers. Both Arab American men and women are represented in these occupations. Other Arab American women stay home raising children and running households.

Following the events of 9/11, Arab Americans have experienced not only increased discrimination but also increased awareness and interest in their lives, traditions, and cultures. Some Arab Americans felt a backlash in their workplace as a result of the fear and ignorance about their culture. In contrast, others report that the events of 9/11 have had little effect on their lives at work. It is hoped that like other minorities who experience discrimination in America's workplaces, Arab Americans will be able to combat these stereotypes and misperceptions. One way this can be done is by teaching others about the histories, cultures, religions, and traditions of Arab Americans while highlighting the similarities and limited differences between all people.

NOTES

1. Interviews conducted by Kathleen Marker between May 5, 2008, and August 20, 2009, as part of her research for a dissertation in progress at the University of California San Diego.

2. Alixa Naff, *Becoming American: The Early Arab Immigrant Experience* (Carbondale: Southern Illinois University Press, 1985), 1–369.

3. Gregory Orfalea, *Before The Flames: A Quest for the History of Arab Americans* (Austin: University of Texas Press, 1988), 82.

4. Arab American National Museum, *Telling Our Story* (Dearborn, MI: Arab American National Museum, 2007), 105.

5. Lee Ann Potter and Wynell Schamel, "The Homestead Act of 1862," *Social Education* 61, no. 6 (October 1997): 359–64, http://www.archives.gov/education/lessons/homestead-act/.

6. Janice Marschner, *California's Arab Americans* (Sacramento: Coleman Ranch Press, 2003), 1–160.

7. Interviews conducted by Kathleen Marker between May 5, 2008, and August 20, 2009, as part of her research for a dissertation in progress at the University of California San Diego.

8. Ivan Light and Steven Gold, *Ethnic Economies* (San Diego: Academic Press, 2000), 111.

9. Interviews conducted by Kathleen Marker between May 5, 2008, and August 20, 2009, as part of her research for a dissertation in progress at the University of California San Diego.

10. Interviews conducted by Kathleen Marker between May 5, 2008, and August 20, 2009, as part of her research for a dissertation in progress at the University of California San Diego.

11. Interviews conducted by Kathleen Marker between May 5, 2008, and August 20, 2009, as part of her research for a dissertation in progress at the University of California San Diego.

12. Arab American Institute, Zogby International, http://www.aaiusa.org/arab-americans/22/demographics. Data based on the U.S. Census Bureau, 2000 Census, file 4.

13. "George F. Addes, 79; Helped Found U.A.W." *New York Times,* June 21, 1990, http://www.nytimes.com/1990/06/21/obituaries/george-f-addes-79-helped-found-uaw.html?pagewanted=1.

14. Arab American Institute, Zogby International, http://www.aaiusa. org/arab-americans/22/demographics. Data based on the U.S. Census Bureau, 2000 Census, file 4.

15. Interviews conducted by Kathleen Marker between May 5, 2008, and August 20, 2009, as part of her research for a dissertation in progress at the University of California San Diego.

16. Study by the League for Economic Empowerment, a group of Arab American professionals, and the Center for Urban Studies at Wayne State University. http://www.lee-usa.org/index.htm.

17. Interviews conducted by Kathleen Marker between May 5, 2008, and August 20, 2009, as part of her research for a dissertation in progress at the University of California San Diego.

18. Jen'nan Ghazal Read, *Culture, Class and Work among Arab-American Women* (New York: LFB Scholarly Publishing, 2004), 64.

19. Read, *Culture, Class and Work,* 64.

20. Interviews conducted by Kathleen Marker between May 5, 2008, and August 20, 2009, as part of her research for a dissertation in progress at the University of California San Diego.

21. Interviews conducted by Kathleen Marker between May 5, 2008, and August 20, 2009, as part of her research for a dissertation in progress at the University of California San Diego.

22. Louise Cainkar, "Thinking Outside the Box," in *Race and Arab Americans Before and After 9/11: From Invisible Citizens to Visible Subjects,* ed. Jamal Amaney and Nadine Naber (Syracuse: Syracuse University Press, 2008), 46–80.

23. Andrew Shryock, "The Moral Analogies of Race," in *Race and Arab Americans Before and After 9/11: From Invisible Citizens to Visible Subjects,* ed. Jamal Amaney and Nadine Naber (Syracuse: Syracuse University Press, 2008), 81–113. Also see Wayne Baker, Sally Howell, Amaney Jamal, Ann Chih Lin, Andrew Shryock, Ronald R. Stockton, and Mark Tessler, *Citizenship and Crisis* (New York: Russell Sage Foundation, 2009).

7

PUBLIC AND POLITICAL LIFE

Helen Hatab Samhan

Over the course of several immigration waves to the United States from the Arab world, generations of Americans of Arab descent have expressed their civic and political identity in ways not unlike other ethnic constituencies but often under unique international and domestic political conditions that have shaped that participation. The contributions of Arab Americans to public life were acknowledged by President William J. Clinton in 1998 when he said,

> I'm honored to be the first sitting president to address an Arab American conference . . . because the Arab American community has made an enormous contribution to this country—with basic values that made us great: love of family and belief in hard work and personal responsibility and a passionate devotion to education, which I hope we will see engulf every single ethnic group in America today.[1]

For more than a hundred years, Arab Americans have engaged in the political process, public service, and debates over policy decisions.

ARENAS OF ARAB AMERICAN POLITICAL PARTICIPATION

Arab American participation in politics as citizens and advocates can be summarized broadly into two arenas: (1) campaigns and elections, where Arab Americans engage in the electoral process as voters, volunteers, political professionals, and donors; and (2) shaping and responding to the debate on public policies that directly impact the welfare of Arab Americans, relations with their ancestral countries, and related peace and justice initiatives. The impact of political engagement by Arab Americans in both these arenas is evident in the recognition of this community as an organized ethnic constituency by both major political parties and in the ability of community leaders to advocate on behalf of the welfare and policy interests of its members. The emergence of an Arab ethnic voice in local and national political discourse was particularly important in the period following September 11, 2001, when unprecedented challenges of discrimination, racial profiling, and cultural intolerance demanded community attention and action.

Campaigns and Elections: From Citizen to Voter

This first level of participation, campaigns and elections, is one in which the largest number of Arab Americans engage by taking

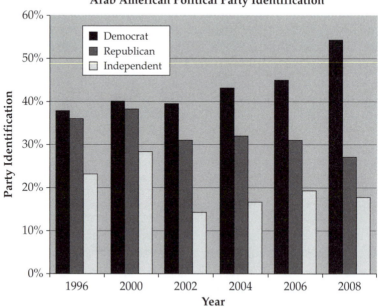

Data compiled from surveys conducted by Zogby International and the Arab American Institute show the shift in Arab American political party identification over the past four U.S. presidential election cycles. (Arab American Institute [AAI]/Zogby International)

part in electoral politics along a spectrum that ranges from voting on Election Day, to joining a political party, and even running for office. As voters, Arab American citizens cannot be identified with any single political party. In national elections, polls show that partisan identification has ranged from being evenly split among Democrats, Republicans, and independents to shifting support to favor one presidential candidate, depending on who is running for office. When surveyed in 2000, the Democratic party held a slight edge in party identification (38 percent vs. 36 percent for the Republican party), yet only 23.5 percent of Arab Americans over-all called themselves liberal, with 37.5 percent defining themselves as conservative. In 2000, the majority of Arab Americans voted for George W. Bush, but in the 2004 election, President Bush received less than 30 percent of the Arab American vote. By 2008, votes were cast overwhelmingly for Barack Obama.[2]

GETTING OUT THE ARAB AMERICAN VOTE

Efforts to increase the number of Arab Americans who register to vote and show up on Election Day began in earnest in the 1980s. Local initiatives in the city of Dearborn, Michigan, home to the highest concentration of Arab Americans in America, followed a racist campaign waged by a mayoral candidate against the increasingly visible Arab presence. The untapped voting power of the city's Arab residents, then at about 20 percent of the population, was the goal of the Arab Voter Registration and Education Committee (AVREC), which was organized to increase Arab American registered voters from the hundreds in the 1970s, to tens of thousands today. After the 1984 presidential elections, the establishment of the Arab American Institute (AAI) as a national political empowerment organization (see below) translated this goal to other communities in states with significant Arab American populations. By the 1990s, a National Registry of Arab American Voters was set up by AAI with the support of Arab American social, cultural, and service organizations.

If registering to vote is the first step to political empowerment, then showing up at the polls is the culmination of that process. Programs to "Get-Out-the-Vote," or GOTV, particularly among immigrants or other first-time voters, have developed over the past three decades, utilizing organizational and community tactics designed to reach a broad spectrum of voters before Election Day. In preparation for the 2008 presidential election, a national campaign was built by the AAI around the theme of "Our Voice, Our Future: Yalla Vote! 2008." *Yalla* is an Arabic expression that means "let's go" or "come on." The GOTV phase, which ran from early October to November 4, 2008, focused on new tools and alliances to encourage more Arab Americans to go to the polls.

The Yalla Vote GOTV project collaborated with the National Association of Latino Elected and Appointed Officials (NALEO), which had designed an online tool to reach ethnic voters regardless of where they live. Through a pool of AAI volunteers who signed up to call lists of registered voters with Arabic surnames in a number of key states, the Yalla Vote "virtual phone bank" reached thousands of voters in the weeks leading up to Election Day. Other GOTV tools in the Yalla Vote campaign included organizing rallies, sending reminder postcards, and sponsoring nonpartisan "robocalls" on Election Day eve, with recorded messages by recognized personalities.

While registering and voting may for most Arab Americans be the extent of their political participation, the involvement of individuals in the process of nominating and electing candidates has transformed a previously invisible constituency into an organized political player in the decisions of both major parties. The foundation of Arab American visibility in the party system was laid in the mid-1980s, with the formation of Arab American Democratic and Republican clubs in various U.S. cities. These clubs became a training ground in party politics, incubating activists who became members and then leaders in local, state, and national party affairs. The clubs were formalized into national federations in 1988 (the National Arab American Democratic Federation and the National Arab American Republican Federation) that helped create a broader profile for ethnic activists, that has culminated in an organized Arab American presence, through delegates and cultural events, at every nominating convention since 1988. By the early 1990s, the federations merged to form a bipartisan Arab American Leadership Council, which has networked the political leadership of Arab Americans ever since.

From Immigrant to Party Leader: Journey of an Arab American Political Activist

Rima Nashashibi, an immigrant from Jerusalem, settled in Orange County, California, and became a U.S. citizen in 1988. In that year, another milestone was being laid by the presidential campaign of

Then California State Assembly candidate for the 67th District, Rima Nashashibi, speaking at the Arab American Institute National Leadership Conference in Washington, D.C., in 1998. (Courtesy of Arab American Institute, photo taken by Dupont Photographers)

Rev. Jesse L. Jackson Jr., whose platform included a statement in favor of statehood for Palestine that electrified Arab Americans from both parties. Looking for people from diverse communities to serve as delegates to the national convention, the Jackson campaign needed gender and ethnic balance in the delegation from California's 39th Congressional District. James Zogby, AAI president, in his capacity as a vice chair of the Jackson campaign, recruited Rima to run for delegate—before she had even voted in a U.S. election. "What's a delegate?" Rima inquired. Coached in the process by AAI staff, Rima was elected as a Jackson delegate to the Democratic National Convention in Atlanta—her first foray into party politics. For the past 20 years, Rima Nashashibi has remained active in the party and was recently elected vice chair of the California Democratic Party. She now serves in the leadership of the Democratic Party in her home community of Orange County.

Shaping the Policy Debate

The second arena for Arab American political involvement is on matters of policy. Arab Americans have been organized around policy issues for many decades, especially since the 1967 Arab-Israeli war. They have worked both to promote their viewpoint and to defend their rights when they are threatened. Many Arab Americans closely follow what the U.S. government says and does about matters in the Middle East. In times of conflict, they worry about the safety and welfare of their relatives and friends in Arab countries, so Arab American groups organize their members and supporters to tell the government what they think about these issues and request certain actions. When government decisions have a direct impact on the lives of Arab Americans, organizations like the American-Arab Anti-Discrimination Committee (ADC) and the Arab American Institute (AAI) become advocates to protect the rights of the ethnic community. Advocacy work can address both individual problems and ones that affect a large group of people. Arab American advocacy has also been proactive on behalf of causes that recognize Arab or Muslim American achievement and contributions to American society or mobilize the public response to events in the Middle East. Examples of proactive advocacy include a city council being asked to proclaim "Arab American Day" so that the community can recognize the ethnic contributions of their Arab American neighbors. Another example is a resolution that passed the U.S. House and Senate in 2003, which condemned bigotry against and supported the rights and contributions of Arab Americans and other groups victimized after 9/11.[3]

Events that have mobilized the strongest response by Arab Americans have typically centered on the politics and conflicts in Middle East and how these events play out in the American political arena. Examples of crisis situations related to the Middle East:

- Arab-Israeli wars, especially in 1967 and 1973
- Israeli incursions into Lebanon in 1982, 1996, and 2006
- uprisings in Palestine in 1987 and 1996 and the attacks on Gaza in December of 2008
- the Gulf War of 1991 and the invasion of Iraq in 2003
- terrorist attacks on September 11, 2001, the backlash, and the national security measures that have lasted until today

The combined impact of these conflicts on the home countries of Arab immigrants and the policies of successive U.S. administrations that have favored Israeli positions resulted in a political environment that left many Arab Americans discouraged and bitter about what they perceived to be unjust, mistaken, and even dangerous U.S. foreign policy decisions. As a small, relatively new political voice, the Arab American perspective can only be heard if it joins with other like-minded political actors. It has been through coalitions with other political activist and advocacy groups that Arab Americans have found the most success in the policy arena.

One example of efforts in the 1980s to shape the policy debate proactively, rather than in direct response to a conflict, came in conjunction with the 1988 presidential elections. In this instance, a "Palestine: Statehood Now!" campaign was introduced at the national nominating convention and became part of the platform debate of the Democratic Party. The vehicle for this effort was the presidential primary campaign of Rev. Jesse Jackson, in support of which Arab American activists ran, many for the first time, as convention delegates. The Jackson delegates introduced planks calling

In 1993, marchers were organized both to commemorate the 30th anniversary of the 1963 March on Washington and to press forward the unfinished business of the struggle for justice. (Courtesy Arab American Institute)

for statehood for Palestinians and an end to the Israeli occupation that began in 1967. The campaign culminated in a debate on the floor of the national convention in Atlanta, during which more than a thousand delegates had signed the platform plank petition. While the plank was not formally voted on, its inclusion as part of the convention agenda represented the first time that the specific issue of Palestinian rights in the context of Middle East peace was discussed at a national party convention.

Arab American advocacy in the 1990s was dominated by several major international events that provoked, and often demanded, an ethnic political response. Perhaps the most dramatic was the Gulf War of 1991, which generated a reaction that reflected competing trends in the policy priorities of organized Arab Americans. One segment of the activist community strongly opposed any U.S. involvement in the conflict created by Iraq's invasion of neighboring Kuwait; another view expressed support for the United States to provide defensive assistance to allies in the Gulf region, while a minority agreed that America was justified in attacking Iraqi forces inside Iraq. Arab Americans who supported this last view tended to be either members of the community of exiled Iraqis who hoped the war would destabilize the regime or those from much-assimilated segments of the Arab American community. The complexities of such an explosive inter-Arab conflict and the competing U.S. interests in that region were fully reflected in these responses generated within the Arab American constituency.

Arab American advocacy reached a pinnacle in the aftermath of the terrorist attacks on America on September 11, 2001. No event in modern times had an equally profound effect on the political, civic, cultural, and religious identity of Arab Americans.

For Arab American institutions, the period immediately following the 9/11 tragedy was dominated by the need to protect against an anti-Arab and anti-Muslim backlash: violence, harassment, and discrimination. National and local organizations cooperated with law enforcement agencies and elected leaders to combat the random attacks on people perceived to be Arab, spread messages of tolerance, and teach those most vulnerable about their rights and legal protections.

Then, the swift, if not prudent, passage of the USA PATRIOT (Uniting and Strengthening America by Providing Appropriate Tools Required to Intercept and Obstruct Terrorism) Act by Congress launched a period where fear, suspicion, and a reduction of constitutional protections would be codified by law. The Patriot

Act commanded the attention not just of organizations that represent Arabs and Muslims, but also those of other ethnic communities, such as Asian Americans, who remember the anti-Japanese excesses of the 1940s, and groups who are committed to defending civil liberties and human rights. The ramifications of such legislative responses, which were passed in the heat of the 9/11 attacks, are still at play today and have empowered the federal government to pursue discriminatory and in some cases unconstitutional policies, which have directly influenced political discourse on national and international affairs in a number of ways.

The sheer weight of the 9/11 tragedy and its pervasive influence on American political and civic behavior resulted in a climate where prejudice against Arabs and Muslims that predated the attacks was allowed to thrive on the new oxygen of fear, ignorance, and an overgeneralized "War on Terror." Arab American advocates were called upon to put out fires of racism and intolerance on multiple fronts: in Congressional discourse, in the sermons of certain national religious figures, in the conduct of employers, in the blatant acts of disparate treatment in airports, or in the detention of those with visa infractions if they came from predominantly Muslim countries.

This Hydra of racism and intolerance in the wake of 9/11 created its own dynamic among community-based organizations: new alliances were forged between Arab American organizations like ADC and AAI and national groups who advocate on behalf of civil and constitutional rights, such as the ACLU, the Leadership Conference on Civil Rights, the Asian American Justice Center, as well as with the civil rights divisions of federal agencies like the Department of Justice, the Transportation Security Administration, and the Department of Homeland Security through advisory boards and community working groups. These new relationships at both the nongovernment organization and government levels also increased the visibility of Arab American organizations before grant-making foundations and helped strengthen the political traction on efforts of individual organizations. Similarly, new entities emerged in the post-9/11 era to expand and deepen the reach of Arab American activism. For those in uniform, the suspicions and questions about Arab American patriotism were the driving forces to form the Association of Patriotic Arab Americans in the Military (see next section), an organization representing more than three thousand Americans of Arab descent who serve in the U.S. armed forces. The need to organize and defend the rights and welfare of the Arab American immigrant population prompted a number of service organizations to be formed, as well as a national coalition to take off. The National Network for Arab American Communities grew out of an AmeriCorps-funded program of the Arab Community Center for Economic and Social Services (ACCESS), headquartered in Dearborn, Michigan, with the goal of building the capacity and training the staff of local organizations that serve Arab immigrants, several of which formed since 2001.

ARAB AMERICANS IN GOVERNMENT

In addition to political participation as voters and advocates, Arab Americans have served at all levels of public office, representing a third arena of public participation that has been crucial to Arab American interests. While most elected officials have been children or grandchildren of immigrants, some naturalized citizens have themselves served in government positions. Since the early 1960s, there have been members of the U.S. Congress of Arab descent; in the late 1980s, the majority leader of the U.S. Senate—George Mitchell—was an Arab American. By 1998, the largest congressional delegation was in place with six U.S. representatives and one U.S. senator who trace their roots to the Arab world. U.S. representative Nick J. Rahall II of West Virginia is the longest-serving Arab American member of Congress.

Outside Congress, Arab Americans have served in cabinet and sub-cabinet positions of various U.S. administrations and as diplomats, judges, governors, and mayors, as well as state and local legislators. The number of Arab Americans serving on boards and commissions has also increased in direct proportion to their greater visibility in local and state political life.

Champion of Rights and Heritage on Capitol Hill: Hon. Nick Joe Rahall II

Representative Nick Joe Rahall II has represented with distinction the third district of West Virginia in the U.S. House of Representatives since 1976. Known for his expertise in transportation, energy, and the environment, he is a committed fighter for coal miners' health and safety and veterans' benefits. He is chair of the House Committee on Natural Resources and was a key architect

U.S. representative Nick Joe Rahall II has represented West Virginia's 3rd Congressional District since 1977. Congressman Rahall is of Lebanese descent. (Courtesy of the office of U.S. representative Nick Joe Rahall II)

of the Transportation Equity Act, which, among other achievements, established the Rahall Transportation Institute to "build jobs through transportation."

As founder and dean of the Arab American congressional delegation, Rahall has chaired bipartisan visits to the Middle East. During difficult times in U.S.-Arab relations, Rahall, who traces his heritage to Lebanon, has worked to build bridges of understanding, making him a much sought-after resource for his congressional colleagues. On the House floor, he has been the leader on issues of Arab American concern, giving voice to those who work for justice and peace, and has been a consistent supporter of Arab American institutions and initiatives.

ARAB AMERICANS IN GOVERNMENT SERVICE

*Selected list; *indicates in office at time of publication*

U.S. Congress

Senator George Mitchell

Senator James Abdnor

Senator James Abourezk

Senator John E. Sununu

Representative Nick J. Rahall II*

Representative Darrell Issa*

Representative Charles Boustany*

Representative Mary Rose Oakar

Representative Chris Johns

Representative Toby Moffett

U.S. Cabinet, White House Staff, and Federal Agencies

Secretary of Transportation Ray LaHood*

Secretary of Energy Spencer Abraham

Secretary of Health and Human Services Donna Shalala

White House Chief of Staff John H. Sununu

White House Chief of Protocol Selwa "Lucky" Roosevelt

Office of Management and Budget Director Mitch Daniels

National Institutes of Health Director Dr. Elias Zerhouni

U.S. Department of Labor: George R. Salem, Michael E. Baroody

U.S. Department of Energy: Randa Fahmy Hudome

U.S. Department of Health and Human Services: Alex Azar

U.S. Department of the Interior: Chris Mansour*

U.S. Department of State: Dina Habib Powell

U.S. Department of Homeland Security: Juliette Kayyem*

U.S. Diplomats

Middle East Envoys: George Mitchell,* Philip Habib, Edmund Reggie

U.S. Ambassadors: Marcelle Wahba,* Yousif Ghafari, * Theodore Kattouf, Edward Gabriel, Thomas Nassif, Sam Zakhem

(Continued)

Federal Courts

Judge George Steeh,* Eastern District Court of Michigan

Judge Jay Zainey,* Eastern District Court of Louisiana

Justice Rosemary Barkett,* Eleventh Circuit Court of Appeals (Miami)

Governors

Mitch Daniels* (Indiana)

John Elias Baldacci* (Maine)

John H. Sununu (New Hampshire)

Victor Attiyeh (Oregon)

Mayors

Francis Slay* (St. Louis, MO)

George Latimer (St. Paul, MN)

Joseph Ganim (Bridgeport, CT)

Thersa Isaac (Lexington, KY)

Tom Hazouri (Jacksonville, FL)

Mike Damas (Toledo, OH)

Arab Americans have also been elected to state legislatures across the country, and the numbers who serve on city councils, school boards, county boards, and commissions continues to grow. In the first decade of the 21st century, three to four dozen Arab Americans on average have run an election campaign every year: these candidates range from elections for municipal office, judgeships, and state legislatures to campaigns for governor or U.S. Congress. Even in presidential politics, Arab Americans are in the news: consumer advocate Ralph Nader, who has run several independent presidential campaigns, is of Lebanese descent.

IMMIGRANTS AND THEIR DESCENDENTS IN MILITARY SERVICE

Like all immigrant groups in the United States, Arab Americans—both foreign and U.S.-born—have served in all branches of the armed forces. According to the Association of Patriotic Arab

Americans in the Military (APAAM), which was founded in the aftermath of the 9/11 terrorist attacks, Arab Americans have served in uniform in every major conflict since, and including, the Revolutionary War. The APAAM cites evidence[4] of soldiers with Arab or Muslim origins serving in the Civil War and in World War I, and the largest deployment from the Arab American community occurred during World War II. At that time, the American-born children of the pioneer immigrants from Greater Syria (1880–1920) joined other descendants of the Great Migration to serve their country in uniform. It is estimated that over 12,000 members of the Arab community were on active duty, augmented by the thousands of volunteers who helped the war effort through local church, community, and cultural institutions. The impact of the war experience greatly contributed to the civic integration of that generation into American society.

It is estimated that today, more than 3,500 Arab Americans serve in the U.S. armed forces, but their contributions have often been invisible, a major reason why APAAM was founded by Marine Gunnery Sgt. Jamal Baadani, a 20-year veteran who grew up in Dearborn, Michigan. In the weeks after the 9/11 attacks, Baadani's uncle sought out his nephew and asked for his photograph in uniform because his coworkers, even those he had known for years, had started to avoid him after 9/11. He hoped a picture of his nephew, a Marine, would remind them that he, too, is an American. His uncle's exposure to suspicion and ostracism convinced Sgt. Baadani that recognition of Arab and Muslim service needed to be more public—and APAAM was born.

PROFILES IN MILITARY SERVICE

LIEUTENANT ALFRED NAIFEH, WORLD WAR II

Alfred Naifeh was raised in Norman, Oklahoma, the son of Lebanese immigrants, and graduated from the University of Oklahoma with a law degree in 1940. When World War II began, Naifeh received a commission as an ensign in the Supply Corps on July 5, 1941. While he was serving on the USS *Meredith* in the Solomon Islands, the ship was struck by a massive Japanese air raid and rapidly sank. Naifeh, lieutenant, junior grade, worked for two days and nights to locate

---

(Continued)

his wounded shipmates and place them aboard life rafts. On the third day, he died of exhaustion, after fighting off shark attacks and rescuing many shipmates. Naifeh was posthumously awarded the Navy and Marine Corps Medal and the Purple Heart for his heroics, and in 1944, the USS *Naifeh* was commissioned and began its career in convoy duty.

GENERAL JOHN ABIZAID, FORMER COMMANDER, U.S. CENTRAL COMMAND

From 2003 until 2008 General John Abizaid, whose family originates in Lebanon, was responsible for American military operations in Iraq and a 25-country region stretching from the Horn of Africa to Central Asia. General Abizaid commanded the 3rd Battalion, 325th Airborne Battalion Combat Team in Vicenza, Italy, during the Gulf War crisis and deployed with the battalion to Kurdistan in northern Iraq. He served as the Assistant Division Commander, 1st Armored Division, in Bosnia-Herzegovina, and Deputy Commander (Forward), Combined Forces Command, U.S. Central Command during Operation Iraqi Freedom. General Abizaid's decorations include the Defense Distinguished Service Medal with one Oak Leaf Cluster, the Distinguished Service Medal, the Defense Superior Service Medal, the Legion of Merit with five Oak Leaf Clusters, and the Bronze Star. He earned the Combat Infantryman's Badge, Master Parachutist Badge with Gold Star, Ranger Tab, and the Expert Infantryman's Badge.

Source: Association for Patriotic Arab Americans in the Military, www.apaam.org.

ORGANIZATIONS SERVING ARAB AMERICAN POLITICAL NEEDS

The role of community organizations in facilitating the political participation of Arab Americans has evolved over time. The experience of the pioneer generation, which arrived in the United States having been Ottoman subjects prior to World War I, was not unlike that of other immigrants of that great wave, most of whom struggled for economic and cultural integration. There is little

General John Abizaid, U.S. Army (Ret.). Former Commander of the United States Central Command. General Abizaid is of Palestinian and Lebanese descent. (Courtesy of the office of General John Abizaid)

evidence, however, that the first wave of Arab immigrants and their children formed the political blocs typical of other larger and more urbanized immigrant communities such as the Italians and the Irish.

The intensely patriotic climate of World War II, when many second-generation males served in the armed forces, created opportunities for Arab Americans to solidify their American civic identity. Postwar veteran benefits, programs, and loans helped increase economic mobility; wartime connections and military service provided the American-born children of the pioneer Arab immigrants with access to assets such as job networks and motivated them to increase their civic awareness and take on more civic responsibilities. Thus, individual Arab Americans were more politically connected, although they were not yet functioning as an organized constituency.

By the 1960s, the Arab American community, like the country as a whole, entered a dramatic new era. The civil rights movement that challenged the conscience of the nation to uphold the rights of black Americans also empowered other racial and ethnic minorities to express more publicly and proudly their unique heritages, needs, and concerns. Advances in civil rights protections laid the foundation for changing social attitudes about diversity and American identity. At the same time, new immigration laws passed in the 1960s allowed immigrants from all regions of the world, including the newly independent nation states of the Arab world, to come to America without country quotas. A wave of newcomers from many Arab countries—students, professionals, workers, and refugees—came to America and revitalized the Arab American community, most of whose members were at that point mostly U.S.-born, assimilated, and had less direct ties to the old country.

With the arrival of a new wave of immigrants came their direct experience with the Arab-Israeli wars and a postcolonial Arab national identity—something the pioneer immigrants did not share. This modern Arab identity, coupled with the anti-Arab political climate in the United States, altered the political environment for Arab Americans of all generations. Arab-born elites who were now settling in the United States worked with the American-born descendants of the pioneer Arab immigrants to establish institutions and ad hoc groups to respond to anti-Arab opinion in America. An era of intolerant political discourse motivated by anti-Palestinian political ideology led Arab Americans to solidify around national pan-ethnic institutions such as the National Association of Arab Americans (NAAA), the Association of Arab-American University Graduates (AAUG), the American-Arab Anti-Discrimination Committee (ADC), and the Arab American Institute (AAI).

The American-Arab Anti-Discrimination Committee (ADC), founded in 1980, and the Arab American Institute (AAI), founded in 1985, helped forge a pan-ethnic identity that crossed generations, national origins, and religious affiliations—a necessary ingredient of an Arab American national constituency. The emergence of organized community activism in electoral politics, supported by the formation of AAI, took the contentious issues of Arab political and human rights beyond academia and the very limited lobbying efforts by Arab governments and into the arena of local and state party politics.

The confluence of dramatic international events and demographic changes in the Arab American community from the mid-1980s to the late 1990s caused a shift in the identity of insti-tutions serving Arab American political aspirations and in their ability to respond to the growing number of issues affecting their constituency. In this period, Arab American institutions were fac-ing additional capacity and identity challenges because Muslim activists were expanding their network of political, academic, and charitable institutions and these were organized not around Arab ethnicity but around the pan-ethnic identity of American Islam. Throughout the same period, Arab American community activ-ism was emerging on the local level in order to meet the needs of record numbers of Arab immigrants and refugees settling in U.S. cities, as well as the desire among business, professional, and country-specific communities to maintain contact and resist the pull of American assimilation. By the turn of the 21st century, scores of organizations were in place to serve the social services, media, religious, charitable, fraternal, and professional needs of Arab Americans. This period also saw the dissolution or downsiz-ing of a number of national policy organizations, among them the National Association of Arab Americans (NAAA) and the Asso-ciation of Arab American University Graduates (AAUG), two of the pioneer organizations that had been created to stimulate and propagate an Arab American identity. The remaining national sec-ular, pan-Arab multi-issue organizations were the beneficiaries of the leadership and reach of these pioneer organizations, which provided networks that could be plugged into national strategies and campaigns.

Crises like the first Palestinian intifada of 1987, the first Gulf War of 1991, the attacks on Qana, Lebanon, and the Oslo Accords of 1993, served both to energize and divide segments of the political community as Middle East issues were thrust to the forefront of American public discourse.

Events surrounding the Oslo Accords of 1993 prompted a period of political détente between leaders of the Arab American and American Jewish communities. In the decades leading up to this event, these two communities had starkly divergent perspec-tives on the causes and solutions for the Arab-Israeli conflict. This adversarial relationship was deepened by the uneven access to policy makers and the media that kept Arab American organiza-tions at a disadvantage. Although the period of public cooperation with the Jewish community around the time of the Oslo Accords dissipated with the deterioration of the peace process, the course

INTERNATIONAL CRISES PROMPTING ARAB AMERICAN ADVOCACY

1987 Intifada: popular uprising in Palestinian territories occupied by Israel since 1967; residents of West Bank and Gaza organized demonstrations and strikes to protest their treatment under occupation. A second more violent intifada erupted in May of 2002, sparked by a controversial visit by former Israeli defense minister Ariel Sharon to Muslim holy places in Jerusalem.

1991 Gulf War I: Following the invasion in August 1990 of Kuwait by Iraq under the leadership of Saddam Hussein, the United States participated in air strikes and a ground war against the Iraqi army and set up military bases in Saudi Arabia to protect it from Iraqi attacks.

1993 Oslo Accords: Agreements signed in Norway between Israeli and Palestinian negotiators on a framework for Palestinian autonomy; hailed as a breakthrough in direct negotiations, the accords were celebrated in Washington with a 1993 signing ceremony between Palestinian leader Yasser Arafat and Israeli Prime Minister Yitzhak Rabin.

1996 Qana Attacks: Israeli air strikes against targets in South Lebanon included a United Nations compound where Lebanese civilians were taking shelter; 106 civilians were killed and 116 were wounded. The same village was also attacked in the summer of 2006 when Israeli forces attacked Lebanon following a kidnapping of Israeli soldiers by *Hezbollah*, a political and religious faction in Lebanon.

of increasing Arab American access to government was now irreversible, and precedents in American political discourse were set that few pioneer activists could have envisioned two decades earlier. The historic significance of the 1993 handshake between PLO chairman Yasser Arafat and Israeli Prime Minister Yitzhak Rabin on the White House lawn, however fleeting, was matched by the unprecedented exposure and participation of Arab American community leaders in parity with their Jewish American counterparts.

In that short, heady period, proponents of a Palestinian state were permitted to move from the margins into the mainstream. Federal officials in Washington found themselves in the unusual position of receiving PLO chairman Arafat not as a terrorist but as a statesman, and those who supported Palestinian aspirations were treated not as discredited or suspect but as legitimate partisans in an historic peace breakthrough. A number of developments since this historic détente have strained the relationship with pro-Israel leaders and organizations and galvanized Arab American political action. Starting in the late 1990s, Arab Americans noted with disappointment the failure of the Oslo Accords to be implemented and then the second intifada erupted shortly before 9/11. More recently, international crises that have helped mobilize Arab American political action have included the 2003 war in Iraq, the Israeli attacks on Lebanon in the summer of 2006, and the 2009 war in Gaza. In each of these political conflicts, Arab American groups worked hard to share their concerns with their elected officials and to highlight in the media the humanitarian impact of these wars on the civilian population of each country. In many ways, the engagement of Arab Americans in the policy debate throughout the 1990s succeeded in shattering political taboos—not permanently, but sufficiently to change the dynamics of the discourse over U.S. Middle East policy.

SCRUTINY, SUSPICION, AND SUPPORT IN THE WAKE OF 9/11

The seismic impact of the September 11 terror attacks still affects the American political sphere and continues to be reflected in the popular culture, with powerful repercussions for Arab American political activity and cohesiveness. The 9/11 tragedy led to a period of nonstop challenges that included fighting backlash, discrimination, and federal policies that were often based on investigating or screening large segments of the community by national origin or religious affiliation. But these challenges have been accompanied by coalition-building, interfaith and community outreach, and the process of making Arab and Muslim American needs visible to the philanthropic community and to federal agencies.

The backlash from the terror attacks on September 11, 2001, was both damaging and empowering for all Arab Americans, but especially those in public or nongovernmental leadership positions.

Arab American leaders were on the front line in the media and with government agencies, and they were often the first to absorb the brunt of residual anti-Arab feelings and suspicions on the part of members of the public. Ethnic political and community leaders took the lead in defending against ethnically based policies and procedures enacted by the government in its efforts to strengthen national security.

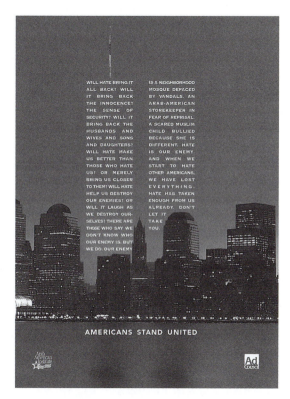

A print advertisement depicting an anti-hate message across a New York City skyline was designed by Brokaw, Inc., and distributed by the Ad Council to 10,000 newspapers and 1,900 magazines. This was the largest public-awareness campaign ever conducted by the Ad Council since World War II. In response to public demand, the Arab American Institute Foundation reproduced the 17" X 24" poster. More than 3,000 posters have been distributed to individuals, universities, community centers, and government offices throughout the country. (Courtesy Brokaw Inc.)

The initial experience of Arab Americans in post-9/11 political life was mixed. The day of the terror attacks, September 11, 2001, coincided with primary elections for local candidates in several states, including Michigan and New York. A number of Arab Americans were on the ballot[5] in Southeast Michigan that day, and there has been speculation that some of the candidates lost because voters may have been turned off by Arabic surnames. In fact, many voters stayed home, including Arab American voters who were less likely to want to be in public that day. Additionally, the fact that several ethnic candidates were competing for the same seats may also explain the poor showing. An interesting contrast was the behavior of candidates for statewide office in Virginia and New Jersey[6] who had been invited to Arab American forums scheduled prior to the attacks. Aware of the intolerance that was surfacing against Arabs and Muslims, candidates for governor from both parties in both states insisted that, rather than cancel the events, they wanted to use these forums as venues to assure their Arab American constituents of their concern for the community's welfare and of their pledge to protect their rights if elected.

Occasionally, Arab ethnicity was used as a negative campaign issue against candidates of Arab origin in the aftermath of 9/11, but this was usually met with a strong response, indicating a new trend. Throughout the 1980s and 1990s, there were instances reported where the Arab origin of certain candidates became a campaign issue—either by their opponents or the voters. During the elections of 2002, Tony Sayegh, a candidate for state assembly in New York, was baited by his opponent for accepting "Arab money." That prompted major organizations in his community of Westchester, including the NAACP, to denounce the smear. When Teresa Isaac ran for mayor of Lexington, Kentucky, that same year, some detractors leafleted an event she spoke at denouncing her for her Palestinian ties. In that case, the local Jewish American leadership also spoke out in her defense. In some ways, the sensitivity to the post-9/11 anti-Arab backlash extended new protections to Arab American candidates.

The biggest challenge to Arab Americans in public and political life in the post-9/11 period was the series of government policies that cast a wide net of suspicion toward large numbers of Arabs and Muslims living in America. These policies have had wide-reaching ramifications for the conduct of government, its checks and balances, and the civil liberties of all Americans, but the impact on the Arab and Muslim communities and their organizations was disproportionate. Viewed broadly, the policies promoted (1) unequal treatment of immigrants and visitors from predominantly Muslim countries, (2) racial profiling, especially in air travel, (3) surveillance and information-gathering on activity not related to terrorism, and (4) the scrutiny of charities that raise funds for Muslim causes.

In the months following 9/11, the Justice Department issued directives about detaining and investigating Arabs and South Asians living in the United States. First there was the detention of nearly 1,000 men in the six weeks after the attacks, who were neither charged nor identified. Most of these men were found to have minor visa violations with no criminal connections, and many were summarily deported.[7] Then in November 2001, voluntary interviews were ordered for 5,000 men, ages 18–33, from countries where terrorists may be harbored, and those with visa violations were arrested and held without bail. By December, the INS announced their plan to locate up to 6,000 absconders: aliens who were in the United States illegally from countries where terrorists were known to reside.

By June of 2002, a new entry-exit system was announced whereby aliens from 26 countries would be required to register, submit to fingerprinting and photographs upon their arrival to the United States, report to an INS field office annually and notify that office of their departure.

The National Security Entry-Exit Registration System (NSEERS) remained in place throughout the George W. Bush administration despite being broadly criticized for allowing discrimination based on national origin, for its waste of resources, and for its ineffectiveness as a law enforcement tool. After its first year in place, close to 80,000 visitors, students, and others had been registered, with not

---

NATIONALITIES COVERED BY THE NATIONAL SECURITY ENTRY-EXIT REGISTRATION SYSTEM (NSEERS)

Afghanistan, Algeria, Bahrain, Djibouti, Egypt, Eritrea, Indonesia, Iran, Iraq, Jordan, Kuwait, Lebanon, Libya, Malaysia, Morocco, Oman, Pakistan, Qatar, Saudi Arabia, Somalia, Sudan, Syria, Tunisia, United Arab Emirates, Yemen. *Note: the Republic of Armenia was originally designated as an NSEERS country but rescinded. Twenty-five countries remain.*

one arrest in the fight against terrorism. By 2003, the government agreed to ease some of the requirements at the request of advocates from Arab and Muslim American organizations who argued that, like all policies based on ethnic profiling, NSEERS was ineffective and counterproductive. Unfortunately, 13,000 of those who registered by the end of 2003 had already been issued deportation notices for minor violations of the visa process.

The discriminatory basis for these immigration-based procedures was also found in the overzealous efforts to tighten airport security in the wake of the attacks. When the President established the Transportation Security Administration (TSA) in November 2001, the new agency was empowered to use information from government agencies to identify passengers who may be a threat to national security. The criteria used included travel history, birthplace, destination, and other factors that resulted in many Arab Americans and their families being caught up in the no-fly screening at U.S. airports. Advocates reported frequent complaints from travelers who were detained, missed flights, and even endured the humiliation of being removed from aircraft. Arab Americans with names similar to those in the databases found themselves on the no-fly list, with little recourse for having their names removed. U.S. airports had become emblematic of the newest form of racial profiling: flying while Arab.

An equally disturbing development in post-9/11 national security measures that unfairly targeted Arab Americans and their organizations was the increase in surveillance and information-gathering on political and religious activity. In late 2004, the Federal Bureau of Investigation (FBI) and Department of Homeland Security (DHS) reportedly launched the so-called October Plan—an initiative including "aggressive—even obvious—surveillance" of individuals "suspected of being terrorist sympathizers, but who have not committed a crime." Furthermore, "other 'persons of interest,' including their family members, may also be brought in for questioning," and "mosques will be revisited and members asked whether they've observed any suspicious behavior."[8] A component of this plan included a massive immigration sweep in major metropolitan areas, with the purpose of detaining those who are "out of status." The Bureau of Immigration and Customs Enforcement (ICE) concentrated its efforts on individuals who had to report as part of the Student and Exchange Visitor Information System (SEVIS), NSEERS, and the US Visitor and Immigrant Status Indicator Technology Program (US VISIT) enacted in 2002. Arab and

Muslim American advocates strongly opposed this additional layer to the already ineffective national origin-based programs put in place since 9/11. The groups charged that the new use of selective enforcement would do little to prevent terrorism but could further alienate Arab and Muslim Americans, the very people with whom law enforcement needed to build trust. According to its electoral research and reports from local political leaders, the Arab American Institute pointed out that the timing of this initiative could have a chilling effect on the voter participation of some segments of the Arab American and American Muslim communities in the 2004 election.

The direct impact of excessive surveillance on community-based institutions was clear and growing. By December of 2005, evidence emerged that the FBI was conducting illegal wiretaps, without warrants, and monitoring Muslim religious institutions. This disclosure prompted calls for a congressional investigation and drew attention to constitutional safeguards that were needed in the reauthorization of the Patriot Act. Surveillance issues had already emerged on college campuses, where university police reportedly were recruited to track individuals and student organizations to look for subversive behavior. And the intense scrutiny of Muslim scholars invited to teach at U.S. universities resulted in some well-publicized cases of interference with academic freedom: when Swiss-born scholar of Islamic theology Tariq Ramadan was appointed to chair the Religion, Conflict, and Peace-Building program at the University of Notre Dame in 2004, the U.S. State Department deemed him to be a national security risk and Professor Ramadan was barred from entry to the United States. This decision alarmed academics and civil liberties advocates alike, spurring a lawsuit in 2006 by the American Civil Liberties Union on behalf of three academic and writers associations.

There is no doubt that Muslim institutions continue to bear the brunt of government security initiatives since 9/11. The most dramatic and politically damaging actions taken against Muslim organizations began with the freezing of assets of several Muslim charities who were accused of financing terrorism. Then in March of 2002, the U.S. Customs Service and other agencies used a sealed search warrant to raid 14 homes and businesses in Northern Virginia, seeking information about possible money laundering and other financial links with terrorist groups. The impact of these actions was far-reaching: charitable giving by American Muslims—which is especially required during the holy month of Ramadan, when *zakat* donations are typically collected to be sent to needy recipients in developing countries—was diminished when donors feared their contributions might be caught up in the government's extra scrutiny of Muslim charities.

Despite their best efforts at transparency and compliance with U.S. Treasury guidelines, Muslim philanthropic organizations, which had not been previously targeted by the government, noticed their donors were fearful of donating. And when the case against one of the accused charities—the Holy Land Foundation—was brought, it included pages and pages naming individuals who were "un-indicted persons of interest," a list that included most national Islamic leaders in America. The stigma of being included on that list, though no legal charges were brought, continues to do damage politically. When Ingrid Matson, the president of the respected Islamic Society of North America (ISNA), was invited to speak at the interfaith prayer breakfast preceding the 2009 inauguration of President Barack Obama, her participation was put in jeopardy by critics who cited her supposed terrorist connections. Fortunately, the detractors did not prevail, and she was part of the ceremony.

The cumulative effect of racial profiling, selective prosecution, religious intimidation, and other post-9/11 national security policies on segments of the Arab and Muslim American communities was profound. But the full brunt of the backlash was absorbed in part by the proactive involvement of community organizations in regular dialogue with federal agencies, law enforcement, local officials, and by strong coalition support from other non-Arab organizations and leaders.

Opening lines of regular communication with agencies of the government, especially those branches dedicated to protecting civil rights and combating hate incidents, was a direct by-product of activism after 9/11. The Office of Civil Rights at the Department of Justice initiated meetings between community advocates and the attorneys assigned to monitor hate crimes in the wake of 9/11. The FBI's Special Agent for the District of Columbia formed a community advisory board for Arab, Muslim, Sikh, and South Asian representatives to report on conditions in their communities and recommend strategies for the prevention of bias crimes. The Equal Employment Opportunity Commission, as they monitored workplace bias in the wake of 9/11, worked with ethnic and religious organizations to teach their members about their rights and recourse when problems occur. Locally, school boards, city councils, and human rights commissions in a number of states took action with community leaders to protect against intolerance, harassment, and discrimination.

Equally important were the alliances formed with other advocacy organizations and coalitions formed specifically to support those whose rights were most threatened. In some ways, the backlash and oppressive federal policies after 9/11 positioned Arab and Muslim Americans squarely on the historic continuum of American civil rights advocacy. As the visibility and empathy for Arab Americans grew, discriminatory treatment toward them under counterterrorism policies forged bonds with members of other profiled minority communities. Asian American leaders were the first to condemn the mistreatment of Arabs and Muslims after 9/11, citing their own painful history of suffering from racist intolerance before and during World War II. They were joined by advocates from black, Hispanic and civil rights organizations, which all recognized the ugliness of racial profiling and spoke out against it.

Another example when allies came to the defense of the community in time of need occurred in the summer of 2004, when it was discovered that the Department of Homeland Security had requested data on Arab Americans' ancestry from the U.S. Census Bureau. In its capacity as a Census Information Center and representative on the Decennial Advisory Committee, AAI circulated a letter of concern about the propriety of such data-sharing that was endorsed by more than 60 organizations, scholars, and community leaders. The regularly scheduled meeting of the bureau's national advisory committees that fall was devoted to a discussion of bureau privacy procedures and how to repair damage to public perceptions. Organizations that took a leading role and drafted resolutions demanding action by the bureau included the National Association of Latino Elected and Appointed Officials (NALEO), the Asian American Justice Center (AAJC), and the American Civil Liberties Union (ACLU).

CONCLUSION

The experience of Arab Americans in public service and political life is not unlike that of other immigrant communities. Throughout their history in this country, Arab Americans continue to step up to positions of leadership, and exhibit bravery and loyalty to the ideals of the United States. As American citizens, they are frequent voters, but do not vote as a single bloc and are active in both major political parties. As public servants, Arab Americans are represented in the

U.S. Congress, in the administration, and as diplomats, judges, governors, and mayors. Thousands of Arab Americans have served with pride in the U.S. armed forces and fought in every American war.

The civic journey of this community has been particularly impacted by the politics of the modern Middle East, and responding to the conflicts and crises that connect the United States with the Arab world continues to be a policy priority for Arab American leadership. Advocacy efforts on behalf of Arab Americans have focused on an array of issues, ranging from concern for victims of conflict in their countries of origin to challenging discrimination and bias against Arabs and Muslims in American society. Promoting policy priorities can take place inside the political parties, in the media, with the White House and in Congress.

Organizations that reflect the priorities, and contradictions, of the Arab American constituency have evolved over the decades and represent a community that is diverse in generation, religious affiliation, country of origin, and political philosophy. Efforts since the 1980s to train activists in the process of American politics and the partnerships that shape public policy have contributed to the resilience of the community, especially in times of crisis. The terror attacks of September 11, 2001, unleashed a period of intolerance, racial profiling, and surveillance that deeply impacted the lives of many Arabs and Muslims in America. In spite of successive federal policies that diminished the rights and protections of Arabs and Muslims, community advocates together with allies from government agencies, civil liberties groups, and other ethnic organizations were able to provide leadership and education to challenge discriminatory policies and promote cultural and religious tolerance and respect.

NOTES

1. Address to Arab American Institute National Leadership Conference, May 7, 1998, in Washington, D.C.; conference proceedings were published by AAI in June 1998 and are available in print version from the Arab American Institute, 1600 K Street, N.W., Washington, D.C. 20006t.

2. Findings taken from national surveys of Arab American voters conducted by Zogby International (www.zogby.com) for the Arab American Institute; survey summaries are available at www.aaiusa.org.

3. House Resolution 234 and Senate Resolution 133 passed by unanimous consent in 2003 during the 107th U.S. Congress. For other examples of resolutions involving Arab and Muslim Americans, see the Congressional Record.

4. See the website of the Association of Patriotic Arab Americans in the Military (www.apaam.org) for details on the history of military service of this ethnic community.

5. Candidates for Dearborn City Council included Bob Abraham, Faye Awada, Fred Berry, Fay Beydoun, George Darany, George Gury, Adel Harb, Edwin Nassar, Tarick Salmaci, and Suzanne Sareini. Of this pool, Bob Abraham, George Darany, and Suzanne Sareini were successful. In neighboring Dearborn Heights, Jumana Judeh and David Turfe competed for city council seats in that primary and both lost.

6. New Jersey gubernatorial candidates were Jim McGreevey (D) and Bret Schundler (R); Virginia candidates were Mark Warner (D) and Mark Early (R). Nominees of both parties attended AAI events in both states.

7. See Dan Eggen and Susan Schmidt, "Count of Released Detainees is Hard to Pin Down," *Washington Post,* Nov. 6, 2001; and "U.S. to Stop Issuing Detention Tallies," *Washington Post,* Nov. 9, 2001.

8. Arab American Institute press release, October 4, 2004, quoting news accounts (http://www.aaiusa.org/press-room/877/pr100404). Accessed February 11, 2010.

8

THE ARTS

Holly Arida

I believe that you are contributors to this new civilization. I believe that you have inherited from your fore-fathers an ancient dream, a song, and a prophecy, which you can proudly lay as a gift of gratitude upon the lap of America.[1]

—Kahlil Gibran

Arab American artists have contributed to the American art scene and American culture for generations. But an actual Arab American art movement has emerged as a result of 9/11. Arab American artists are using their artistic mediums—poetry, literature, visual art, theater, comedy, music, dance, digital arts, film, and television—to reveal what is unknown about the Arab world and people of Arab heritage. The Arab American art movement shares certain motivations, themes, and challenges. Over the last decade, organizations have developed to support Arab American art. The positive and negative attention and curiosity about Arab Americans and the Arab world that came out of the tragedy of 9/11 has moved many Arab American artists and their art into the mainstream.

WHAT IS ARAB AMERICAN ART?

What makes this artistic expression uniquely Arab American is that it is created by artists who are immigrants living in America or Americans of Arab descent. There are also particular subjects and themes that are common to Arab American art, such as cross-cultural identity and migration, family, war, and homeland. Frequently, Arab American art transcends the boundaries of immigrant art by treating universal themes such as love, loss, injustice, and the human experience. Arab American art sometimes fuses together several themes and genres, but it can also be completely abstract and not adhere to any identifiable themes whatsoever. Like all artists, Arab Americans are devoted to their craft, to innovation, and to individual freedom of expression.

THE IMPACT OF 9/11 ON ARAB AMERICAN ART

Anti-Arab stereotyping and Islamophobia have been pervasive and, to some extent, tolerated in America. This has had a profound effect on the Arab American experience. These negative perceptions have been perpetuated for several reasons: (1) a lack of knowledge about the Arab world and Islam, (2) acts of terrorism committed by a very small number Arab Muslims who are perceived as representing all Arabs and Muslims, (3) the prevalence of derogatory depictions of Arabs in American movies, television, and other media, (4) American political and military activity in the Arab world, and (5) resentment over American dependence on Arab countries for oil supplies. The acts of terrorism that occurred on 9/11 profoundly impacted all Americans, but for Arab Americans, the tragedy brought a double burden. Arab Americans were, like all Americans, concerned for their personal safety and that of their loved ones as they boarded planes and went about their everyday living. But they also felt the weight of collective blame directed at them or felt subjected to heightened scrutiny, which created in many the impetus to respond to the denigration and misrepresentation of their ethnicity, culture, or religion.

An ethnic consciousness began to permeate the work of many Arab American artists, some of whom had never previously identified in their professional life as Arab or treated their identity in their work in any way. The post-9/11 period brought about an urge to make a difference by telling their own story. Arab American artists have used their artistic mediums to counter the negative images of

Arabs and Muslims. Rather than being defined by those who commit violence in the name of Arabs or Islam, or by those who consign collective blame to Arabs and Muslims for 9/11, artists have chosen instead to define themselves. The tragedy of 9/11 left many people angry and afraid, but a positive ramification is that it also created curiosity and a thirst for knowledge about Islam and the Arab world among many Americans, who wondered, "Who are these Arabs and Muslims and what are they about?" As Arab American artists responded to the post-9/11 dynamic through their work, an Arab American art movement emerged.

THE EMERGENCE OF THE ARAB AMERICAN ART MOVEMENT

To constitute an actual artistic movement, a group of artists needs to be similarly motivated to action. In response to 9/11, many Arab American artists have been motivated to use their artistic expression to contemplate the Arab American experience, battle ignorance and stereotypes, and tell their own story in order to connect with their audience on a common level of human understanding. The forging of a strong Arab identity in many Arab Americans also brought about a flattening of national identities carried over from the Arab world. So for example, before 9/11, an artist may have identified as a Lebanese or Palestinian American, rather than as an Arab American. In many cases, the reaction to 9/11 brought together for the first time artists whose roots trace back to particular nations in the Arab world—to collaborate in art festivals, exhibitions, and gatherings, to work together in artistic production, and to share their common interest of exploring and asserting their own image of what being an Arab or Muslim American means. This newfound level of collaboration is evidenced by the emergence of several Arab American art collectives as well as publications that cover Arab American art.

ARTISTIC MEDIUMS

Arab American Artists are involved in the full range of mediums in artistic expression. The four main categories of artistic production are:

Visual Arts: artistic works that the audience experiences primarily through sight, such as drawing, painting, sculpture, architecture, or the modern visual arts of photography, video, and filmmaking.

Performing Arts: artistic works where the artists use their face, body, and actual presence as a means of expression, often before a live audience, such as music, dance, theater, and comedy.

Literary Arts: nontechnical fiction and nonfiction writing using the written word as the medium in novels, epics, short stories, and poems.

Digital Art: an emerging contemporary art form, created through the use of computer graphics, software, and technology that sometimes transforms the traditional art forms of painting, drawing, and photography or creates new forms, including installation art, virtual reality, or Web-based art.

Certain mediums, such as Arabic music and dance, mainly adhere to traditional styles, although fusion and modern forms of music, such as Arab American hip-hop, have come on the scene over the last decade. Through other mediums such as poetry, literature, and painting, Arab Americans have made significant and recognized contributions to American culture. Since 9/11, mediums such as theater, comedy, film, and digital arts have really expanded in terms of artist and audience participation.

Table 8.1 Arab American Contributions to Artistic Mediums

Artistic Medium	Arab American Artistic Contributions
Poetry	Historically, rhythmic verse has been a medium where Arab Americans have drawn mainstream attention, most notably with Kahlil Gibran. Over the last decade, Arab American poets have received national and international awards, published in anthologies and individually, and have even appeared in popular venues like HBO's *Def Poetry Jam* and at the Kennedy Center. Spoken word poetry has also become a popular poetic form.
Literature	Since 9/11, novels, short stories, and children's books written by Arab Americans have garnered more attention from publishers as the American public's interest in the Arab world has increased.
Visual Art	Painting, sculpture, and drawings by Arab Americans can be found in collections such as those of the Smithsonian Institution and the White House and in exhibits at museums and galleries around the country. Photography has become a growing medium among Arab American visual artists.

Theater	Arab American playwrights have garnered much more attention and exposure in post-9/11 America, working individually or with collective theatrical projects. In particular, the one-woman show, where female playwrights and actors portray Arab or Arab American experiences, has become quite popular; many have toured the country being performed in multiple venues.
Comedy	In response to misperceptions about Arab Americans and the Arab/Muslim world that peaked with 9/11, there has been an increase in the visibility of Arab American comedians, who have performed in festivals or on the national comedy circuit.
Music	Arabic music is a traditional art form that is performed in public venues at cultural arts festivals and at parties or celebrations. Some Arab American musicians have enhanced and fused Arabic music in some innovative ways. Recently, Arab American hip-hop that addresses social injustice has flourished, particularly in urban ethnic enclaves.
Dance	Arabic dance is performed by Arab Americans but more frequently by non-Arabs in America. Traditional Arab line dancing called *dabkah* and solo performances are commonly performed at cultural festivals, nightclubs, and parties or celebrations.
Film	Films that deal with Arab American life and the Arab world have been produced increasingly since 9/11. Some of these films have reached mainstream audiences, although in limited distribution. Arab Americans are increasingly writing screenplays and directing and acting in films. Communications expert Dr. Jack Shaheen has served as a consultant on several Hollywood films to ensure that film portrayals of Arabs and Arab Americans are more balanced, realistic, and less stereotypical.
Television	Arab Americans are increasingly visible in television roles and the Arab/Islamic world has become the subject of television shows. Slowly, film roles are expanding beyond terrorists and the subject of terrorism toward more diversity for Arab actors and subjects.
Digital Media	Art by Arab Americans that has been produced and manipulated through computer software has grown over the last decade. Virtual experiences, video, and media imagery are being used to powerfully address Arab American issues as well as portray conditions in the Arab World.

CHALLENGES

The struggle for artistic freedom, finding an audience, and maintaining financial support for their career are customary challenges for all artists, and Arab American artists are no different in this respect. But simply by virtue of being Arab American, some artists encounter other difficult challenges to performing or showing their work, particularly if it addresses political issues. The political reality of post-9/11 includes the War on Terror, the Iraq War, and the deterioration in the Palestinian-Israeli peace initiatives, as well as the violation of Arab American civil liberties. Artistic expression is often controversial, but with raised public fears about Muslims and Arabs supporting terrorism, political art, particularly when produced by Arab Americans, is more provocative than ever. Like many artists, Arab American artists sometimes use their mediums to address social injustice—this may mean disagreeing with American foreign policy in the Arab world, criticizing Arab regimes, promoting peace, or addressing problems in the American society in which they live.

Among the challenges Arab American artists face are misinterpretation of their work, having to defend against false claims of being "sympathetic to terrorism," or even having shows cancelled. If their work pertains to the Palestinian-Israeli conflict, museums and galleries and their constituencies may exert pressure on artists to show "the other side" in order to balance perspectives. Sometimes artists who do not even deal with political content get categorized as controversial due simply to their Arab or Muslim sounding name.

ART COLLECTIVES AND FESTIVALS

Sharing a common purpose and similar challenges has brought many Arab American artists together in collectives, collaborative shows, and organizations. Using a variety of art forms, Arab American artists have grouped together to support one another. While this coming together, or in Arabic, *diwan,* began as a response to the pressures exerted on the Arab American community of artists after 9/11, the cooperation and networking that has come out of this period has created a long-lasting cohesiveness among artists from different home countries and artistic mediums. Arab American art collectives arose in various forms, including (1) artists who collaborate and produce a shared work, (2) artists who perform individually but in a shared program, (3) artists who share a virtual or actual workspace but produce individual works, or (4) a combination of these various collective arrangements.

Several Arab American art collectives emerged in the United States after 9/11, and although most are no longer operational, their existence has cultivated lasting cooperation among the artists. In Detroit, a number of local artists came together in June 2004 to collaborate on two projects that eventually set into motion the creation of the group OTHER: Arab Artists Collective. The first of their collaborations was *Detroit Unleaded,* a film written and directed by Rola Nashef, which was followed by an invitation by the Arab American National Museum for OTHER to create a permanent installation on the stereotyping of Arab Americans in the United States. The collective mission of OTHER was to create a supportive organization that provided a collaborative environment for aspiring artists of Arab heritage. Despite continuous material challenges, their collectivization allowed them to establish a studio that operated for more than four years, functioning as an artists' forum and working space for a variety of Detroit-based artists who otherwise would not have had the exposure, opportunity, or facility to collaborate. The studio became a hub of intellectual, artistic, and political engagement for many Detroiters and artists, including Adnan Charara, painter and sculptor, who also has his own nearby studio, Christina Dennaoui, painter and digital artist, Sarah Khazem, photographer, Michael Mansour, audio-based artist, Marwan Nashef, musician, Jackie Salloum, filmmaker, and many others. Although OTHER has since closed its studio, the collective's members are actively engaged in personal projects and continue to support, critique, and inspire one another.[2]

Similarly, a number of performance art collectives evolved out of the Arab American art scene in New York City. Nibras, which in Arabic translates to "lantern," was a theater company founded in June 2001 by a group of early-career theater artists, primarily actors and writers. While the collective was formed prior to 9/11, the experience of being Arab American in New York during and after that day gave the group a heightened sense of urgency and inspired them to dedicate the years following to creating and staging theatrical work that reflected and responded to the challenges, gifts, and questions of being Arab in America. *Sajjil* (*Record*), Nibras's documentary theater piece based on interviews about "What comes to mind when you hear the word Arab?" won Nibras the Best Ensemble Performance award in the 2002 New York Fringe

Festival. Many Nibras projects included readings, performances, and workshops by Nibras members. For several years, Nibras was a company-in-residence at New York Theatre Workshop; this culminated in collaboration with New York University on *ASWAT: Voices of Palestine*—a highly successful public presentation of eight plays about Palestine. Another theater collective, Nisa'a, which in Arabic means "women," worked together for just over a year in 2006. Nisa'a comprised seven women who came together to write, perform, and produce *The Panel*, a satirical-theatrical exploration of the challenges of representing Arab women. Although these theater collectives are no longer operational, their former members perform together on occasion and continue to support each other's work.

In addition to art collectives, various festivals around the country have celebrated Arab American art. Cultural centers and organizations routinely sponsor cultural arts festivals to highlight Arab and Arab American performers, particularly dancers and musicians. Prestigious venues such as Carnegie Hall and the University of Michigan Musical Society have featured Arabic music performances. Film festivals have been held by universities and museums to highlight cinematic contributions from the Arab world and Arab Americans. An area of performance art that has grown tremendously over the last decade is Arab American comedy.

The famous 17th-century French playwright Molière said, "The duty of comedy is to correct men by amusing them." Arab American comedians are attempting to heal misunderstandings and misperceptions about Arabs, and especially Islam, through humor. Comedy shows that contemplate the Arab American experience have played to mixed audiences on both coasts and in the Arab American ethnic enclave of Dearborn, Michigan. The most established is the annual Arab American Comedy Festival in the New York area, which was founded in 2003 by comedian Dean Obeidallah and actress/comedienne Maysoon Zayid, in an effort to combat stereotypes and racism through the healing power of humor. The festival showcases the talents of dozens of Arab American performing artists and writers through comedic plays, stand-up routines, and short films that have given the participants national and international exposure. The festival garners publicity for the artists, while answering audiences' post-9/11 curiosity about the Arab world and Arab Americans. Many of the artists featured in the Arab American Comedy Festival are crossing over into mainstream media outlets.

This is the 2009 promotional poster for the annual Arab American Comedy Festival in New York City. This continued collaboration among Arab American Artists has endured and the continued popularity of this event demonstrates that laughter is the best medicine. (Courtesy New York Arab American Comedy Festival)

While the Arab American Comedy Festival remains an annual production, the OTHER, Nibras, and Nisa'a collectives are no longer formally operative. The explanation for this could lie in the fact that the intensity of the post-9/11 period that galvanized these artists to cooperate has waned. Also, many of the founding artists of these collectives were at the time early in their careers but are now well established and the demands of their individual work schedules may not allow for the investment of time, energy, and creativity required to support and sustain a collective project. Although certain strength is derived from a shared artistic community where common goals, ideas, and challenges energize artistic output, there are also benefits in Arab American artists telling multiple stories in different spaces in order to multiply the reach of those stories, while continuing to maintain creative relationships in a broad network of support in the Arab American community.[3]

The coming together of organized collectives in the nascent stage of the Arab American art movement was significant, but the com-

"Whirling in Damascus," a photograph by Doris Bittar

Martyrdom, Violence, and the Passion for Sanctity
by Elie Haddad
Thirteen Hours of Interrogation
by Mohammed Ali Atassi
Cairo's Fourth Pyramid: Reflections on Naguib Mahfouz
by Amin Malak
A Father to the Point of Tears
by Faraj Bayrakadar

This cover of Al Jadid from Winter/Spring 2006 features the photograph "Whirling in Damascus," by renowned visual artist Doris Bittar, a piece that in part explores the ideas of Syria's role and influence over Arab culture in general. At a deeper level, the frozen state of the dancer refers to the frozen state, the inability to move forward or change. (Doris Bittar/ Courtesy Al Jadid)

ing apart of some these collectives also indicates a new wave of creativity. All of these collectives resulted in informal collaborative networks, where Arab American artists exchange ideas and continue to work together, although in smaller numbers. Many of the founders of these collectives have gained momentum in their individual careers, allowing them to reach out to a mainstream audience and collaborate with non-Arabs. Within this system of more organic collaboration, as well as in the remaining collectives like the Arab American Comedy Festival or the online networking resources such as AART (Arab Artists Resource and Training), there is still opportunity for early-career artists to work together among their ethnic counterparts and to follow in the path of pioneering Arab American artists in many mediums. An artistic community remains.

ARAB AMERICAN ART ORGANIZATIONS, INSTITUTIONS, AND PUBLICATIONS

In the aftermath of 9/11, both mainstream and Arab American cultural organizations and institutions, including museums, community centers, and universities, had an increased interest in promoting the understanding of Arab and Arab American art and culture. There was also a surge of organizations, institutions, and publications dedicated entirely to supporting Arab American art that were either initiated or significantly expanded in this period, another key indicator of the rise of an actual Arab American art movement. These organizations, institutions, and publications provide a wide range of support for artists: networking, venues for exhibiting work, curatorial services, organization of conferences and exhibits, publication of artistic works, and documentation of the achievements of Arab American artists. The exhibitions, conferences, and publications generated through these organizations are highly professional and have given the Arab American art movement a voice. They share the mission of promoting awareness of artistic expression from Arab America, and they cover the full range of artistic mediums.

An important function of these organizations and institutions is the ability to draw artists together to examine their craft, their successes, and their challenges. The Arab American National Museum (AANM), which opened in 2005, has the mission of preserving and documenting the history of Arab Americans in the United States. In addition to sponsoring an annual Arab American Book Award

Table 8.2 Arab American Art Organizations

Arab American Art Organization	Mission
Al Jadid: A Review & Record of Arab Culture and Arts Los Angeles, California http://www.aljadid.com	*Al Jadid* ("the news") was founded in 1994 by Professor Elie Chalala. This print and Web-based publication analyzes cultural and artistic production from the Arab world and Arab America in English, with contributors from around the world, including only original material.
Al Jisser Group New York City http://www.aljisser.org	Al Jisser ("the bridge") began in 2001 through artists and supporters of the arts who primarily curate and organize exhibitions and projects around Palestinian art and artists around the country.
Arab American National Museum (AANM) Dearborn, Michigan http://www.arabamericanmuseum.org	Established in 2005, AANM is the first museum in the world dedicated to displaying and documenting Arab American history and culture, as well as sponsoring regular exhibits of Arab American art and a biennial *DIWAN*, "gathering," of Arab American artists across artistic mediums from around the country.
Arab Artists Resources & Training (AART) Seattle, Washington http://www.aart.ws	This website, created in 2001, provides resources for Arab American artists, including possible venues to show their work and job opportunities. AART also provides a comprehensive list of organizations in America that support Arab American art.
ArteEast, Inc. New York City http://www.arteeast.org	Launched in 2003, ArteEast raises the profile of Arab and Arab American artists through their online gallery and resource site as well as their sponsorship of a biennial film festival and other art events open to the public.
Bidoun: Arts and Culture from the Middle East Brooklyn, New York http://www.bidoun.com	This nationally recognized glossy art magazine chronicles art culture of the Middle East as well as Arab American artists and was begun in 2003.

Jerusalem Fund Gallery Washington, D.C. http://www.thejerusa lemfund.org/	Founded after 2000, the gallery includes a physical space and website that exhibits fine art, often around Palestinian themes and culture, as well as a film series and juried art competition.
MIZNA Minneapolis, Minnesota http://www.mizna.org	Begun in 1999, MIZNA has produced a prestigious journal of Arab American litera- ture but has now expanded its operations to include a physical space to host cultural events.
Radius of Arab Ameri- can Writers, Inc. (RAWI) http://www.rawi.org/ CMS/	Set in motion in 1992, RAWI provides a professional support network for both estab- lished and aspiring writers of Arab heritage who work in the English language, with a commitment to coalition building and social justice.

Source: Information adapted from Fayeq S. Oweis, "Resources on Arab American Artists and Arab Culture in the United States," in *Encyclopedia of Arab American Artists: Artists of the American Mosaic* (Westport, CT: Greenwood Press, 2008), 273–279.

that honors several literary categories, the AANM hosts a biennial conference called *DIWAN: A Forum for the Arts* that brings together Arab American artists from across the nation and different medi- ums for discussion panels, exhibitions, and performances. It also hosts an annual Arab American Film Festival. In its temporary gal- leries, the AANM regularly hosts exhibits of Arab American art. Additionally, in the short while since its inception, the AANM has published three books that document the work of Arab Americans, and artists in particular, a crucial step in garnering recognition for their contributions to American culture.

Similarly, the Radius of Arab American Writers (RAWI) has held two national-level conferences, in 2005 and 2007, drawing writ- ers together from around the country to discuss their work and to network with publishers, who for the first time addressed Arab American writers as a collective group. Membership in RAWI includes writers from multiple genres, including memoir, poetry, fiction, blogs, journalism, academic scholarship, and playwriting, as well as from various levels of professional distinction, ranging from award-winning writers to novice, aspiring writers. Their most recent conference theme, "Writing While Arab: Politics, Hyphens,

DIWAN: A Forum for the Arts draws creative Arab Americans from across the country to the Arab American National Museum. This 2009 panel, "From Beirut Hills to Muslim! The Musical: What's So Funny About Arab Americans?" was comprised of comic writer/actors (from left) Tamar Vezirian, Alia Tarraf, Negin Farsad, and Mike Mosallam. (Devon Akmon/ Arab American National Museum)

and Homelands," focused on the polemics of writing during the War on Terror, and the challenges writers face in balancing their impulse to fight prejudice and raise awareness about their ethnicity, with the marketability and circulation of their work. As an organization, RAWI is dedicated to increasing the visibility of its members and their writings in journals and on their website.[4]

The influence of Arab American writers radiates in many directions, as illustrated in the logo of RAWI (Radius of Arab American Writers). This organization continues to grow its network to support its members' needs and foster writing by and about Arab Americans. (Courtesy RAWI [Radius of Arab American Writers]. Logo design by Joe Naimy)

By formalizing and professionalizing these gatherings of artists, AANM, RAWI, and other organizers have galvanized a community of artists to work together. Garnering greater exposure and documenting the artistic contributions of Arab Americans has also been crucial to this community of artists, in order to preserve their lasting contributions to American culture. Arab American organizations and publications have drawn recognition in the mainstream for these artists as a formidable professional group with shared interests and genres.

COMMON THEMES IN ARAB AMERICAN ART

Certain themes are common to Arab American art. Arab American artists very much identify as Americans, and so the ideals and institutions of the United States as a country and society are also a common theme in their art. Some of these artists have used their artistic expression as a form of political activism or to contemplate the post-9/11 climate directly. The life experience of many Arab Americans and their families includes cross-cultural identity, which derives from migration from an Arab country to the United States, often against a backdrop of war in the home country. Also, a strong sense of family, including extended family, predominates in the lives of many Arab Americans. War and homeland are prominent themes as well, particularly since military conflicts have recently engulfed Lebanon, Iraq, and Palestine. Arab American artists certainly treat subjects outside of this range, but these common themes are central to the Arab American art movement that galvanized after 9/11.

On America

In spite of the fact that an ethnic consciousness was raised in many Arab American artists in the aftermath of 9/11, a strong sense of "American-ness" has always existed and continues to be strongly felt by Arab Americans. While many Arab Americans may feel connected to their country of origin, America is very much home. Arab Americans whose families have sought refuge in America, leaving war-torn homelands to seek safety, freedom, and economic and educational opportunities, can have a profound appreciation for their American homeland and a deeply felt American identity. For this

"Capitol Building" (2002) is painted with gouache and ink on board. It is one of many depictions of Washington, D.C., in a collection by Helen Zughaib, the talented Beirut-born painter and U.S. cultural envoy to the West Bank and Switzerland. (Courtesy of the artist)

reason, quintessential American themes and the American experience permeate Arab American art. Patriotism, empathy toward fellow Americans, and an appreciation for the values and symbols of America are exhibited frequently in Arab American art, as in Helen Zughaib's rendition of the Capitol Building in Washington, D.C. The building is a symbol of American government and its commitment to the rule of democratic law; Zughaib's painting highlights American symbols and ideals, demonstrating her belief that art can transform dialogue between cultures and promote understanding.[5] As citizens and members of American society, Arab American artists identify with their fellow Americans, and through their art they may exercise their freedom of speech to call attention to the government response to a humanitarian crisis in America.

The spoken word poet and political activist Suheir Hammad was born in Jordan to Palestinian refugee parents and later raised in Brooklyn. Here she reflects on an American tragedy: Hurricane Katrina

OF REFUGE AND LANGUAGE

I do not wish
To place words in living mouths
Or bury the dead dishonorably
I am not deaf to cries escaping shelters
That citizens are not refugees
Refugees are not Americans
I will not use language
One way or another
To accommodate my comfort
I will not look away
All I know is this
No peoples ever choose to claim status of dispossessed
No peoples want pity above compassion
No enslaved peoples ever called themselves slaves
What do we pledge allegiance to?
A government that leaves its old
To die of thirst surrounded by water
Is a foreign government
People who are streaming
Illiterate into paperwork
Have long ago been abandoned
I think of coded language
And all that words carry on their backs
I think of how it is always the poor
Who are tagged and boxed with labels
Not of their own choosing
I think of my grandparents
And how some called them refugees
Others called them non-existent
They called themselves landless
Which means homeless
Before the hurricane

(Continued)

No tents were prepared for the fleeing
Because Americans do not live in tents
Tents are for Haiti for Bosnia for Rwanda
  Refugees are the rest of the world
  Those left to defend their human decency
Against conditions the rich keep their animals from
Those who have too many children
Those who always have open hands and empty bellies
Those whose numbers are massive
Those who seek refuge
From nature's currents and man's resources
  Those who are forgotten in the mean times
  Those who remember
  Ahmad from Guinea makes my falafel sandwich and says
So this is your country
  Yes Amadou this my country
And these my people
  Evacuated as if criminal
Rescued by neighbors
Shot by soldiers
  Adamant they belong
  The rest of the world can now see
What I have seen
  Do not look away
  The rest of the world lives here too
In America

Post-9/11

The shifts brought on by 9/11 in terms of suspicion, profiling, and stereotyping that confronted Arab Americans have been treated directly in some high-profile artistic endeavors, particularly in two emerging mediums of Arab American art: theater and film. Two very distinct films, director and co-writer Hesham Issawi's *American East* (2007) and writer/director Cherien Dabis's acclaimed *Amreeka* (2009), as well as the off-Broadway production of playwright Yussef El-Guindi's *Back of the Throat* (2006), all look at what it means to be Arab American and pursuing the American Dream in the complicated post-9/11 climate.

Arab American theater has blossomed since 9/11. The title of *Back of the Throat* comes from antagonist Khaled's attempts to get the government agents who raided his home to pronounce his name with the proper beginning Arabic sound. Taking on the controversial issue of heightened government scrutiny and questioning of Arab Americans, the play depicts the tension of this period when many Arab Americans felt guilty until proven innocent.[6] When *Back of the Throat* appeared at the Flea Theater in TriBeCa in 2006, the play received national attention, indicating the way heightened curiosity about the Arab experience has increased the demand for and marketability of the work of Arab American playwrights.

The film *American East* relays a similar experience and is reminiscent of Spike Lee's *Do the Right Thing,* when racial tensions escalated over the course of a hot Los Angeles summer. The Egyptian-born immigrant Mustafa draws the attention of the FBI when he loses his son, who no longer wants to be a Muslim, while picking up a relative at the Los Angeles International Airport. Set in his steamy falafel store with a broken air conditioner, things get hot as Mustafa's fate spirals downward. His commitments to his family in Egypt result in his wiring money back to Egypt to pay for land, which draws the suspicions of the FBI. He has also promised his daughter, Leila, in marriage to a cousin from back home, but Leila is not cooperating. The underlying theme of the film is how assimilation into American culture has become all the more difficult for Arab immigrants in the post-9/11 era. The film is notable for the fact that it not only tackles anti-Muslim stereotyping but, through a confrontation between two of the main characters, addresses anti-Semitism in the Arab Muslim community as well.

The critically acclaimed and award-winning film *Amreeka* is more subtle in its contemplation of the Arab American experience, tracing the immigration of Muna, a single mother, and her son, who arrive from the West Bank as the American-led 2003 Iraq War begins. Their story of migration tests the promise of the American Dream in small-town Illinois. Dabis's characters confront an American culture that is rife with misunderstanding about their Arab homeland. But through heartfelt humor, Muna and her son transform those who touch their lives, as they, too, are transformed. The fact that *Amreeka* was screened at Sundance and Cannes, distributed through the National Geographic Society, and opened in limited release throughout the United States is indicative of the trend toward greater exposure and attention for quality films by Arab American filmmakers focusing on the Arab American experience.

Migration and Cross-Cultural Identity

Arab American life has been characterized by what has been termed as "doubleness," the sense of being part of two different places at the same time. The experience of Arab Americans as they migrate, settle, and assimilate often informs the subject of Arab American art. The theme of migration and cross-cultural identity is central to Arab American art for two reasons. First, although Arabs have been migrating to the United States for centuries, the heaviest waves of immigration occurred during the 20th century. Consequently, many Arab American artists are still close to the immigrant experience, either through their own relocation to the United States or that of their parents or extended family. Second, many art forms (poetry, literature, music, and dance among them) have strong stylistic roots in the Arab world, which Arab American artists sometimes adapt into something new.

As is the case with all immigrant groups, the process of assimilation and creating a life somewhere new can be alienating. Historically, many ethnic groups have experienced stereotyping and discrimination as they have settled in the United States. In the case of Arab Americans, their ethnic group has often been portrayed negatively within the dominant culture, and, for some, their sense of otherness has been made more acute through the heightened scrutiny and reinforcement of stereotypes that resulted from 9/11. Therefore, the hyphenated identity of Arab Americans has become a prominent theme in Arab American art over the last decade.

As Leila Buck demonstrates in the excerpt from her play *Hkeelee,* rifts between generations are commonplace as families transition to America. Young people may want to blend in and fully assimilate into American culture, while older generations may try to maintain their Arab heritage and traditions in their new homeland. Arab American art that deals with cross-cultural identity often depicts the tension between the parents and grandparents who want to instill in the youth a pride in their heritage, while the youth feel shame about being different, and are embarrassed by their parents' accents and the family traditions that make them stand out from mainstream American culture. Although this is a common struggle for all immigrant groups as they assimilate in America's melting pot, for Arab American youths, this tension has been exacerbated in the post-911 climate.

SCENES FROM THE FIRST DRAFT OF ARAB AMERICAN PLAYWRIGHT LEILA BUCK'S 2009 PLAY-IN-PROGRESS, *HKEELEE* (TELL ME A STORY)

Beirut, 1968

MOTHER and FATHER in a nightclub, laughing and dancing to Arabic, then French music.

Beirut, 1976

MOTHER, FATHER, and MONA (age 4) in their home. Gunfire outside.

FATHER shoves belongings into suitcases.

MOTHER returns them to shelves, drawers.

They argue. MONA cries.

Washington, D.C.

1989

MOTHER, FATHER, and MONA (age 17) at home.

FATHER wears a sanitation worker's uniform.

MONA is helping them study for the citizenship exam.

MONA: OK . . . who said "Give me Liberty or Give me Death?"

FATHER: I did.

MONA: C'mon, Papi, be serious.

MOTHER: Patrick Henry.

MONA: Right. Are we done?

FATHER: Done? There are 25 more questions! Dey can ask any one of dem. You want your parents to be "aliens" forever?

(MONA sighs impatiently)

MOTHER: Come on, habibti, you can go see Jessica when we're done.

FATHER: NO, when we are done I will test YOU on your calligraphy.

MONA: Papi, I told you I'm going over to Jessica's tonight.

FATHER: And I told YOU, after you do your Arabic homework.

MONA: Papi—

FATHER: Yallah, next question.

(Continued)

(MONA reluctantly continues)

MONA: "What holiday was celebrated by the American colonists?"

MOTHER/
FATHER: Thanksgiving!

MONA: "Who helped the Pilgrims in America?"

FATHER: The red Indians!

MONA: *(rolling her eyes)* NATIVE AMERICANS.

FATHER: Den why dey call de football team de Redskins?

MONA: I dunno, OK? Just please don't say red Indian or people will think you're racist, or ignorant.

(A pause)

FATHER: Who told you I was ignorant? Was it dis boy at school who calls you dese names??

MONA: Papi—

FATHER: Do YOU tink I'm ignorant? Because of dis uniform?

MOTHER: Sharif . . .

FATHER: You know in Beirut your fader was chief of police. You tell dem that at school next time they boder you.

(FATHER starts to close the exam)

MONA: Papi–

FATHER: Khalass ya binti. Go play wiz your friends.

(A moment—MONA looks to MOTHER, who nods. Grabs her bag, and leaves.)

FATHER: *(under his breath)* Ask dem if DEY are native American.

Family

There is much diversity among Arab Americans, but the centrality of family transcends generational, religious, socioeconomic, and geographic differences. As outlined in chapter 3, because of chain migration, the development of ethnic enclaves, and the retention of culture from the homeland, Arab American families have a propensity toward close relationships among nuclear and extended families, a connection to Arab traditions, and a strong sense of respect for elders. Therefore, Arab American art is often concerned with familial themes, whether the struggle against conformity to traditional family roles or an embrace or contemplation of their family's stories of migration and culture. In their work, many Arab American artists reflect on their families' expectations for career success, gender roles, and values.

WON'T YOU STILL LOVE ME WHEN I'M DEAD?

—Naomi Shihab Nye

That stopped the room.
Then Yes! Yes!
Impossible to arrange your pillows
any comfortable way. Tangled sheets,
other people's lives going on outside.
Where else could we have taken you?
On your last day we left the hospital
for a brief walk under leaves. You
refused final dinner tray, ate only
junk I'd hidden upon your command.
So unlike you, Dad. At least I had a small can
of *hummus* in my purse. You tasted it.
Everything hurt by then. There was no inch
that didn't hurt.
Electric lines buzzed with birds. The sky
looked ominous.
You called your oldest
friend, said goodbye. I turned my back
to check e-mail. Who was I expecting
a message from? You were right
there. Cracking thunder the moment
you left. We'll still love you
when we're dead too.

Perhaps no other Arab American artist is as renowned for capturing the intimacy and deep connection of family in Arab American life as the award-winning poet Naomi Shihab Nye. Nye is a Palestinian American, and several of her works of poetry and prose have crossed over many genres. As Nye memorializes her father, the late reporter and writer Aziz Shihab, she not only captures a quintessential element of Arab American life but also the universal bond between parent and child. Depicting the universality of family is one way artists have normalized Arab American culture to combat stereotypes perpetuated after 9/11.

War and Homeland

Art can be a conduit by which to address injustice, reveal the heartbreak and destruction of war, or express a longing for homeland. Certainly many Arabs migrated to the United States for opportunity, but very often they left behind their family, land, and traditions, impelled by political instability, economic strife, or potential danger to their well-being or that of their family. Many Arab Americans have come from war-torn countries with peaks of migration from specific Arab regions—Palestine, Lebanon, Yemen, Iraq—corresponding to periods of war. Some Arab Americans return to visit or resettle in their homeland to find it war-torn or forever altered, and some stay connected to their home country through family, the media, or political activism. For this reason, a longing for homeland, protest against political conditions, and a preoccupation with the strife of war, displacement, and homelessness are common themes among Arab American art.

The *Landscapes of Desire* series by the activist/artist John Halaka fits squarely within this theme, reflecting the ongoing destruction of Palestinian culture and history by Israel and the persistent struggle of the Palestinians to return to and rebuild their homeland. Halaka's Palestinian identity has led him to focus on human oppression and homelessness; for many Palestinians, their villages and their way of life no longer exist except through memory. The very recollection of these memories, their depiction in Halaka's art, is a form of resistance. Through his work "he attempts to initiate a dialogue with the viewer that could hopefully instigate transformation, one person at a time."[7]

Visual artist John Halaka considers memories of destroyed Palestinian villages in "Landscapes of Desire" (2009). The images are rendered with oil paint, ink, and rubber-stamped words. The repeated stamping of the words defines the forms, textures, and tones of the landscapes, but most importantly, the repeated words employed by Halaka to construct the drawings become a visual mantra, compelling us to "remember, resist, desire, rebuild and forgive." ("Landscapes of Desire," Number p06. Memory. 2009. Ink and Rubber Stamped ink on paper. 22" x 30" . Courtesy of the artist)

ARAB AMERICAN ART AS POLITICAL ACTIVISM

By the very nature of their work, artists tend to contemplate the human experience in a more profound way than many other professions. Particularly for artists whose families came from countries rife with warfare, whose histories may include conflict and displacement, and who have a heightened sense of otherness because of the immigrant experience and the aftermath of 9/11, there is a propensity toward political subjects or themes. Some artists have taken their art beyond a passive contemplation of political issues to a means of political activism. The goal of their artistic expression is to raise awareness, send a particular political message, or inspire a call to action in their audience, with relation to a political concern. Political causes that have motivated Arab American artists to take action are the demand for Palestinian rights and opposition to military action against Arabs, most recently in Iraq, Lebanon, and Gaza.

For these artists, political action can take several forms. Artists can produce an individual work of art or band together in a collective work that expresses their political position. Artists can show individual works together in a single exhibit or group together multiple pieces of their own work that support their political viewpoint or speak to the same political issue. The post-9/11 period has

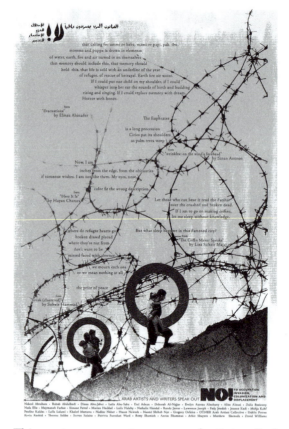

This poster represents a group of artists called "Arab Artists and Writers Speak Out: NO to OCCUPATION, INVASION, and COLONIZATION AND DISPLACEMENT" who protest injustices in the Arab World. The artists came together behind this message during the 2006 Lebanon War. (Joe Namy)

brought many Arab American artists in contact with each other to network and collaborate. It has been a period rich in organized political activities among artists.

GOING MAINSTREAM

The curiosity about the Arab world and Arab Americans that arose from 9/11, as well as the Arab American art movement's response through combating misinformation and stereotypes, has resulted in increased visibility and demand for Arab American artistic expression. Individually, many Arab American artists have broken through barriers to achieve crossover appeal and are well-regarded by mainstream audiences. More importantly, Arab American art as a collective voice has recently gained access to new venues and publications.

For example, in their fall 2008 issue, *PMLA,* the prominent journal of the Modern Language Association (MLA) that has been published since 1884, included a series of essays from a panel of well-respected Arab writers and professors. They had been featured at the 2007 RAWI conference on a panel presentation, entitled "Writing while Arab." The essays covered topics related to Arab American writing, such as race, Islam, and diasporic identities, as well as an analysis of contemporary poets. The forum in *PMLA* even addressed controversial topics such as the torture that took place in the Abu Ghraib Prison in Iraq. This level of attention to Arab American writers in leading scholarly journal is without precedent and indicates that Arab American art is moving into the mainstream.[8]

There is perhaps no better example of Arab American art moving into the mainstream than "Arabesque: Arts of the Arab World," a three-week festival that took place at the Kennedy Center in the winter of 2009. The festival focused on artistic expression from 22 countries throughout the Arab world in a vast array of performances, including music and dance, theater, film, literature, and spoken-word poetry. "Arabesque" also featured several Arab American artists and scholars of the arts. The festival is an example of a federally funded institution fostering American citizens' understanding of the Arab world. The financial support for "Arabesque" came from Arab and American foundations, governments, and individuals. The rich program was developed by Alicia Adams, Kennedy Center vice president for international programming and dance, in collaboration with artists from the Arab world, such as the renowned Egyptian novelist Ahdaf Soueif and Arab arts advocate/promoter Basma El Husseiny.[9] As part of an ongoing international series that has highlighted other regions of the world, the performances at "Arabesque" were met with critical acclaim and receptive audiences.

CONCLUSION

Arab American Art has come together as an artistic movement that shares common genres, themes, and interests. Although 9/11 acts of terrorism brought about stereotyping and profiling of Arabs, 9/11 also engendered a curiosity about the Arab world and Arab Americans. In order to affirm Arab American identity and promote understanding, many Arab American artists have collaborated with each other both formally and informally, working in a wide range of mediums in the visual, performing, literary, and digital arts. While artists are innovating in traditional art forms, other exciting new mediums are being explored in Arab American Art, including digital arts, hip-hop, comedy, filmmaking and one-woman shows. Arab American artists face challenges common to all artists but also some that are unique to their Arab heritage. Since 2001, there has been a proliferation and expansion of organizations, institutions, publications, and collectives to support Arab American artists to meet those challenges. Festivals, exhibitions, and conferences have taken place across the nation to give exposure to Arab American artists. Mainstream venues, organizations, and publications are featuring Arab American artists and their work.

Arab American artists share common themes that convey what is unique about the Arab American experience, with a concentration on family, migration and cross-cultural identity, war and homeland. While many Arab American artists remain connected to their Arab ancestry and homeland, they also truly identify as Americans, and many contemplate American themes, ideals, and values in their work. Because war and political strife are common in many countries in the Arab world, numerous Arab Americans have used their artistic expression as a form of political activism, and have sometimes issued political statements collectively. Some Arab American artists have taken on the post-9/11 climate directly, making it the featured subject of their work.

The post-9/11 period has been a time of prodigious output from Arab American artists. A movement has come together, sharing a common concern. Over the last decade, some of the energy that galvanized the movement has been rechanneled into artists' individual careers, although networks and relationships among Arab American artists remain strong. As they continue to work together informally, collaborate, and share their message with non-Arabs, they build on the contributions of Arab American artists who came before them. In America, a flourishing artistic community of Arab heritage thrives.

NOTES

1. Kahlil Gibran, "I Believe In You (to the Americans Of Lebanese Origin)," in *This Man from Lebanon: A Study of Kahlil Gibran,* by Barbara Young (New York: Knopf, 1945), 136.

2. Joe Namy, e-mail interview by author, June 29, 2009.

3. Leila Buck, telephone interview by author, July 23, 2009.

4. Khaled Ahmad Mattawa, telephone interview by author, July 16, 2009.

5. Helen Zughaib, interview by author, Arab American National Museum, Dearborn, Michigan, March 27, 2009.

6. Dinitia Smith, "For Arab-American Playwrights a Sense of Purpose," *New York Times,* February 11, 2006, http://www.nytimes.com/2006/02/11/theater/ newsandfeatures/11thro.html?scp=3&sq=arab%20american%20writers&st=cse (accessed August 15, 2009).

7. John Halaka, e-mail interview by author, August 3, 2009.

8. Khaled Ahmad Mattawa, telephone interview by author, July 16, 2009.

9. Alicia Adams, e-mail interview by author, August 4, 2009.

GLOSSARY

agrarian—Agriculturally dependent, used to describe a society or a sector of the economy.

aliens—Individuals, also referred to as nonimmigrants, who live in the United States but are not citizens, including temporary workers, students, visitors, as well as undocumented workers.

Allah—The word meaning God in Arabic; used by both Muslim and Christian Arabs.

Al Qaeda—Literally translated as "the base," this terrorist network was led by Osama bin Laden and based in Afghanistan and the tribal areas of Pakistan. Al Qaeda espouses an extreme political and religious ideology and has launched attacks worldwide, most notably the 9/11 attacks on the United States. While Al Qaeda targets Americans in the United States and abroad, many of its victims are actually Muslim civilians. Although Al Qaeda uses Islam to justify its actions, the overwhelming majority of Muslims around the globe condemn these acts and resent having these crimes committed in the name of their religion.

American Dream—The ideals of freedom, equality, and opportunity traditionally held to be available to every American. The possibility of achieving such a dream is what attracted many immigrants to come to the United States.

anti-Arab stereotyping—A distorted or oversimplified and negative characterization of all Arabs as a group that can lead to prejudice and discrimination.

anti-Semitism—Discrimination, prejudice, or hostility toward Jews.

Arab American studies—The field of research dedicated to the study of Arab Americans.

Arab world—The 22 Arabic-speaking countries in North Africa and West Asia that stretch from Morocco on the Atlantic to Iraq and the countries of the Arabian Peninsula and the Arab/Persian Gulf.

artistic movement—A group of artists who adhere to a common style or purpose during a specific time period.

Ashura—Observed by Muslim Shi'a during the first 10 days of the lunar month of Muharram to commemorate the death of Hussein, the prophet Muhammad's grandson.

azza—A three-day mourning period, held after a funeral when people come to visit and pay their condolences.

baklava—A traditional dessert made of thin sheets of pastry layered with honey and butter and stuffed with nuts.

bilingual—The ability to speak two languages, especially with equal fluency. This can refer to persons, institutions, or media outlets that use two languages of expression.

bilingual education—The use of more than one language in schools to ease the transition of newly immigrant students from using their native language to using English.

brain drain—The phenomenon that takes place when a large number of educated and highly skilled citizens of a developing country migrate to a developed country that offers a higher standard of living.

chain migration—The process whereby members of a group immigrate and are then followed by other members of the same group who may belong to the same family or village. The first migrants will often help subsequent immigrants move to their area. Sometimes entire villages from an Arab country have relocated to the same towns in the United States.

Chaldeans—An indigenous ethnic group from northern Iraq whose members speak a distinct language and trace their ancestry to ancient Babylon.

Christian missionaries—Christians sent by churches to different parts of the world to convert the indigenous people and establish churches of their specific denomination. In some instances, missionaries open schools and clinics that benefit the local population.

civil rights movement—The national grassroots movement of African Americans and their supporters that in the 1950s and 1960s sought to eliminate segregation and institutionalized discrimination and to gain equal rights. Among its most famous leaders is Reverend Dr. Martin Luther King Jr.

co-ethnic population—People who share the same ethnicity.

colonization—The occupation and political and economic control of one country over another. It often refers to European control of many African and Asian countries.

Coptic—An Egyptian Christian domination whose followers are Egyptian and Ethiopian; the patriarch is located in Alexandria, Egypt.

diaspora—A dispersion of a people from their original homeland to resettle in a new location.

discrimination—Negative behavior or policies toward individuals or groups because of their national origin, race, gender, sexual orientation, or physical challenges.

Druze—A small branch of Islam that developed in the 11th century. The largest Druze community in the Arab world is in Lebanon.

due process of law—The legal principle that government must respect all of the rights guaranteed to an individual by law.

Eastern Orthodox—A branch of Christianity that split from the Roman Catholic Church in the seventh century. It includes the Middle Eastern or Arab Antiochan, Coptic, Syrian, and Assyrian Orthodox churches.

eid—The Arabic word for holiday or celebration.

Eid al-Adha—The Muslim holiday that commemorates Abraham's attempted sacrifice of his son and takes place at the end of the hajj or pilgrimage to Mecca.

Eid al-Fitr—The Muslim holiday that commemorates the end of Ramadan.

ethnic economy—An economy that consists of the self-employed, their co-ethnic employees, and unpaid family workers who earn a living and run businesses within an ethnic community. Such an economy often exists in an ethnic enclave because the community is often spatially clustered, with a high concentration of people from the same ethnic or national background.

ethnic enclaves—A neighborhood, district, or suburb that is culturally distinct from a larger, surrounding area. It is usually home to a group of people who have same cultural, racial, national, or religious background and can consist of recently arrived immigrants, second-generation residents, or a mix of both.

ethnicity—An identity linked to a shared sense of heritage or history.

ethnographic research—A participant-observation research method in which the researcher lives and participates with the group he or she studies.

evil eye—In many traditional cultures there is a superstitious belief that a jealous look or attitude toward a person or object can result in derogatory effects. To ward off these evil spirits, many people, particularly babies, wear a blue glass or ceramic representation of an eye to keep them in good health.

falafel—Croquettes made of chickpeas and/or fava beans, spices, and parsley. It is usually served in a pita bread sandwich with a sauce made from sesame seeds, accompanied by turnip pickles and tomato.

faseekh—A salted, gray mullet fish that is served during Sham el-Nassim, a national nonreligious Egyptian festival that marks the beginning of spring.

filial duty—The duty of a son or daughter toward their parents.

glass ceiling—Barriers to advancement in the workplace due to bias or discrimination based on gender, race, or ethnicity. They are called "glass" ceilings because they reflect no official policy, and it is thus hard to "see" them.

Great Depression—The worst and longest worldwide economic collapse in the history of the modern industrial world, which began in October 1929, when the U.S. stock market crashed, and lasted until 1932. High levels of unemployment and poverty became rampant and the U.S. economy did not totally recover until 1940.

Greater Syria—An area ruled by the Ottomans until the early 20th century; it comprised the present-day countries of Syria, Lebanon, Jordan, Palestine, and Israel.

Great Migration—The period between 1880 and 1924, when more than 20 million immigrants entered the United States. Most of these immigrants came from southern and eastern Europe, but close to 100,000 Arabs also arrived, mainly from Syria, Lebanon, and Palestine.

Gulf War—A 1991 war launched by a U.S.-led international coalition in response to the Iraqi occupation of Kuwait under Saddam Hussein.

hafla—A party or social gathering.

hajj—The Muslim pilgrimage to the city of Mecca, birthplace of the prophet Muhammad. The hajj is a mandatory religious requirement of those who are physically and financial capable. It is one of the five Pillars of Islam.

halal—Actions or objects that are permissible according to Islamic law, often used to describe foods prepared according to Islamic code.

Hart-Cellar Act—A law passed by Congress in 1965 that lifted earlier immigration restrictions, in place between 1917 and 1924, limiting the number of non-European immigrants who were allowed to enter the United States.

hate crime—An assault or a direct threat against a person or an institution because of race, religion, ethnicity, nationality, gender, sexual orientation, or disability. Such acts are considered crimes against the whole group and therefore incur severe legal penalties.

hijab—Head covering sometimes worn as a display of modesty by Muslim women.

Holy Land—The geographical region of the Levant where important religious sites that are sacred to the three monotheistic, Abrahamic religions, Judaism, Christianity, and Islam, are located.

homestead—The act of settling on a piece of property to make it a permanent home. In 1862, the U.S. government passed the Homestead Act, granting freehold titles of up to 160 acres to people who agreed to cultivate and live on the land.

hummus—A popular Arabic dish of pureed cooked chickpeas, tahini sauce, garlic, lemon juice, salt, and olive oil.

hyphenated identity—A way of expressing one's origins or regional culture or ancestry along with one's new American identity, often through the use of a hyphen, as in Asian-American or African-American.

iftar—The sunset meal that ends the day-long fast during Ramadan.

imam—A Muslim religious leader.

immigrant—Person who leaves one country to settle permanently in another. Term also refers to American citizens or communities who came to the United States from other countries.

immigrant art—Artistic expression and works created by foreign artists who have resettled in the United States or by Americans of foreign descent.

immigration centers—U.S. government facilities that newly arrived immigrants must pass through for processing by immigration authorities.

intifada—The Arabic term for a popular uprising or revolt, used internationally to describe the 1987 Palestinian uprising to protest the ongoing Israeli occupation of their land.

Iraq War—The invasion and subsequent occupation of Iraq launched under the military name "Operation Iraqi Freedom" on March 20, 2003, when the United States and Great Britain led a multinational force to invade Iraq and remove the government of Saddam Hussein. The Bush administration justified the preemptive invasion by asserting that Iraq was developing weapons of mass destruction and had links to the Al Qaeda 9/11 attacks on the United States, although both of these claims turned out to be based on faulty intelligence.

Islamism—A term used loosely to refer to a range of modern and political versions of Islam. Some of them are moderate reform movements that work within parliamentary systems, as in Turkey, while others, such as Osama bin Laden's Al-Qaeda or the Taliban, are extremist in their goals and violent in their methods.

Islamofascism—A pejorative term that suggests there is a similarity between Muslim extremist movements and European fascist regimes, such as Mussolini's Italy or Hitler's Germany. The term is often used by anti-Muslim ideologues in a way that implies that most Muslims, including most American Muslims, support terrorism.

Islamophobia—Fear of Muslims based on prejudice and lack of information. Islamophobia often results in attempts to marginalize or exclude Muslims from public life or justify discrimination against them on the pretense that Muslims and Islam are violent and cannot be trusted. The term came into wider usage as anti-Muslim attitudes became more widespread in Europe in response to the growth in Muslim populations and in the United States in the aftermath of 9/11.

Japanese internment camps—The guarded camps in various parts of the country to which nearly all persons of Japanese ancestry living in the United States were forcibly relocated following the Pearl Harbor attacks in December 1941. The overwhelming majority of these individuals were U.S. citizens or legal residents. Later, the U.S. government acknowledged its wrongdoing by apologizing and paying Japanese victims symbolic reparations.

kafiyyeh—A white and black or white and red checkered scarf worn by Arab men, particularly Palestinian peasants, over the head or around the shoulders, which became a symbol of Palestinian nationalism and cultural identity. During the first intifada, young men and women around the world began to wear a kafiyyeh as a sign of political support for Palestinians and later as a global fashion statement.

Kahlil Gibran—The renowned Arab American novelist, poet, and artist who was born in Lebanon in 1883 and died in the United States in 1931. Among his most famous publications is *The Prophet*, which has been translated into tens of languages and taught in schools and universities around the world.

Kitab al-kittaab—The Muslim marriage ceremony in which the couple recites the first verse of the Qur'an with the imam, or religious leader. It literally translates to "the writing of the book."

kofta—A popular Arabic dish, also known as kebob, composed of ground lamb and/or beef, mixed with onion, parsley, sumac, garlic, and spices, and grilled on skewers.

mahr—The dowry or wedding gift from the groom and his family to the bride.

mansaf—A traditional dish that is popular in Jordan and parts of Palestine. It is usually served on a large round platter for communal eating at holidays and feast days. It is made of a thin layer of flatbread, rice, lamb, roasted almonds, and/or pine nuts and topped with a sauce made of dried fermented yogurt.

Marshall Plan—A program under which the United States gave substantial economic aid to European countries to help them rebuild after the devastation of World War II.

Middle East—This term has no precise definition and has been used historically to refer to very different geographic areas. Its origins reflect the orientation of British colonial officials in London, who saw China and Japan as the "Far East." The "Middle East" is sometimes defined to include both North Africa and southwest Asia as far as Afghanistan but more often refers to the countries from Egypt or Libya east to the Arabian Peninsula and Iran. "Middle East conflict" is often used by journalists and politicians to refer specifically to the Palestinian-Israeli conflict.

Middle East studies—The field of scholarship dedicated to the study of the language, culture, history, and politics of the peoples of this geographical region.

migrant workers—Individuals who relocate to find work and often travel back and forth throughout the year between their jobs and their country or area of origin in order to make a living and maintain their relationships with family and friends.

Model T Plant—A Ford Motor Company automobile factory located in Highland Park, Michigan, which was open from 1908 to 1927.

monotheism—The belief in one God.

mosque—The Muslim place of worship, similar to the church or synagogue.

moughli—A pudding, also called *karawya*, served after the birth of a newborn that is made of crushed rice or cornstarch, sugar, cinnamon, and crushed caraway seeds, then topped with raw peeled nuts such as almonds, walnuts, and pistachios. It is served either hot or cold in small dessert bowls and is said to help the mother produce breast milk and ease the after-birth bleeding period.

Mount Lebanon region—A mountain range in Lebanon that under the Ottoman Empire was considered part of the province of Syria.

muta'akhir—The part of a dowry whose payment is delayed until the death or divorce of a spouse.

nationality—An identity linked to a person's country of origin or citizenship in a nation, which can be complicated for many Arab Americans. For example, Palestinian Americans do not have a state, while the nationality of immigrants whose ancestors came from villages that were once Syrian and are now part of Lebanon has changed even though their place of origin remains the same.

nativism—Attitudes or policies originating with the native population of a country that are hostile toward immigrants because of real or perceived ethnic, racial, cultural, or religious differences. Nativists believe that foreigners cannot or should not be assimilated into the mainstream population. The term has a neutral, scholarly meaning, but it has also been used in a pejorative sense. Nativists usually see themselves as defending the integrity of their national or cultural group.

naturalized citizens—Individuals of other nationalities who become U.S. citizens by immigrating and submitting a citizenship application, rather than by being born in the United States.

nonimmigrants—(see *aliens*)

NSEERS—National Security Entry-Exit Registration System set up by the Department of Justice in June 2002, which compelled aliens (noncitizens) from 25 predominantly Muslim countries to register and submit to fingerprints and photographs upon arrival in the United States, report to the Immigration and Naturalization Service (INS) annually, and notify the INS prior to departure.

Ottoman Empire—Turkish Muslim dynasty that emerged in the 14th century; its capital was in Constantinople (now Istanbul). At their most powerful, the Ottomans controlled many parts of southeastern Europe and most of the Arab world until after their defeat in World War I; many of the territories the empire occupied were subdivided by the European victors into the Middle Eastern nations that exist today.

Ottoman subjects—Residents of areas from the eastern Mediterranean, North Africa, and parts of Europe that were ruled by the Ottoman sultan based in Istanbul, Turkey, until World War I.

Palestinian-Israeli conflict—The ongoing struggle between Arabs and Jews over the land that was historic Palestine. The conflict began under the British Mandate following World War I.

peddlers—Individuals who sell goods door to door, traveling mostly in areas not served by stores. Peddling was a common trade for early Arab American immigrants because it yielded good profits, without requiring capital or knowledge of the English language.

Pen League—A literary organization that was founded in New York City in 1920 by a number of Arab American writers, among them Kahlil Gibran, author of the famous book *The Prophet*.

Persian Gulf—A body of water, also known as the Arabian Gulf, the surrounding coastline of which provides much of the world's crude oil. The oil-rich countries in this region include Bahrain, Kuwait, Oman, Qatar, Saudi Arabia, the United Arab Emirates, Iraq, and Iran.

profiling—The use of a set of criteria by law enforcement officers to determine the likelihood that an individual will engage in a specific type of criminal act. In practice, it has sometimes meant the targeting of minority individuals because of an assumed propensity toward certain types of crimes. This is known as "racial profiling."

pull factor—Desirable living conditions that draw people to immigrate to a new place.

push factor—Undesirable living conditions that encourage or force people to leave their country, city, or neighborhood.

Qur'an—The sacred text of Islam, also spelled Koran or Quran, that is comparable to the Christian Bible or Jewish Torah. Muslims believe that it is the inspired word of God that was revealed to the prophet Muhammad by the archangel Gabriel over a 23-year period. The term literally means "recitation."

Ramadan—The ninth month of the Islamic calendar, when Muslims fast from sunrise to sunset in observance of one of the Five Pillars of Islam.

Revolutionary War—One of the most significant events in American history, also referred to as the American Revolution following the Continental Congress's Declaration of Independence in 1776 and culminating in the official defeat of the British forces in 1783.

Rouge Plant—A Ford Motor Company automobile factory located in Dearborn, Michigan. Completed in 1928, it ultimately replaced the Model T Plant (see above) and became the largest integrated industrial complex in the world.

Salaat al-Janazah—A special group funerary prayer in Islam.

SEVIS—Student and Exchange Visitor System, which became law on January 30, 2003, and tracks foreign student enrollment, academic status, and disciplinary actions.

Sham el-Nassim—A national nonreligious Egyptian festival that marks the beginning of spring.

sheikh—A Muslim religious or tribal leader.

Shi'a—Followers of a branch of Islam that believes the descendents of the prophet Muhammad (through Ali, Muhammad's cousin) should be the leaders of the Islamic community. Also known as Shi'a, this sect has a significant following in Lebanon and southern Iraq. In the non-Arab country of Iran, they are the majority.

shwarma—A popular sandwich consisting of slow-roasted chicken or beef served in pita bread with lettuce, tomato, and garlic sauce.

Sunni—The branch of Islam followed by the majority of Muslims worldwide.

tabbouli—A Lebanese salad of parsley, onion, tomato, bulgur, olive oil, garlic, and lemon juice.

terrorism—The use of violence or threat of violence against unarmed civilians in order to achieve a political purpose.

transnationalism—The flow of people, ideas, and goods across national boundaries that has escalated through expanded technology and globalization.

USA PATRIOT Act—An act of Congress, the full title of which is "Uniting and Strengthening America by Providing Appropriate Tools Required to Intercept and Obstruct Terrorism," passed on October 25, 2001. The Patriot

Act gave law enforcement agencies sweeping powers of surveillance and was signed into law by President George W. Bush.

US-VISIT—The United States Visitor and Immigrant Status Indicator Technology Program is a U.S. immigration and border management system that collects and analyzes biometrics such as fingerprints, which are then checked against a database to track individuals deemed by the United States to be terrorists, criminals, and illegal immigrants.

War on Terror—The military response to the terrorist attacks against the United States on September 11, 2001, that was conceptualized under the Bush administration. Described by its leaders as a political, military, legal, and ideological effort to eradicate militant Islamism, the War on Terror has been used to justify military operations against both state and nonstate actors; it is also known as the Global War on Terrorism. Under the Obama administration the effort has been referred to as the Overseas Contingency Operation.

wudu—A ritual cleansing of the body that Muslims practice before prayer.

yalla—A term in colloquial Arabic used to mean "let's go" or "hurry up."

zakat—The religious obligation of Muslims to give annually of their income or wealth to charity for the less fortunate; one of the Five Pillars of Islam.

BIBLIOGRAPHY

CHAPTER 1   ARAB AMERICAN IMMIGRATION

Books

Abraham, Sameer, and Nabeel Abraham. *Arabs in the New World: Studies on Arab American Communities.* Detroit: Wayne State University, Center for Urban Studies, 1983.

Ameri, Anan, and Yvonne Lockwood. *Arab Detroit: A Pictorial History.* Chicago: Arcadia Publishing, 2001.

Ameri, Anan, and Dawn Ramey, eds. *The Arab American Encyclopedia,* Woodbridge, CT: U.X.L, 2000.

Arab American National Museum. *Telling Our Story.* Dearborn, MI: Arab American National Museum, 2007.

Aswad, Barbara. "Yemeni and Lebanese Muslim Immigrant Women in Southeast Dearborn, Michigan." In *Muslim Families in America,* ed. Earle H. Waugh, Sharon McIrvin Abu-Laban, and Regula Qureshi, 256–81. Edmonton, AB, Canada: University of Alberta Press, 1991.

Behdad, Ali. *A Forgetful Nation: On Immigration and Cultural Identity in the United States.* Durham, NC: Duke University Press, 2005.

Benson, Kathleen, and Philip Kaya, eds. *A Community of Many Worlds: Arab Americans in New York City.* New York: Museum of the City of New York, 2002; and Syracuse: Syracuse University Press, 2002.

Blakley, J.R. *Acculturation and the Use of Media among Arab Women Immigrants Living in Metropolitan Detroit.* PhD diss.: Regent University, Virginia. 2006.

Boosahda, Elizabeth. *Arab-American Faces and Voices: The Origins of an Immigrant Community.* Austin: University of Texas Press, 2003.

Dummett, Michael A. E. *On Immigration and Refugees.* London and New York: Routledge, 2001.

Hooglund, Eric, ed. *Crossing the Waters: Arabic-Speaking Immigrants to the United States before 1940.* Washington, DC: Smithsonian Institution Press, 1987.

Kayyali, Randa A. *The Arab Americans.* Westport, CT: Greenwood Press, 2006.

Naff, Alexa A. *Becoming American: The Early Arab Immigrant Experience.* Carbondale: Southern Illinois University Press, 1985.

Orfalea, Gregory. *The Arab Americans: A History.* Northampton, MA: Olive Branch Press, 2006.

Orfalea, Gregory. *Before the Flame: A Quest for the History of Arab Americans.* Austin: University of Texas Press, 1988.

Read, Jen'nan Ghazal. *Culture, Class, and Work among Arab-American Women.* New York: LFB Scholarly Publishing, 2004.

Shakir, Evelyn. *Bint Arab: Arab and Arab American Women in the United States,* Westport, CT: Praeger, 1977.

Shryock, Andrew, and Nabeel Abraham. *Arab Detroit: From Margin to Mainstream.* Detroit: Wayne State University Press, 2000.

Suleiman, Michael, ed. *Arabs in America: Building a New Future.* Philadelphia: Temple University Press, 1999.

Articles

Ajrouch, Kristine. "Arab-American Elder Views about Social Support." *Aging & Society* 25, no. 5 (2005): 655–73. http://www.proquest.com. proxy.lib.wayne.edu/ (accessed November 17, 2009).

Al-Hajal, Khalil. "Local Imam Traces History of Arab Immigrants from Tibnin." *Arab American News* (Dearborn, MI), April 17, 2009. http:// www.arabamericannews.com/news/index.php?mod=article&cat= Artamp;Culture&article=2116.

American Historical Association. "Autobiography of Omar ibn Said, Slave in North Carolina, 1831." *American Historical Review* 30, no. 4 (July 1925): 787–95.

"The Arab Immigrants." Special issue, *Saudi Aramco World* (September–October 1986).

Morse, Kitty. "Esteban of Azemmour and His New World Adventures." *Saudi Aramco World* (March–April 2002).

Seymour-Jorn, Caroline. "Arab Language Learning among Arab Immigrants in Milwaukee, Wisconsin: A Study of Attitudes and Motivations." *Journal of Muslim Minority Affairs* 24, no. 1 (2004): 109–22.

Journals

International Journal of Middle Eastern Studies: http://journals.cambridge.org/action/displayJournal?jid=mes.

International Migration Review: http://www.cmsny.org/. Published by the Center for Migration Studies of New York, Inc. Searchable.

Journal of Immigrant and Minority Health: http://www.springer.com/public+health/journal/10903.

MELUS (The Society for the Study of Multi-Ethnic Literature in the United States): http://webspace.ship.edu/kmlong/melus/.

Websites

Arab American Institute (AAI): http://www.aaiusa.org/.

Arab American National Museum (AANM): http://www.arabamericanmuseum.org/.

The Immigration History Research Center: A Guide to Collection. University of Minnesota: http://catdir.loc.gov/catdir/toc/becites/genealogy/immigrant/91016262.idx.html or http://www.loc.gov/rr/genealogy/bib_guid/immigrant/.

National Arab American Medical Association: http://www.naama.com/.

The Urban Institute [main page]: http://www.urban.org/immigrants/index.cfm.

The Urban Institute. Immigrants Section: http://www.urban.org/UploadedPDF/901292_immigrationtrends.pdf. This site includes a fact sheet with a few charts that include Middle Eastern immigrant statistics, particularly those relating to children (see pages 3 and 4).

US Department of Homeland Security [immigration statistics]: http://www.dhs.gov/files/statistics/immigration.shtm.

CHAPTER 2   THE IMPACT OF 9/11, MIDDLE EAST CONFLICTS, AND ANTI-ARAB DISCRIMINATION

Books

Baker, Wayne, Sally Howell, Amaney Jamal, Ann Chih Lin, Andrew Shryock, Ron Stockton, and Mark Tessler. *Citizenship and Crisis: Arab Detroit After 9/11.* New York: Russell Sage Foundation, 2009.

Bayoumi, Moustafa. *How Does It Feel to Be a Problem? Being Young and Arab in America.* New York: Penguin Press HC, 2008.

Bennis, Phyllis. *Understanding the Palestinian-Israeli Conflict: A Primer.* Northampton, MA: Olive Branch Press/Interlink Publishing, 2007.

Bennis, Phyllis, and Noam Chomsky. *Before and After: U.S. Foreign Policy and the September 11th Crisis.* Northampton, MA: Interlink Publishing, 2002.

Cainkar, Louise. *Homeland Insecurity: The Arab American and Muslim American Experience after 9/11.* New York: Russell Sage Foundation, 2009.

Chomsky, Noam. *Pirates and Emperors, Old and New: International Terrorism in the Real World.* Rev. ed. Cambridge, MA: South End Press, 2003.

David, Ron. *Arabs and Israel for Beginners.* New York: Writers and Readers Publishing, 1993.

El Rassi, Toufic. *Arab in America.* Illustrated ed. San Francisco: Last Gasp, 2008.

Lee, Michael S. *Healing a Nation: The Arab American Experience after September 11.* Washington, DC: Arab American Institute, n.d.: http://adc. org/index.php?id=3302 (accessed February 2009).

Neff, Donald. *Fallen Pillars: U.S. Policy towards Palestine and Israel since 1945.* Rev. ed. Washington, DC: Institute for Palestine Studies, 2002.

Salaita, Steven. *Anti-Arab Racism in the USA: Where It Comes From and What It Means for Politics Today.* London: Pluto Press, 2006.

Shaheen, Jack G. *Guilty: Hollywood's Verdict on Arabs After 9/11.* Northampton, MA: Interlink Publishing, 2007.

Shaheen, Jack G. *Reel Bad Arabs: How Hollywood Vilifies a People.* Northampton, MA: Interlink Publishing, 2002. (DVD version, director Jad Jhally. Media Educational Foundation, 2006, 50 minutes).

Articles and Reports

Cainkar, Louise. "No Longer Invisible: Arab and Muslim Exclusion after September 11." *Middle East Report* 224 (Fall 2002): http://www. merip.org/mer/mer224/224_cainkar.html (accessed March 3, 2009).

Cainkar, Louise. "Reel Bad Arabs: How Hollywood Vilifies a People." Democracy Now Radio, October 19, 2007: http://74.125.47.132/search? q=cache:Q0um0PmrSfgJ:www.democracynow.org/2007/10/19/ reel_bad_arabs_how_hollywood_vilifies+%22jack+shaheen%22+%22 the+kingdom%22&hl=en&ct=clnk&cd=2&gl=us (accessed February 28, 2009).

Halper, Jeff. "The Key to Peace: Dismantling the Matrix of Control." Israeli Committee Against House Demolitions (n. d.): http://www.icahd. org/eng/articles.asp?menu=6&submenu=3 (accessed March 7, 2009).

Ibish, Hussein, ed. *1998–2000 Report on Hate Crimes and Discrimination against Arab Americans.* Washington, DC: American-Arab Anti-Discrimination Committee, 2001: http://adc.org/index.php?id= 3302 (accessed February 2009).

Ibish, Hussein, ed. *2003–2007 Report on Hate Crimes and Discrimination against Arab Americans.* Washington, DC: American-Arab Anti-

Discrimination Committee, 2008: http://adc.org/index.php?id=3302 (accessed February 2009).

Ibish, Hussein, ed., and Ann Stewart, principal researcher. *Report on Hate Crimes and Discrimination against Arab Americans: The Post-September 11 Backlash.* Washington, DC: ADC Research Institute, 2002: http://adc.org/index.php?id=3302 (accessed February 2009).

Khouri, Ghada, ed. *1996–97 Report on Hate Crimes and Discrimination against Arab Americans.* Washington, DC: American-Arab Anti-Discrimination Committee, 1997.

Middle East Research and Information Project. "Palestine, Israel, and the Arab-Israeli Conflict: A Primer." http://www.merip.org/palestine-israel_primer/toc-pal-isr-primer.html (accessed February 2009).

1991 Report on Anti-Arab Hate Crimes: Political and Hate Violence Against Arab-Americans. Washington, DC: American-Arab Anti-Discrimination Committee, 1992.

Sajid, Imam Abduljalil. "Islamophobia: A New Word for an Old Fear." OSCE Conference on Anti-Semitism and Other Forms of Intolerance, Cordoba, June 8 and 9, 2005: http://www.osce.org/documents/cio/2005/06/15198_en.pdf.

CHAPTER 3   THE FAMILY

Books

Bilgé, Barbara, and Barbara C. Aswad, eds. *Family and Gender among American Muslims: Issues Facing Middle Eastern Immigrants and Their Descendants.* Philadelphia: Temple University Press, 1996.

Cainkar, Louise. *Homeland Insecurity: The Arab American and Muslim American Experience after 9/11.* New York: Russell Sage Foundation, 2009.

Ewing, Katherine Pratt. *Being and Belonging: Muslims in the United States Since 9/11.* New York: Russell Sage Foundation, 2008.

Joseph, Suad. *Intimate Selving in Arab Families: Gender, Self, and Identity in Arab Families.* Syracuse, NY: Syracuse University Press, 1999.

Kayyali, Randa A. *The Arab Americans.* Westport, CT: Greenwood Press, 2006.

Read, Jen'nan Ghazal. *Culture, Class, and Work among Arab-American Women.* New York: LFB Scholarly Publishing, 2004.

Shakir, Evelyn. *Bint Arab: Arab and Arab American Women in the United States.* Westport, CT: Praeger, 1997.

Sharabi, Hisham. *Neopatriarchy: A Theory of Distorted Change in Arab Society.* New York: Oxford University Press, 1988.

Suleiman, Michael W., ed. *Arabs in America: Building a New Future.* Philadelphia: Temple University Press, 1999.

Articles and Reports

Ajrouch, Kristine. "Arab-American Immigrant Elders' Views about Social Support." *Aging and Society* 25, no. 5 (2005): 655–73.

Brittingham, Angela, and Patricia de la Cruz. 2003. *The Arab Population: 2000.* Washington, DC: U.S. Census Bureau.

Kayyali, Randa A. "The People Perceived as a Threat to Security: Arab Americans Since September 11." *Migration Information Source* (July 2006): http://www.migrationinformation.org/Feature/display.cfm?ID=409.

Read, Jen'nan Ghazal, and Sharon Oselin. "Gender and the Education-Employment Paradox in Ethnic and Religious Contexts: The Case of Arab Americans." *American Sociological Review* 73, no. 2 (2008): 296–313.

CHAPTER 4   RELIGIOUS LIFE

Books

Ahmed, L. *Women and Gender in Islam: Historical Roots of a Modern Debate.* New Haven: Yale University Press, 1992.

Ameri, Anan, Arab Community Center for Economic and Social Services (ACCESS), and Dawn Ramey, eds. *The Arab American Encyclopedia,* Woodbridge, CT: U.X.L., 2000.

Bayoumi, Moustafa. *How Does It Feel to Be a Problem? Being Young and Arab in America.* New York: Penguin Press HC, 2008.

Cainkar, Louise. *Homeland Insecurity: The Arab American and Muslim American Experience after 9/11.* New York: Russell Sage Foundation, 2009.

Dickinson, Eliot. *Copts in Michigan.* East Lansing: Michigan State University Press, 2008.

Esposito, John. L. *What Everyone Needs to Know about Islam.* Oxford: Oxford University Press, 2002.

Ewing, Katherine P. *Being and Belonging: Muslims in the United States since 9/11.* New York: Russell Sage Foundation, 2008.

Haddad, Yvonne Y. *The Muslims of America.* New York: Oxford University Press, 1993.

Haddad, Yvonne Y., and John. L. Esposito. *Muslims on the Americanization Path?* New York: Oxford University Press, 2000.

Hassoun, Rosina J. *Arab Americans in Michigan.* East Lansing: Michigan State University Press, 2005.

Hunter, Shireen, and Huma Malik. *Islam and Human Rights: Advancing a U.S.-Muslim Dialogue.* Significant Issues 27, no. 5. Washington, DC: Center for Strategic and International Studies, 2005.

Jamal, Amaney, and Nadine Naber. *Race and Arab Americans before and after 9/11: From Invisible Citizens to Visible Subjects.* Syracuse, NY: Syracuse University Press, 2008.

Jones, Richard. R. ".2." In *Arab Detroit: From Margin to Mainstream*, edited by Nabeel Abraham and Andrew Shryock, 219–40. Detroit: Wayne State University Press, 2000.

Kayyali, Randa A. *The Arab Americans*. Westport, CT: Greenwood Press, 2006.

McCarus, Ernest N. *The Development of Arab-American Identity*. Ann Arbor: University of Michigan Press, 1994.

Sengstsock, Mary C. *Chaldeans in Michigan*. East Lansing: Michigan State University Press, 2005.

Strum, Philippa. *Muslims in the United States: Identity, Influence, Innovation*. Washington, DC: Woodrow Wilson International Center for Scholars, 2005.

Strum, Philippa, and D. Tarantolo. *Muslims in the United States: Demography, Beliefs, Institutions*. Washington, DC: Woodrow Wilson International Center for Scholars, 2003.

Suleiman, Michael W. *The Arab-American Experience in the United States and Canada: A Classified, Annotated Bibliography*. Ann Arbor, MI: Pierian Press, 2006.

Suleiman, Michael W. *Arabs in America: Building a New Future*. Philadelphia: Temple University Press, 1999.

Walbridge, Linda S. *Without Forgetting the Imam: Lebanese Shi'ism in an American Community*. Detroit: Wayne State University Press, 1997.

Articles

Ajrouch, Kristine J. "Gender, Race, and Symbolic Boundaries: Contested Spaces of Identity among Arab American Adolescents." *Sociological Perspectives* 47, no. 4 (2004): 371–91.

Cainkar, Louise. "No Longer Invisible: Arab and Muslim Exclusion after September 11." *Arabs, Muslims and Race in America: Middle East Report* 224 (2002).

Naber, Nadine. "Ambiguous Insiders: An Investigation of Arab American Invisibility." *Ethnic and Racial Studies* 23, no. 1 (2000): 37–61.

Read, Jen'nan Ghazal. "The Sources of Gender Role Attitudes among Christian and Muslim Arab-American Women." *Sociology of Religion* 64, no. 2 (2003): 207–22.

Online Resources

The Center for Muslim-Christian Understanding: http://cmcu.georgetown.edu/.

Oxford Islamic Studies Online: The Essential Reference for Islamic Studies: www.oxfordislamicstudies.com.

CHAPTER 5   ARAB AMERICANS AND
THE AMERICAN EDUCATIONAL SYSTEM

Books

Bakalian, Anny, and Mehdi Bozorgmehr. *Backlash 9/11: Middle Eastern Americans Respond.* Berkeley: University of California Press, 2009.

Bayoumi, Moustafa. *How Does It Feel to Be a Problem? Being Young and Arab in America.* New York: Penguin Press, 2008.

Cainkar, Louise. *Homeland Insecurity: The Arab American and Muslim American Experience after 9/11.* New York: Russell Sage Foundation, 2009.

Council on Islamic Education. *Teaching about Islam and Muslims in the Public School Classroom.* 3rd ed. Fountain Valley, CA: Council on Islamic Education, 1995.

Jamal, Amaney, and Nadine Naber, eds. *Race and Arab Americans before and after 9/11: From Invisible Citizens to Visible Subjects.* Syracuse, NY: Syracuse University Press, 2007.

Kadi, Joanna. *Food for Our Grandmothers: Writings by Arab-American and Arab-Canadian Feminists.* Boston: South End Press, 1994.

Oweis, Fayeq S. *Encyclopedia of Arab American Artists: Artists of the American Mosaic.* Westport, CT: Greenwood Press, 2008.

Salaita, Steven. *Anti-Arab Racism in the USA: Where it Comes From and What It Means for Politics Today.* London: Pluto Press, 2006.

Saliba, Theresa. "Resisting Invisibility: Arab Americans in Academia and Activism. " In *Arabs in America: Building a New Future,* ed. Michael W. Sulieman, 304–19.Philadelphia: Temple University Press, 1999.

Shabbas, A., C. El-Shaieb, and A. An-Nabulsi. *The Arabs: Activities for the Elementary School Level; The Things That Make for Peace: Empowering Children to Value Themselves and Others* (Berkeley: Awair, 1991).

Shaheen, Jack G. *Reel Bad Arabs.* Northampton, MA: Olive Branch Press, 2001.

Shakir, Evelyn. *Bint Arab: Arab and Arab American Women in the United States.* Westport, CT: Praeger, 1997.

Strum, Philippa, ed. *American Arabs and Political Participation.* Washington, DC: Woodrow Wilson International Center for Scholars, 2006.

Strum, Philippa, and Danielle Tarantolo, eds. *Muslims in the United States.* Washington, DC: Woodrow Wilson International Center for Scholars, 2003.

U.S. State Department. *Being Muslim in America.* Washington, DC: Author, 2009: http://www.america/gov/media/df/books/being-muslim-in-america.pdf.

Articles and Reports

American Arabs: History, Identity, Assimilation, Participation. Special Report #2.1. Washington, DC: Woodrow Wilson International Center for Scholars, 2001.

Hanley, D.C. "Protecting Arab-American Students Becomes a Priority: Arab American Literature Panel." *Washington Report on Middle East Affairs.* Washington, DC: American Educational Trust (AET), August 2009.

Read, J.G., and S. Oselin. "Gender and the Education-Employment Paradox in Ethnic and Religious Contexts: The Case of Arab Americans." *American Sociological Review* 73, no.2 (April 2008): 296–313.

Terry, Janice J., and Elaine Hagopian, eds. "The AAUG Experience: Achievements and Lessons Learned." *Arab Studies Quarterly* 29, nos. 3 and 4 (Summer and Fall 2007): i-xii, 1–172.

2003–2007 Report on Hate Crimes and Discrimination against Arab Americans. Washington, DC: American-Arab Anti-Discrimination Committee, 2007.

U.S. Department of Commerce, Economics, and Statistics Administration. "We the People of Arab Ancestry in the United States: Census 2000 Special Report." Washington, DC: U.S. Census Bureau, 2000.

CHAPTER 6   PROFESSIONAL LIFE

Abraham, Nabeel, and Andrew Shyrock, eds. *Arab Detroit: From Margin to Mainstream.* Detroit: Wayne State University Press, 2000.

Amaney, Jamal, and Nadine Naber, eds. *Race and Arab Americans before and after 9/11: From Invisible Citizens to Visible Subjects.* Syracuse, NY: Syracuse University Press, 2008.

Arab American National Museum. *Telling Our Story.* Dearborn, MI: Arab American National Museum, 2008.

Hassoun, Rosina J. *Arab Americans in Michigan.* East Lansing: Michigan State University Press, 2005.

Light, Ivan, and Steven Gold. *Ethnic Economies.* San Diego: Academic Press, 2000.

Marschner, Janice. *California's Arab Americans.* Sacramento: Coleman Ranch Press, 2003.

McCarus, Ernest, ed. *The Development of Arab-American Identity.* Ann Arbor: University of Michigan Press, 1994.

Naff, Alixa. *Becoming American: The Early Arab Immigrant Experience.* Carbondale, IL: Southern Illinois University Press, 1985.

Orfalea, Gregory. *Before the Flames: A Quest for the History of Arab Americans.* Austin: University of Texas Press, 1988.

Read, Jen'nan Ghazal. *Culture, Class and Work among Arab-American Women.* New York: LFB Scholarly Publishing, 2004.

Suleiman, Michael W., ed. *Arabs in America*. Philadelphia: Temple University Press, 1999.

CHAPTER 7   PUBLIC AND POLITICAL LIFE

Books

Ameri, Anan, and Ramey Dawn, eds. *The Arab American Encyclopedia*. Dearborn, MI: Arab American National Museum, 2000.

Bakalian, Anny, and Mehdi Bozorgmehr. *From Backlash to Mobilization: Middle Easterners and Muslims in Post-9/11 America*. University of California Press, 2009.

Strum, Philippa, ed. *American Arabs and Political Participation*. Washington, DC: Woodrow Wilson International Center for Scholars, 2006: www.wilsoncenter.org.

Zombie, James J. 2001. *What Ethnic Americans Really Think*. Utica, NY: Zombie International.

Articles and Reports

American Civil Liberties Union (ACLU), 2002. "Civil Liberties after 9/11: A Historical Perspective on Protecting Liberty in Times of Crisis." New York: ALCU: http://www.aclu.org/files/FilesPDFs/911_report.pdf.

Arab American Institute. *Healing the Nation: The Arab American Experience after September 11*. Washington, DC: AAI, 2002: www.aaiusa.org.

Arab American Institute. *Roster of Arab Americans in Public Service and Political Life*. Washington, DC: AAI, 2008: http://www.aaiusa.org/arab-americans/3923.

Arab American Institute. *2008 Election Report*. Washington, DC: AAI, 2008: http://www.aaiusa.org/resources/400/campaigns-elections.

Association of Patriotic Arab Americans in the Military website: www.apaam.org.

Ibish, Hussein, ed., and Ann Stewart, principle researcher. *Report on Hate Crimes and Discrimination against Arab Americans: The Post-September 11 Backlash*. Washington, DC: ADC Research Institute, 2002: http://adc.org/index.php?id=3302 (accessed February 2009).

Jamal, Amaney. "Religious Identity, Discrimination and 9/11: The Determinants of Arab American Levels of Political Confidence in Mainstream and Ethnic Institutions." Paper presented at the Middle Eastern Diasporas: (In)visible Minorities Symposium, Yale University, New Haven, CT, 2005.

CHAPTER 8   THE ARTS

Books

Ameri, Anan, and Holly Arid, eds. *Etching Our Own Image: Voices from within the Arab American Art Movement.* Newcastle, UK: Cambridge Scholars Publishing, 2007.

Arab American National Museum. *In/Visible: Contemporary Art by Arab American Artists.* Dearborn, MI: Arab American National Museum, 2005.

Arab American National Museum. *Telling Our Story.* Dearborn, MI: Arab American National Museum, 2007.

Kaldas, Pauline, and Khaled Mattawa, eds. *Dinarzad's Children: An Anthology of Contemporary Arab American Fiction.* Fayetteville, AK: University of Arkansas Press, 2004.

Kanazi, Remi. *Poets for Palestine.* Astoria, NY: Al Jisser Group, 2009.

Oweis, Fayeq. *Encyclopedia of Arab American Artists.* Westport, CT: Cambridge Scholars Press, 2008.

Shaheen, Jack. *Reel Bad Arabs.* Northhampton, MA: Olive Branch Press, 2001.

Shihab, Aziz. *Does the Land Remember Me? A Memoir of Palestine.* Syracuse, NY: Syracuse University Press, 2007.

Journals, Articles, and Online Resources

ALJADID: A Review and Record of Arab Cultural Arts: http://www.aljadid.com.

Arab Artists Resources & Training (AART): http://www.aart.wshttp://www.aart.ws/.

Arabesque: Arts of the Arab World Festival at Kennedy Center: http://www.kennedy-center.org/programs/festivals/08–09/arabesque/.

Smith, Dinitia. "Arab American Authors, Uneasy in Two Worlds." *New York Times,* February 19, 2003: http://www.nytimes.com/2003/02/19/books/19WRIT.html?scp=1&sq=arab%20american%20writers&st=cse.

Smith, Dinitia. "For Arab-American Playwrights, a Sense of Purpose." *New York Times,* February 11, 2006: http://www.nytimes.com/2006/02/11/theater/newsandfeatures/11thro.html?scp=3&sq=arab%20american%20writers&st=cse.

INDEX

ABOUT THE EDITORS AND CONTRIBUTORS

The Arab American National Museum (AANM) is the only institution among America's 17,500 museums that documents, preserves and presents Arab American history, culture and contributions. Since opening in Dearborn, Michigan in May 2005, the Museum has enlightened hundreds of thousands of visitors, both Arab and non-Arab, from across the U.S. and around the world, through thought-provoking exhibitions, engaging on-site and off-site programs and informative websites. The AANM Library & Resource Center contains the single largest collection of materials by and about Arab Americans. Learn more at ww.arabamericanmuseum.org.

EDITORS

Anan Ameri, PhD, is the founding director of the Arab American National Museum. She holds a PhD in sociology from Wayne State University and was a visiting scholar at Harvard University's Center for Middle Eastern Studies in 1996. Dr. Ameri has close to 30 years of experience in working with Arab American communities in the United States. She is the author and editor of several books and articles about Arab Americans, including the *Arab American Encyclopedia* and *Telling Our Story: The Arab American National Museum.*

Holly Arida is an educator and writer who specializes in Middle Eastern and Arab American affairs. She developed a new method for teaching about the Middle East and consults for schools and universities on global education strategies. She has authored several articles and co-edited the book *Etching Our Own Image: Voices from within the Arab American Art Movement* for the Arab American National Museum, where she serves as an advisor. Arida is a graduate of the Center for Modern Middle Eastern and North African Studies at the University of Michigan and teaches at Cranbrook Kingswood Upper School.

CONTRIBUTORS

Randa A. Kayyali is the author of *The Arab Americans,* which received an award from the Arab American National Museum in the nonfiction book category and was translated into Arabic by the Arab Institute for Research and Publishing. She received her MA in sociology/ anthropology from the American University in Cairo and is currently pursuing her PhD in cultural studies at George Mason University.

Kathleen Marker is a PhD candidate in the department of sociology at the University of California, San Diego, where her dissertation research focuses on the relationship between identities and the economy. With the support of grants from the National Science Foundation and Kauffman Foundation, she has conducted interviews of Arab American entrepreneurs around the country investigating the role of religion and ethnicity in business networking.

Helen Hatab Samhan is a senior executive with the Arab American Institute, which focuses on Arab American issues in politics, leadership training, and public policy. She lectures and publishes on the immigrant experience of Arabs in the United States, Arab American identity and demographics and political involvement, and Arab American women. Samhan serves on numerous boards and holds an MA in Middle East studies from the American University of Beirut.

Janice J. Terry is a professor emeritus at Eastern Michigan University and a graduate of the School of Oriental and African Studies, University of London. She is coauthor of *The Twentieth Century:*

A Brief Global History and has published widely on various aspects of Arab American and Arab history. She is also the former editor of the *Arab Studies Quarterly*.

Marvin Wingfield was for many years the director of education and outreach for the American-Arab Anti-Discrimination Committee (ADC). His educational work includes the development of many lesson plans and teachers' resources, as well as numerous articles on Arab Americans, anti-Arab discrimination, Arab culture, and Islam. He has an MA in religious studies from the Earlham School of Religion.